Modernist Afterlives in
Irish Literature and Culture

ANTHEM IRISH STUDIES

The Anthem Irish Studies series brings together innovative scholarship on Irish literature, culture and history. The series includes both interdisciplinary work and outstanding research within particular disciplines and combines investigations of Ireland with scholarship on Irish diasporas.

Series Editor
Marjorie Howes – *Boston College, USA*

Editorial Board
Síghle Bhreathnach Lynch – *National Gallery of Ireland, Ireland*
Nicholas Canny – *National University of Ireland, Galway, Ireland*
Brian Ó Conchubhair – *University of Notre Dame, USA*
Elizabeth Butler Cullingford – *University of Texas at Austin, USA*
R. F. Foster – *University of Oxford, UK*
Susan Cannon Harris – *University of Notre Dame, USA*
Margaret Kelleher – *University College Dublin, Ireland*
J. Joseph Lee – *New York University, USA*
Riana O'Dwyer – *National University of Ireland, Galway, Ireland*
Diarmuid Ó Giolláin – *University of Notre Dame, USA*
Kevin O'Neill – *Boston College, USA*
Paige Reynolds – *College of the Holy Cross, USA*
Anthony Roche – *University College Dublin, Ireland*
Joseph P. Valente – *University at Buffalo, SUNY, USA*

Modernist Afterlives in Irish Literature and Culture

Edited by Paige Reynolds

ANTHEM PRESS

Anthem Press
An imprint of Wimbledon Publishing Company
www.anthempress.com

This edition first published in UK and USA 2019
by ANTHEM PRESS
75–76 Blackfriars Road, London SE1 8HA, UK
or PO Box 9779, London SW19 7ZG, UK
and
244 Madison Ave #116, New York, NY 10016, USA

First published in the UK and USA by Anthem Press 2016

© 2019 Paige Reynolds editorial matter and selection;
individual chapters © individual contributors

The moral right of the authors has been asserted.

All rights reserved. Without limiting the rights under copyright reserved above,
no part of this publication may be reproduced, stored or introduced into
a retrieval system, or transmitted, in any form or by any means
(electronic, mechanical, photocopying, recording or otherwise),
without the prior written permission of both the copyright
owner and the above publisher of this book.

British Library Cataloguing-in-Publication Data
A catalogue record for this book is available from the British Library.

ISBN-13: 978-1-78527-186-1 (Pbk)
ISBN-10: 1-78527-186-5 (Pbk)

This title is also available as an e-book.

CONTENTS

List of Figures vii

Acknowledgements ix

Introduction
Paige Reynolds 1

Section One: LITERATURE AND LANGUAGE

Chapter 1. 'A World of Hotels and Gaols': Women Novelists and the Spaces of Irish Modernism, 1930–32 11
Anne Fogarty

Chapter 2. 'I Knew What It Meant / Not to Be at All': Death and the (Modernist) Afterlife in the Work of Irish Women Poets of the 1940s 23
Lucy Collins

Chapter 3. 'Whatever Is Given / Can Always Be Reimagined': Seamus Heaney's Indefinite Modernism 35
Leah Flack

Chapter 4. James Joyce and the Lives of Edna O'Brien 49
Ellen McWilliams

Chapter 5. Modernist Topoi and Late Modernist Praxis in Recent Irish Poetry (with Special Reference to the Work of David Lloyd) 61
Alex Davis

Chapter 6. 'Amach Leis!' (Out with It!): Modernist Inheritances in Micheál Ó Conghaile's 'Athair' ('Father') 75
Sarah McKibben

Section Two: INSTITUTIONS, ART AND PERFORMANCE

Chapter 7. 'Make a Letter Like a Monument': Remnants of Modernist Literary Institutions in Ireland 93
Andrew A. Kuhn

Chapter 8. Storm in a Teacup: Irish Modernist Art 111
Róisín Kennedy

Chapter 9. 'Particles of Meaning': The Modernist Afterlife in Irish Design 125
Linda King

Chapter 10. Animal Afterlives: Equine Legacies in Irish Visual Culture 141
Maria Pramaggiore

Chapter 11. Choreographies of Irish Modernity: Alternative 'Ideas of a Nation' in Yeats's *At the Hawk's Well* and Ó Conchúir's *Cure* 153
Aoife McGrath

Chapter 12. The Modernist Impulse in Irish Theatre: Anu Productions and the Monto 163
Emilie Pine

Afterword: The Poetics of Perpetuation 175
David James

Notes on Contributors 183

Index 187

LIST OF FIGURES

1.1	Eileen Gray, Exterior of E.1027, 1926–29.	14
1.2	Eileen Gray, Interior of E.1027, 1926–29.	14
7.1a	Title page, Padraic Colum, *Ten Poems* (Dublin: Dolmen, 1957).	99
7.1b	Title page, W. B. Yeats, *In the Seven Woods* (Dundrum: Dun Emer, 1903).	100
7.1c	Title page, W. B. Yeats, *The Cat and the Moon and Certain Poems* (Dublin: Cuala, 1924).	101
7.1d	Title page, Liam Miller, ed., *The Dolmen Press Yeats Centenary Papers MCMLXV* (Dublin: Dolmen, 1968).	102
7.2	Thomas Kinsella, trans., *The Táin*, illus. Louis le Brocquy (Dublin: Dolmen, 1969).	104
7.3	Stéphane Mallarmé, *Dice Thrown Never Will Annul Chance*, trans., Brian Coffey (Dublin: Dolmen, 1965).	104
8.1	Dorothy Cross, *Teacup*, 1997, DVD PAL, 3-minute loop.	112
8.2	Michael Farrell, *Madonna Irlanda*, 1977, lithograph, 45 x 61.88 cm. (17.7 x 24.4 in.).	114
8.3	Louis le Brocquy, *A Family*, 1951, oil on canvas, 147 x 185 cm.	115
8.4	Sean Scully, *Figure in Grey*, 2004, oil on linen, 299.7 x 256.5 cm.	117
9.1	Michael Scott, Irish Pavilion at the 1939 New York World's Fair.	131
9.2	Stella Steyn, *Rn nnn*, 1931–32.	133
9.3	Jan de Fouw, *Britain*, 1959, screenprinted poster.	135
9.4	Alvin Lustig, book jacket for *Exiles* by James Joyce (New Directions Books, 1947).	137

ACKNOWLEDGEMENTS

Modernist Afterlives in Irish Literature and Culture stems from the March 2014 symposium 'Modernist Afterlives in Irish Literature' convened in Dublin at Boston College – Ireland. Designed and organized as part of my tenure as the William B. Neenan Visiting Fellow, this symposium brought together academics from Ireland and abroad working in modernism across a variety of disciplines to consider how Irish artists from the mid-twentieth century forward have engaged and recalibrated high modernism's formal innovations, thematic concerns and cultural practices. This collection arose from a desire to extend and share the symposium's exhilarating conversations. The interdisciplinary nature of modernist and Irish studies – exemplified by the audience in attendance that day – as well as the analytical possibilities generated by comparative essays from among different fields, invited further considerations of a wider array of cultural institutions, objects and practices in order to flesh out more fully the topic of 'modernist afterlives'.

For the opportunity to serve as the 2013 Neenan Visiting Fellow at Boston College – Ireland, I thank Thomas Hachey, then executive director, Center for Irish Programs at Boston College, and Mike Cronin, academic director, Boston College – Ireland. Along with Mike, Thea Gilien, head of programmes, and Claire McGowan, programmes coordinator, enriched my tenure as the Neenan Fellow with their generous support and warm company – attributes showcased during our beautifully orchestrated symposium staged with help from Laoise Ní Dhonnchú. For the success of the symposium, my thanks to the faculty and students in attendance, who shared their intelligence and thoughtful engagement with the topic. My particular appreciation goes out to our opening keynote, David James, as well as to the day's speakers, Lucy Collins, Alex Davis, Anne Fogarty, Patrick Lonergan, Ellen McWilliams and Emilie Pine. Thanks as well to Margaret Kelleher and Claire Connolly, who chaired the two panels. And of course, tremendous thanks to the volume's contributors, who have produced remarkable essays for this collection.

Marjorie Howes, editor of the Anthem Irish Studies series, offered early and ongoing support for this project, and anonymous readers provided valuable suggestions for improvement. The staff at Anthem Press helped to make the publication process a smooth one, and Steve Csipke eased the final stages of publication with his adept indexing of the contents. The College of the Holy Cross, through support from the Committee for Faculty Scholarship and the Arthur J. O'Leary Fellowship, awarded financial assistance to this collection. Sean Scully Studio and Dublin City Gallery The Hugh Lane generously granted permission to reproduce Sean Scully's *Figure in Grey* for the collection's cover image.

Finally, as always, thanks to Mario and Asher Pereira for supporting my enthusiasm for Irish literature and culture and the complicated travel plans it sometimes engenders, as well as to Margaret Kelleher for her generous hospitality and always enlivening friendship.

INTRODUCTION

Paige Reynolds

Modernist Afterlives in Irish Literature and Culture explores how the themes, forms and practices of high modernism are manifest in Irish literature and culture produced subsequent to that cultural movement. In a bracing set of essays – ranging not only among literary genres, but also among practices such as dance, publishing, design and film – this collection considers how Irish writers and artists from the mid-twentieth century forward engage with modernism as they endeavour to forge new modes of expression.

The character and chronology of modernism continue to be subjects of heated debate, though critical consensus defines literary modernism broadly as a quest to 'make it new' (in the words of Ezra Pound) and frequently locates its heyday between 1880 and 1939 – an endpoint coinciding with the start of World War II and the publication of James Joyce's *Finnegans Wake*. Since the advent of the 'new modernist studies' in the 1990s, we have come to accept that modernism spans disciplines and did not unfold exclusively between 1890 and 1922 in a Paris salon, London drawing room or Manhattan gallery.[1] Critics have decisively rebutted the notion that modernism was strictly an Anglo-European or American phenomenon, later adopted elsewhere by 'marginal' cultures, by demonstrating that modernist vocabularies, forms and practices emerged in different places at different moments – a recalibration manifest in a new wave of transnational, Atlantic, global and even planetary modernisms. Consequently, not only has the Western derivation of modernism been questioned, but also the temporal boundaries of the movement have blurred as we acknowledge what modernism borrowed from its historical precursors and granted its heirs. When trying to pinpoint the modernist place and the modernist moment, it is hard to get it entirely right, but refreshingly difficult to be wholly wrong. For example, Pascale Casanova has been criticized for her Eurocentric history of literary formations in *The World Republic of Letters* (2004), a comparativist study invoked by critics of Irish modernism for its account of

Irish exceptionalism. But Casanova's traditional understanding of locale is countered by a progressive conception of time when she bounds across historical periods and cites the medieval courts as a point of origin for modern Anglo-European literatures.[2]

As part of these expansions, scholars are beginning to explore how, and to what ends, late modern and contemporary writers have invoked modernist forms and practices, thus refining or even rejecting longstanding notions of the postmodern. As Laura Marcus notes, these studies trouble 'the literary-historical narrative in which "high modernism" gave way (after the extreme experimentation of *Finnegans Wake* in 1939 and with the coming of the second world war) to postwar realism, and cosmopolitanism to parochialism'.[3] A number of critics have exposed how modernism trickles into the novel of the mid-twentieth century, coining terms such as 'late modernism' (Tyrus Miller) or 'intermodernism' (Kristin Bluemel), while James Smethurst has identified in African-American poetry of the 1940s a popular and a high 'neomodernism'.[4] Other scholars have elongated the period even further, suggesting that we can enhance our understanding of literature produced after the mid-twentieth century by reading modernism as continuous and adaptive into the present moment.[5] David James and Urmila Seshagiri make a compelling argument for containing modernism's sprawl by 'returning to the logic of periodization' through what they label 'metamodernism', which 'offers a rubric for reading contemporary literature's relationship to modernism but also generates a retrospective understanding of modernism as a moment as well as a movement'.[6]

The creative appropriation of previous aesthetic traditions has been in evidence since at least the classical era. Yet, during the twentieth century, as perceptions of modernism began to coalesce, the poet and critic T. S. Eliot specifically identified in Irish literature the modern-day prototype for this tactic of recapitulation and reworking. In '*Ulysses*, Order, and Myth' (1923), Eliot famously praised Joyce's 'mythical method': his use of myth in *Ulysses* to produce 'a continuous parallel between contemporaneity and antiquity' that controls, orders and gives 'a shape and a significance to the immense panorama of futility and anarchy which is contemporary history'.[7] Eliot advocates copying this mythical method: those who follow in Joyce's footsteps 'will not be imitators, any more than the scientist who uses the discoveries of an Einstein in pursuing his own, independent, further investigations' (177). He goes on to praise Yeats for this same practice of borrowing from the past, and to adumbrate: 'Mr. Joyce is pursuing a method which others must pursue after him' (177). This parallelism, adapting the mythic past to the contemporary present, also has roots in the Irish revivalism of the early twentieth century, highlighting the congruities between revivalism and modernism. Emily Lawless in her novel *Grania* (1892) and Lady Gregory in her play *Grania* (1912) grafted the ideals of the sexual and independent New Woman onto this determined mythic figure.[8] The 1902 premiere of Gregory and Yeats's *Cathleen ni Houlihan* placed myth expressly in dialogue with contemporary politics when it cast the political activist Maud Gonne in the role of the old woman of Ireland, highlighting the tension between 'contemporaneity and antiquity' through performance choices. And in their handcrafted artefacts, Elizabeth and Lily Yeats's Cuala Industries reproduced Celtic dragon designs and other symbols drawn from Irish myth.[9] Examples such as these demonstrate the crucial role that Irish women played in creating and sustaining modernism, an irrefutable fact substantiated by this collection.

Irish Modernist Afterlives in Space and Time

In a moment when the critical spotlight has turned on the global circulation of capital, people and culture, attention to a single national tradition may appear regressive. However, the present collection demonstrates that modern Irish cultural production has always moved across national and ethnic boundaries. The international character of Irish modernism was long typified by European exile, by narratives depicting the native geniuses Joyce and Beckett escaping a homeland mired in outdated aesthetics and beliefs. Within this selective framework, mid-twentieth-century Irish culture was, in turn, represented as constrained and burdened by parochialism, and the more recent past regarded as a moment suddenly alert to the world beyond the island's borders, thanks to factors such as membership in the European Union, the rise and fall of the Celtic Tiger, and other manifestations of a belated modernity. This collection undermines these pat narratives and simplified chronologies, in part by revealing that global influences register throughout Irish modernism as well as in culture produced in its wake. The deployment of modernist vocabularies, practices and tropes by Irish artists inevitably means that their work is rarely strictly 'national' in character. As these essays demonstrate, Irish modernism and its afterlives are shaped not only through cultural interaction with the United Kingdom and the United States, but also with Russia, Holland and Japan, among others.

The topic of 'afterlives' also complements ongoing conversations about uneven or disrupted temporalities in modern Irish literature and culture. The invocation of modernist forms and tropes subsequent to the modernist era appears, on one level, as yet another instance of the Irish cultural 'belatedness' examined by critics such as Declan Kiberd and Joe Cleary.[10] However, the artists discussed in this collection were highly alert to the aesthetic innovations of the early twentieth century, even deploying them in concert with high modernism's 'banquet years'. They were also, as these essays demonstrate, early and enthusiastic champions of the metamodernism identified by James and Seshagiri, disproving the notion that experimental Irish writers and artists categorically lagged behind artistic innovators elsewhere. Nonetheless, these essays confirm – as Eliot suggested roughly a century ago – that Irish cultural production often abides by an anomalous timeline, thanks in part to the country's colonial past. As David Lloyd notes, colonial modernity contributes to the distinctive nature of cultures, since 'modern forms and institutions emerge always in differential relation to their nonmodern and recalcitrant counterparts'.[11] The offbeat temporality of Irish culture thus may be partially responsible for its continued fruitful engagement of modernist forms and themes presumed depleted.

Further, if postcolonial theory, according to Lloyd, has a larger political purpose to 'represent the possibility of as yet unexhausted alternatives to the unidirectional progress of modernity' (76), modernist afterlives may well be regarded as part of that endeavour. A refusal to relinquish modernism in Ireland suggests that the modernist project is not complete; its quest to 'make it new' lives on in a present-day Ireland marked by its formidable commitment to nostalgia, to memory, to commemoration. This 'backwardness' (to invoke Lloyd's term) ironically testifies to the enduring potentiality of modernist forms, themes and practices, as evident in the upsurge of Irish fiction by contemporary writers such as Eimear McBride or Sara Baume – fiction that overtly and knowingly recapitulates modernist technique. Here, old modernist form provides women writers with a valuable new tool for the critique of abusive patriarchal structures and practices.

Modernist Afterlives and Interdisciplinarity

The interdisciplinary nature of *Modernist Afterlives in Irish Literature and Culture* showcases the range of international and historical influences on Irish culture and exposes how Ireland has informed experimental cultural practices beyond its borders. We learn that Irish modernists and their inheritors enthusiastically drew from traditions native – such as the Book of Kells, Celtic orthography and the writing of Jonathan Swift – and foreign, including the poetry of Homer and the paintings of Kose Kanaoka. Many of the essays productively invoke Yeats, Joyce, Bowen and Beckett, those predictable agents of Irish modernism, to reveal new and nuanced ways these writers helped to mould subsequent manifestations of modernism. Contributors introduce, as well, surprising yet profound inspirations for twentieth- and twenty-first-century Irish artists. For instance, Alex Davis in his account of procedural verse, Andrew Kuhn in his study of print culture and Aoife McGrath in her analysis of modern dance all demonstrate how French symbolist Stéphane Mallarmé affected various modes of Irish cultural production, while Anne Fogarty and Linda King elucidate how architect and designer Eileen Gray shaped our understanding of space in twentieth-century fiction and design. The collection reveals that distinctive temporalities define modernism in different fields, further complicating and enriching discourses about periodization. If literary studies cautiously accepts 1890–1939 as the modernist moment, then modernism in design, as King demonstrates in her essay, spans from the late nineteenth century into the 1970s in three stages. Further complicating matters, she reminds us that, whereas literary modernism was largely directed at elites, modernism in design was geared toward the masses.

Even as these essays engage with various cultural practices, *Modernist Afterlives in Irish Literature and Culture* keeps literature as its touchstone, exploring the work of major figures from Yeats to Heaney, while ranging among other practices from contemporary theatrical production to architecture. In part, this is a legacy of the ambit of the 'Modernist Afterlives in Irish Literature' symposium that preceded this collection, but it also gestures to the formidable role that literature plays in shaping not only Irish self-understanding, but also the country's global identity. Irish literature is seen, perforce, as a significant influence on international modernism. As a result, its literary figures and works continue to appear in eclectic forms ranging from tourism branding to course syllabi – thus generating new audiences for, and even practitioners of, contemporary work inflected with traits distinctive to Irish modernism.

In their analyses of contemporary poetry, Alex Davis and Leah Flack approach 'modernist afterlives' in contemporary Irish poetry from provocatively different perspectives. Davis notes that poets such as Trevor Joyce and Catherine Walsh primarily have appropriated modernist forms rather than themes or topics traditionally associated with the movement. By focusing on the procedural verse of David Lloyd, whose scholarly insights into temporality were mentioned earlier in this preface, Davis exposes the crucial need to acknowledge the radically diverse ways in which modernism plays out in Irish poetry. He reveals how Lloyd's procedural compositions, with their 'rigorous' invocation of methods 'adopted' from high modernism, can powerfully 'reflect and critique' aspects of contemporary culture. Davis avers that his argument does not consign Seamus Heaney or Derek Mahon to a thematically driven 'modernism lite', and his point is driven home by the astute reading of Heaney provided by Flack, who attends to the poet's 'exultant model of modernism that depended on reading Joyce and Eliot in dynamic relation to Mandelstam'. Heaney summons this Russian poet consciously to extend the legacies of modernism, while maintaining a critical position of enthusiasm and ambivalence about their utility.

Essays here also reflect the attention now focused on the contributions of Irish women writers to modernism and its afterlives.[12] Lucy Collins takes the notion of an 'afterlife' quite literally, studying how Rhoda Coghill, Mary Devenport O'Neill and Sheila Wingfield – three experimental women poets writing in the 1940s – represented death and mourning in the aftermath of two world wars and years of violent conflict within Ireland. How, she asks, could women poets adopt the fragmented subjectivity characteristic of high modernism in a historical moment when the place of female artists and their legacy was so precarious? Anne Fogarty draws attention to novels – written during the 1930s by Elizabeth Bowen, Kathleen Coyle and Pamela Hinkson – that represent the complex symbolic role the home and the domestic held for their female protagonists. By reading these novels through Hannah Arendt and Eileen Gray's ruminations on the public and private, Fogarty identifies the 'restless subjectivity' these women struggled to depict and the value of inwardness upon which they insisted.

Throughout the collection, contributors challenge sacred truths about modernism through their thoughtful readings of contemporary texts that explicitly or implicitly acknowledge modernism as an antecedent. Ellen McWilliams traces the influence of James Joyce on Edna O'Brien, demonstrating how in her life writing O'Brien dances with the legacy of her admired progenitor, engaging and redirecting accepted perceptions of him, at once accentuating his inspiration and casting him in her shadow, laying claim to 'her' Joyce. Sarah McKibben studies the relationship of twentieth-century Irish-language authors to modernism, undermining hackneyed perceptions of these writers as strictly anxious about modernity and resistant to formal experimentation. Her analysis of Micheál Ó Conghaile's short story, 'Athair', a contemporary coming-out narrative, showcases the author's command of modernist irony and ambiguity, in part through close attention to his playful engagement with the word *gay* in Irish.

Other contributions highlight the important role that cultural institutions play in sustaining and remoulding the legacies of modernism. Róisín Kennedy recounts the enthusiastic embrace of Irish modernist art by contemporary collectors and institutions in Ireland, which stands in contrast to the ambivalent reaction of contemporary artists such as Dorothy Cross or Nevan Lahart, who found more useful tactics in subversive continental modernism. Lucy Collins and Alex Davis both note the influence poetry presses have on thwarting or advancing, respectively, the aims of the poets they study. Andrew Kuhn offers a rich case study of this logic by revealing how Dolmen Press invoked the ideals and practices of its modernist precursor, Cuala Press, to situate Irish poets within a high modernism that was necessarily cosmopolitan.

Linda King likewise attends to the book as object to demonstrate that design provides a powerful example of how Irish art moves across borders. In her study of Irish design throughout the twentieth century – as manifest in branding, architecture and book design, among others – she highlights the importance of emigration and immigration to the development of modern and contemporary Irish design. Maria Pramaggiore traces representations of the horse in visual media, including painting, sculpture, film, television and video, to expose how 'animal afterlives' can alter our sense of modernist temporality since the horse embodies both a 'a backward-looking nostalgia and a forward-looking aspiration'. Her opening discussion of eighteenth-century writer Jonathan Swift confirms the 'jagged' temporality of modernism she sees embodied in the horse; high modernism's purported last gasp produced several experimental Irish dramas invoking Swift, including Yeats's *The Words upon the Window Pane* (1930), Lord Longford's *Yahoo* (1933) and Denis Johnston's *The Dreaming Dust* (1940). Horses, like the spirits studied by Lucy Collins, suggest that Irish nationalism offered modernism and its afterlives potent symbols that could be harnessed in the service of revolutionary politics and revolutionary aesthetics.

Emilie Pine and Aoife McGrath consider how contemporary performances in Ireland echo modernism in their quest to represent trauma to audiences. Pine examines the 2012 Anu production of *The Boys of Foley Street*, a site-specific play set in the Monto, famously where the 'Circe' episode in Joyce's *Ulysses* unfolds. McGrath turns her attention to the resonances of W. B. Yeats's dance play *At the Hawk's Well* (1916) in Feargus Ó Conchúir's *Cure* (2013), a solo performance that engages the personal and societal after-effects of economic and religious collapse in contemporary Ireland. In both essays, the authors vividly describe their personal responses to these performances, exposing how present-day manifestations of modernism can profoundly affect the audience emotionally and kinesthetically. These productions, as Pine notes, point to how live performance and the avant-garde theatrical tactics of Brecht and Jarry can undermine the aesthetic distance often attributed to literary modernism as they seek to engage empathy in audience members in a critique of contemporary Irish culture.

These rich essays, in tandem with David James's thoughtful afterword, highlight the particular contribution that the study of Irish literature and culture has made, and continues to make, to the critical concern with aesthetic afterlives. By attending to the relationships among and between material texts, aesthetic objects, ephemeral performances and cultural institutions, the collection as a whole sheds welcome light on questions related to transnational cultural exchange, modernity's intricate temporalities, the value of attending closely to aesthetic form and the ethical potential embodied by literature and the arts.

Notes

1 Doug Mao and Rebecca Walkowitz, 'The New Modernist Studies', *PMLA* 123, no. 3 (2008): 737–748.
2 Laura Doyle, 'Modernist Studies and Inter-Imperiality in the Longue Durée', in *The Oxford Handbook of Global Modernisms*, eds. Mark Wollaeger and Matt Eatough (Oxford: Oxford University Press, 2012), 673.
3 Laura Marcus, 'The Legacies of Modernism', in *The Cambridge Companion to the Modernist Novel*, ed. Morag Shiach (Cambridge: Cambridge University Press, 2007), 82.
4 Tyrus Miller, *Late Modernism: Politics, Fiction and the Arts Between the World Wars* (Berkeley: University of California Press, 1999); Kristin Bluemel, ed. *Intermodernism: Literary Culture in Mid-Twentieth-Century Britain* (Edinburgh: Edinburgh University Press, 2009); James Smethurst, *The New Red Negro: The Literary Left and African American Poetry, 1930–1946* (New York: Oxford University Press, 1999). See also Marina MacKay and Lyndsey Stonebridge, eds. *British Fiction after Modernism: The Novel at Mid-Century* (Basingstoke: Palgrave Macmillan, 2007).
5 See Michael D'Arcy and Mathias Nilges, eds., *The Contemporaneity of Modernism: Literature, Media, Culture* (New York: Routledge, 2016); Amy Hungerford, "On the Period Formerly Known as Contemporary," *American Literary History* 20, nos. 1–2 (Spring/Summer 2008): 410–19; David James, ed. *The Legacies of Modernism: Historicising Postwar and Contemporary Fiction* (Cambridge: Cambridge University Press, 2012); David James, *Modernist Futures: Innovation and Inheritance in the Contemporary Novel* (Cambridge: Cambridge University Press, 2012).
6 David James and Urmila Seshagiri, 'Metamodernism: Narratives of Continuity and Revolution', *PMLA* 129, no. 1 (2014): 88. For an example of this approach, see Stephen Watt, *Beckett and Contemporary Irish Writing* (Cambridge: Cambridge University Press, 2009).
7 T. S. Eliot, '*Ulysses*, Order and Myth', in *Selected Prose of T. S. Eliot*, ed. Frank Kermode (New York: Harcourt, Brace and Co., 1975), 177. Subsequent references parenthetical.
8 Heather Edwards, 'The Irish New Woman and Emily Lawless's *Grania: The Story of an Island*: A Congenial Geography', *English Literature in Transition* 51, no. 4 (2008): 421–38; Heidi Hansson, *Emily Lawless 1845–1913: Writing the Interspace* (Cork: Cork University Press, 2007).
9 On this topic, see Kennedy and Kuhn in this volume.
10 Declan Kiberd, *Inventing Ireland: The Literature of a Modern Nation* (New York: Vintage, 1996); Joe Cleary, 'Toward a Materialist-Formalist History of Twentieth-Century Irish Literature', *Boundary* 2, no. 31 (2004): 207–41. See Pramaggiore in this volume for further discussion of Irish temporalities.
11 David Lloyd, *Irish Times: Temporalities of Modernity*, Field Day Files 4 (Dublin: University of Notre Dame, 2008), 4.
12 Gerardine Meaney, 'Regendering Modernism: The Woman Artist in Irish Women's Fiction', *Women: A Cultural Journal* 15, no. 1 (2004): 67–82; Anne Fogarty, 'Women and Modernism', in *The Cambridge Companion to Irish Modernism*, ed. Joe Cleary (Cambridge: Cambridge University Press, 2014), 147–60; Aintzane Legarreta Mentxaka, *Kate O'Brien and the Fictions of Identity: Sex, Art and Politics in Mary Lavalle and Other Writings* (London: McFarland & Company, 2011); Paige Reynolds, 'Colleen Modernism: Modernism's Afterlife in Irish Women's Writing', *Éire-Ireland* 44, nos. 3 & 4 (Fall/Winter 2009): 94–117.

Section One
LITERATURE AND LANGUAGE

Chapter 1

'A WORLD OF HOTELS AND GAOLS': WOMEN NOVELISTS AND THE SPACES OF IRISH MODERNISM, 1930–32

Anne Fogarty

The current impetus to historicize modernism, to break it into phases or periods and to see it as a congeries of nonconcurrent developments, permits an opening up of the ramifying pathways of Irish literary modernism and a recognition of the contribution of women writers to the always-contested accounts of the modern and of the plural and quarrelsome artistic modes that this movement spawns. In particular, interest in what Kristin Bluemel has dubbed *intermodernism* or others conceive of as *late modernism*, facilitates a detailed investigation of the work of women writers and an assessment of the novelty and inventive facets of their creations.[1] David James has made a cogent case for the revalidation of British novels written in the 1930s through a sympathetic reconsideration of the seemingly realist frameworks they espouse and a recognition of the political challenges involved in their concentration on the local and the regional.[2]

In a similar spirit, this essay sets out to examine three texts by Irish women writers published in the early 1930s: Pamela Hinkson's *The Ladies' Road* (1932), Elizabeth Bowen's *To the North* (1932) and Kathleen Coyle's *A Flock of Birds* (1930).[3] All three authors may be construed as belonging to a transnational modernism, as they lived outside of Ireland and were part of different artistic milieux in Europe, the United Kingdom and the United States. My purpose is to assess how they remould the novel and query the imperatives of modernism – such as internationalism and mobility – by focusing on the social position of women, the import of the home and the domestic and the place granted to their unorthodox heroines in the psychic, sexual and affective spaces of the modern. My endeavour is not to co-opt these texts into a canon of experimental modernism, but rather to explore thematic links between them in order to discern how feminist writers continue the business of deconstructing social and mythic sanctities, how they work to topple male-defined symbolic codes and how they rethink the formal possibilities of the novel in order to depict the dislocations and the restless subjectivities attendant on the modern. Specifically, a wager of this essay is that microhistories of the modern are necessary in order to achieve a more nuanced account of the ways in which women writers engaged with the structures of modernism and selectively and purposefully made their own of them. Only through such particularist and comparativist frameworks can we begin to take stock not only of the difference of their works, but also of their subtly textured questioning of social norms and values and of their retooling and reshaping of artistic form. Above all, my concern is to identify and tease out aspects of a late phase of Irish women's modernism in the 1930s, to track how it is in overt dialogue with the achievements of artists active in the 1910s and 1920s and to unearth overarching aesthetic patterns and philosophical metadiscourses that typify it.

Elizabeth Bowen, deploying characteristically unsettling double negatives, averred that '[n]othing can happen nowhere' in the novel.[4] This essay seeks to read the symbolic dimensions of the varying houses and nonplaces represented in the texts by Hinkson, Bowen and Coyle. It will address their preoccupation with architecture and spatiality, with movement, with the sites of the domestic and with the problematic lines of division between the private and the public. David Spurr has contended that built spaces should not be seen simply as supplying analogies in modern texts. Rather, it will be proposed that houses and indoor spaces in the novels by Hinkson, Bowen and Coyle constitute conceptual cruxes and guiding metaphors, especially with regard to the disruptive but devalued position of the feminine in the modern.[5] Recurrent iterations of tropes of movement and of spatial and temporal images capture the shifting essence of modernity and permit a calibration of the changes that it wrought in women's place in the world and in their association with the home and the desire to belong to a public sphere. The struggle to be part of a modern 'world of hotels and gaols' (145), as enunciated by Kathleen Coyle's heroine, bridges these texts. In order to draw out the peculiar dimensions of this nexus of concerns in these fictions, Hannah Arendt's reflections on the problem of inwardness in the modern era and Eileen Gray's articulation of the importance of the private and of screened recesses in her radical reordering of modernist interiors and structures, are useful for deciphering the metaphysics of dwelling and of the restless subjectivity with which they struggle.

The necessity of preserving the public sphere as a space for democratic action is a keystone of Hannah Arendt's thinking. The public arena is for her a site of action, political praxis and enacted stories.[6] Yet, that arena appears to be resolutely masculinist in nature. Seyla Benhabib, however, in her study of Arendt's thinking, tracks how her elucidation of the functions of the public world also allowed her to philosophize notions of the domestic, to address the problem of subjectivity and implicitly to suggest how women could contest relegation to the private sphere. She shows how Arendt's concept of the public sphere has its roots in her first work, a biography of the Jewish intellectual Rahel Varnhagen (1771–1833). Varnhagen found only an intermittent outlet for her intellectual energies in a salon she ran and, after its demise, she fell prey to Romantic yearning and introspection – states in which, for Arendt, the public and private are falsely blurred. Benhabib uncovers continuities between Arendt's early reflections on how the individual veers between feelings of worldlessness and attempts to create a home in the world and her later insistence on the necessity for privacy as a means of offsetting the demands and strictures of the public sphere.[7] In Benhabib's feminist retooling of Arendt's philosophy, this latter zone depends on a simultaneous reconstruction of the private sphere and a querying by implication of the binary oppositions between male and female. The heroines in the texts considered in this chapter, it will be argued, are torn between a desire for a place in the world and feelings of worldlessness as articulated by Arendt and, although often refused a space in the public sphere, insist on inclusion in it and on the validity of inward states and the domestic worlds to which they are attached.

Eileen Gray (1878–1976), increasingly recognized as a key proponent of Irish modernism, was born in Enniscorthy, trained in the Slade School of Fine Art in London and spent most of her life in Paris where she practised lacquer work, carpet weaving, painting, photography and furniture design.[8] Gray was a self-taught architect, one of whose masterpieces is E.1027, a South of France coastal villa that encapsulates her unique and challenging aesthetic (Figure 1.1). Contra Le Corbusier, Gray averred that 'a house is not a machine to live in' and noted that 'external architecture seems to have absorbed avant-garde architects at the expense of the interior [...] which leads to an impoverishment of the inner life by suppressing all intimacy'.[9] The interior that Gray designed for E.1027 featured the spare, exposed spaces favoured by modernist design, but broke them up so that they also corresponded with the functions of those living in them and made use of multiple thresholds and screens (Figure 1.2).[10] In its conjoining of sensual objects, multipurpose adjustable pieces of furniture and clean lines, it thus flew in the face of Le Corbusier's precepts for the interior, which aimed to exorcize it of anxieties raised by the private, the domestic and the feminine.[11] Gray's interiors emphasized separations and concealments and allowed for geometrical precision and withdrawal simultaneously, thus fluidly interlinking public and private spaces. The domestic is not banished but rather becomes the medium by which unworkable divisions between male and female and public and private can be undone. Such quarrels, it will be seen,

14 MODERNIST AFTERLIVES IN IRISH LITERATURE AND CULTURE

Figure 1.1 Eileen Gray, Exterior of E.1027, 1926–29. Image courtesy of National Museum of Ireland.

Figure 1.2 Eileen Gray, Interior of E.1027, 1926–29. Image courtesy of National Museum of Ireland.

over the meaning of the architectural interior and the tension between inner and outer are played out in different ways in the novels of Hinkson, Bowen and Coyle and are linked with the quest of their heroines to negotiate the existential dilemmas of modernity.

The daughter of writer Katherine Tynan, Pamela Hinkson (1900–1982) was raised as a Catholic and spent parts of her childhood in London, Dublin and Claremorris, County Mayo. Her early fictional output includes popular genres such as school stories for girls and novels about World War I, written under the pseudonym Peter Deane. *The Ladies' Road* conflates several genres, being at once a boarding-school story, an Irish 'Big House novel', a narrative about World War I, a Bildungsroman and a modernist fiction in the manner of Virginia Woolf and Elizabeth Bowen.[12] Time and space are its dominant subjects; their changing nature and often corrosive effects define the consciousness and fate of the main protagonist, Stella Mannering. The novel correlates three domiciles with which Stella is associated: Cappagh, a 'Big House' demesne in the West of Ireland, the home of her aunt, Nancy Creagh; Winds, the British country estate on which she grew up; and Maythorpe, the boarding school she attends. In particular, Cappagh and Winds are opposed yet fluidly intertwined. The ramshackle, shadow-laden nature of the Anglo-Irish estate and house, with its ominous horizon of dark woods, 'a black wall of trees' (50), cutting it off from the real Irish world beyond, is endowed with the fairy tale–like allure of a seemingly unchanging world, remote from politics and time. As Edmund Urquhart, a visitor to Cappagh, reflects, 'You couldn't tell inside these houses what was happening out there' (32). Winds, by contrast, is depicted as an orderly domain dominated by the affairs of the nursery and the reassuring rhythms of riding and hunting in the landscape it commands. Stella's recollections of both houses are patterned by her memories of movements from their differently ordered interiors to the circumambient natural world.

However, the opposition of the two houses proves illusory as time, politics and loss undo their seeming equilibrium. Hinkson's lyrical, recursive style, which constantly replays leitmotifs to depict the fluctuations of her heroine's thought processes, also captures the instability of a war-torn world. The novel dwells particularly on the way in which World War I liberates women only to heighten their social exclusion and state of worldlessness. Stella resents the separation and sense of being 'shut outside' (95) that result as her brother David trains to be a soldier and eventually departs for the front in France. Correlations are posited in the text between the restiveness of men awaiting deployment, the alienation of returned soldiers and the privations of women, 'shut out from an experience [...] they] had not shared' (278). Yet, these equivalences are also subtly refuted to highlight the existential isolation of women manacled to their private griefs and rebuffed by the public sphere. The crushing news of the death of David in May 1918 in the Third Battle of the Aisne fulfils Stella's worst fears and leads to her piercing awareness that she no longer has a home in the world.

Le chemin des dames, the ladies' road, is the name of a ridge in Picardy on the Western Front around which the three catastrophic Battles of the Aisne were fought in a vain attempt to repel German advances.[13] It becomes emblematic in Hinkson's text, which obsessively cross-connects moments of childhood bliss and of adult loss and scenes of arrival and departure in houses or on railway platforms, of the thwarted longing of women to partake in a public sphere from which they are debarred. Homes shorn of their ability to provide security and continuity, resonant shards of landscape and the inarticulate mourning of family dogs longingly sniffing the reeking uniforms returned to next of kin affectingly project the intense privacy of the placeless grief experienced by Stella, who recognizes that 'she must live always in a No Man's Land left by the War with a country on either side that was not hers' (313). Yet, she cleaves to the image of the road, which redolently bespeaks her quest for world and her overwhelming sense of worldlessness, despite the image's tragic associations.

The final section of the novel, echoing Woolf's rendering of the depredations of time in *To the Lighthouse* (1927), describes a return to Cappagh in 1921 and its ominously changed nature brought about by the hostilities of the War of Independence. Wounded rebels hiding in the stable loft, 'their blood staining the hay' (305), now add to the darkened nature of the place. Like Danielstown in Bowen's *The Last September* (1929), Cappagh is burnt to the ground at the end of the novel and left 'a pile of blackened ruins smoking under the sky' (320). The text signs off with this image of ruination but appends the detail of rabbits creeping out to take over the garden. A pastoral idyll returns to a state of nature and becomes part of the symbolic nonplaces and the interzones of no man's land that epitomize the social upheavals on which the text dwells. The obliteration of this house beloved of the heroine concretizes her sense of worldlessness and grief-stricken devastation but also gestures toward the possibilities of renewal that might still arise from the ruptures of the modern era.

Elizabeth Bowen (1899–1973) came from a Protestant Ascendancy background and was the last inheritor of her family demesne at Bowenscourt in North Cork. Her quirky, obliquely narrated novels combine many different modes, including the Gothic, melodrama, the Bildungsroman, comedies of manners, women's romance and spy fiction, bending syntax and deploying unsettling scenarios in which objects and subjects interpenetrate to capture the charged psychosocial conditions of twentieth-century living.

Speed and travel are predominant motifs in *To the North*, a novel that opens in an express train speeding through northern Italy and ends with a fatal, homicidal car crash.[14] The two central characters, Cecilia and Emmeline Summers, are sisters-in-law who for reasons of expedience have set up house together on the fictitious Oudenarde Road, in St John's Wood, London. Both are in perpetual nervous motion and pursue erratic and fateful attachments. Cecilia is addicted to going out, travel and flighty communication, overspending regularly on taxis and phone bills, while Emmeline, 'the map of Europe [...] never far from her mind' (26), runs an idiosyncratic travel agency in Bloomsbury, which has the motto 'Move dangerously' (23). Her company aims to reintroduce uncertainty into travel, albeit furnishing fully the data needed, and to induce people when abroad 'to use their own wits' (23). This latter necessity is enforced by their chaotic provisions, as in the case of a client who spent a 'frightful fortnight in Silesia' (92) when he had expected a holiday in Sicily. Emmeline, despite her profession, is too busy to travel but moves at headlong speed around London in her car, with her foot invariably on the accelerator. Lady Waters, a tutelary relative of both women, who runs a salon in which she seeks to psychoanalyse her friends, laments that this 'age [...] is far more than restless: it is decentralized'(170), while her vicar opines that motoring has ceased to be a pleasure since its 'whole incentive [...] seems an anxiety to be elsewhere' (64).

Bowen pits her heroines against each other as lethal opposites: Cecilia's predatory capriciousness acts as a foil to Emmeline's virginal innocence. Fateful collusions, misprisions and crossed circumstances abound in the plot, especially in the realm of sexual relations. Emmeline falls compulsively for the caddish Markie Linkwater, who inevitably cheats on her, while the widowed Cecilia struggles with her inability to fall in love with the portentously named Julian Tower. Journeys and interiors act as metaphors for the women's fractious liaisons with these men and their unrealized desires. In an essay published in 1949, Bowen lamented the fact that the 'romantic privacy' and bohemianism of St John's Wood, a place once replete with villas and secluded gardens, had been wiped out in the Blitz and were now threatened by the intrusion of blocks of flats.[15] It seems no accident that the house shared by Cecilia and Emmeline is in this area of London and that it exudes the idealized values Bowen associated with the location. Even though it at times reflects the conflicts between them, it also acts as a site of otherness, female subversiveness and a queer devotion that cannot otherwise be voiced. Their drawing room mantelpiece, on which the 'ornaments smiled at each other', is a pleasing 'gala of femininity' (20) and the gardens and leafy glades of the district are described as possessing an 'airy superurbanity' (94). By contrast, Markie lives in a sealed-off apartment in his sister's house 'in which one [...] might have lain gassed for days before the other became suspicious' (66); here, he communicates via unnerving whistles through a 'speaking-tube' (67) with his cook, who delivers his meals in a dumb waiter.

The crisis of the novel hinges on a double betrayal, Markie's affair with Daisy and Cecilia's decision to marry Julian Tower after all. Although the text has counterpoised the callous Cecilia, 'a social Columbus' (87), with the guileless Emmeline, it intimates that the latter, too, has a 'splinter of ice in the heart' (47) and has an affinity with the frozen North, to which she is magnetically attracted. The incompatibility between Markie and Emmeline is exposed during excursions that go comically but resoundingly wrong. On a trip to Paris, Markie fails to partake in Emmeline's joy in the 'exalting idea of speed' (135) and her appetite for sightseeing and is appalled by the 'passionless entirety of her surrender' (142) to him – while on a romantic weekend in Devizes he similarly refuses to play the role of complaisant suitor.

The larger betrayal in the novel, however, is that of Cecilia, and it is likewise captured in conspicuously spatial terms. When Emmeline learns of Cecilia's proposed marriage, she is shaken by a vision of their shared home falling apart, timber by timber, 'as small houses are broken up daily to widen the roar of London' (207). Earlier, she had realized that 'this house is Cecilia' and that she herself left nothing there 'but steam in the bath' (192). The novel concludes with Emmeline's anguished but determinedly lethal drive north, in which she ploughs herself and the still-faithless Markie into oncoming traffic. 'An immense idea of departure' (244), we are told, consumed her on this fatal journey. *To the North* depicts Emmeline and Cecilia as enjoying the velocity of the modern and restlessly moving between the domestic and the public. Their joint household falls asunder because Cecilia, in particular, refuses to acknowledge the happiness she derives from its defiant femininity and queer seclusion. Equally, the difficulty of reconciling public and private roles (we learn at the end that Emmeline's business is bankrupt) and of carving out a space for female desire appears to doom Bowen's fatefully allied protagonists to play out, but also be consumed by, the self-obliterating forces and drives of the modern metropolis and its spatial regimes.

Kathleen Coyle (1886–1952) was born in Derry to a Protestant family 'in a *Cherry Orchard* condition', as she acerbically recorded, and lived in London, Paris, Antwerp, Greenwich Village and Philadelphia.[16] Often forced to produce work to earn a living, she wrote popular romances and children's books as well as literary fiction that drew on modernist structures and motifs. *A Flock of Birds*, a novel of tormented waiting and self-reflection, is focalized from the viewpoint of Catherine Munster, whose son Christy is about to be hanged in a Belfast gaol for a republican murder.[17] The scenario is knowingly in dialogue with Lady Gregory's *The Gaol Gate* and James Joyce's *A Portrait of the Artist as a Young Man*, and with Irish nationalist archetypes of the self-immolating mother.

Catherine is torn between detachment and empathy, picking up on but distancing herself from the pain of her children and especially of Cicely, Christy's lover. Catherine conceives of herself as both inside and outside their lives, at once liminal and absolutely central. In the twin impetuses that define her thoughts and emotions, her disengagement is of a piece with her intent fully to embody and thereby to deconstruct maternal pain. As she reflects aphoristically, 'Women hated sacrifice as they hated child-birth but they had to face it' (9). But what seems like Christian stoicism is, in fact, a modernist revaluation of things. Catherine is a devotee of Nietzsche and, like Zarathustra, is concerned with finding the right moment to die and with pursuing the goal of self-overcoming.[18] Unlike the others around her, she does not hope for a reprieve for Christy, but rather worries about his guilt and his readiness for death. For her, Christy is less a Christ-like figure than a potentially transfigured Zarathustra. He is also her alter ego and her inward self, turned inside out. Ultimately, she is reassured that he is ready to die, and that he is honourably shielding others, so is not a murderer.

Catherine's battle to realize her own death through that of her son involves a painful meditation on the meaning of existence, as illuminated by the double subject of mother and son and a debate about the problematic of modernist revolt. She disputes the value of Joyce with her daughter Kathleen – a writer who has lived in Paris – observing that he had begun so differently, '[l]ike Lucifer', and that 'he had not been born like other people, and he had never been re-born' (17). The novel tracks her several visits to her son in gaol in his final days and her return to Gorabbey, the family home in Southern Ireland in which she gave birth to him. She reflects that she never liked the houses she had shared with her deceased husband, Luke, and that Gorabbey represented 'her own intimate minute world' (17). It is associated for her with not only her all-consuming love for Christy but also her unrealized passion for Mitchell, a childhood friend who had introduced her to Eastern philosophy and whose orientalist interests ultimately took him to China. However, even though she derives solace from the beauty and seclusion of Gorabbey, she decides by the end of the novel to abandon it, embracing worldlessness and choosing to live in exile in Provence. The temporary, anonymous spaces with which Catherine is associated in the novel – hotel bedrooms, the courthouse, taxis, Belfast streets and her son's cell – function as objective correlatives for the 'terrible feeling of dislodgement' (105) that constantly besets her. As she steelily lives through the death of Christy, she recognizes that she herself now moves irretrievably 'in a world of hotels and gaols' (145).

A Flock of Birds takes place during World War I. Catherine's second son, Valentine, has fought in the war, and Kathleen is having an affair with André Grenier, a French soldier. Different forms of militarism are thus juxtaposed in this world, which is inherently self-divided but also open and cosmopolitan. The heroine's philosophy of suffering, acceptance and Nietzschean self-supersession is counterpointed by her sharp refutations of heroism and masculine bravado. At one point, she divulges to Cicely that Christy was always good at history: 'all the heroes in turn – from William Tell to the Lord Mayor of Cork' (35). Her stream of consciousness following this disclosure calls up a scrambled quotation from James Joyce: 'Kathleen had said that somebody had said: a sow that eats her own farrow. The lapine that had eaten her young from fright. If they had to be destroyed they were better destroyed at birth' (35). Stephen Dedalus's scornful adage that 'Ireland is the old sow that eats her farrow' is here appropriated and given a feminist cast.[19] In Coyle's reimagining of things, the mother, far from being rapacious and cannibalistic, changes from a sow to a rabbit or wolf and performs an act of savage clemency, killing her young in order to forestall later pain and violence. Coyle purposefully rewrites Joyce, intimating that her oblique and condensed fiction about a mother's anguish, as she psychically enacts her son's execution and strives to rebirth herself through and beyond the cultural and sexual archetypes available to her, is a necessary rescripting of the early achievements of modernism.

The Ladies' Road, *To the North* and *A Flock of Birds* belong irrefutably to a belated phase of Irish feminist modernism in the 1930s. The patterns of recursiveness that they trace out, and their concern with repeating and working through aspects of World War I and the Irish nationalist revolution and their immediate aftermath, self-consciously signal their position in a modernism that comes after. In so doing, they can reflect on and contest aspects of an aesthetic and a radicalism with which they still align themselves. These works of fiction, too, depict women as quintessentially modern subjects operating in the in-between sphere of 'hotels and gaols', and who embody, but also struggle with, the condition of worldlessness that is an ineluctable by-product of the social, economic, sexual and political changes that abound in the twentieth century. Strikingly, these novels posit the difference of femininity as an alternative site of the modern and shine a light on women's quest for different roles as a consequence of altered relations between the public and private spheres. They show that the recesses of the private and inward are not to be feared but can be embraced, plumbed and reconfigured in the artifices and devices of narratives that marry modernist and popular modes. Above all, even though themes of loss, mourning and dislodgement are core elements of these fictions, they coincide in depicting the feminine as a key driver of the restless, but revivifying, energies of modernity.

Notes

1 For varying conceptualizations of *intermodernism* and *late modernism*, see Kristin Bluemel, ed., *Intermodernism: Literary Culture in Mid-Twentieth-Century Britain* (Edinburgh: Edinburgh University Press, 2009); Tyrus Miller, *Late Modernism: Politics, Fiction and the Arts between the World Wars* (Berkeley: University of California Press, 1999) and Tim Armstrong, *Modernism: A Cultural History* (Cambridge: Polity Press, 2005), 35–41.

2 David James, 'Localizing Late Modernism: Interwar Regionalism and the Genesis of the Micro Novel', *Journal of Modern Literature* 32, no. 4 (2009): 43–64.
3 Pamela Hinkson, *The Ladies' Road* (Harmondsworth: Penguin, 1932); Elizabeth Bowen, *To the North* (1932; repr., London: Penguin, 1945); and Kathleen Coyle, *A Flock of Birds* (1930; repr., Dublin: Wolfhound Press, 1995). All further references to these texts will be noted in parentheses.
4 Elizabeth Bowen, *Afterthought: Pieces about Writing* (London: Longmans, 1962), 253.
5 David Spurr, *Architecture and Modern Literature* (Ann Arbor: University of Michigan Press, 2012), 1–49.
6 Hannah Arendt, *The Human Condition* (Chicago: University of Chicago Press, 1958). For a feminist re-evaluation of Arendt's philosophy of action, see Julia Kristeva, *Hannah Arendt: Life Is a Narrative*, trans. Frank Collins (Toronto: University of Toronto Press, 2001).
7 Seyla Benhabib, *The Reluctant Modernism of Hannah Arendt* (London: Sage Publications, 1996). On the concept of worldlessness, see Hannah Arendt, 'What Is Existential Philosophy?', in *Arendt: Essays in Understanding: 1930–1954*, ed. Jerome Kohn (1946; repr., New York: Harcourt Brace and Company, 1994), 163–87.
8 An exhibition of Gray's work hosted by the Pompidou Centre, Paris, 20 February–20 May 2013 and the Irish Museum of Modern Art, Dublin, 12 October 2013–19 January 2014, has drawn renewed attention to it, as have the novel *The Interview* (Dublin: New Island, 2014) by Patricia O'Reilly, reimagining Bruce Chatwin's lost interview with Gray, and Mary McGuckian's biopic of Gray, *The Price of Desire* (POD Film Productions, 2014). On Gray's biography, see Peter Adam, *Eileen Gray: Her Life and Work* (London: Thames and Hudson, 2009) and Jennifer Goff, *Eileen Gray: Her Work and Her World* (Dublin: Irish Academic Press in association with the National Museum of Ireland, 2015).
9 Quoted in Jasmine Rault, *Eileen Gray and the Design of Sapphic Modernity* (Aldershot: Ashgate, 2011), 45.
10 Ibid., 45–49. For room plans and images of the exterior and interior, see Goff, *Eileen Gray*, 262–81.
11 Notoriously, Le Corbusier painted murals on the walls of E.1027 in 1938–39, thus defacing it. Yet, he remained obsessed with the building and strove to have it preserved. See Goff, 282–83.
12 For analyses of the novel, see John Wilson Foster, *Irish Novels 1890–1940: New Bearings in Culture and Fiction* (Oxford: Oxford University Press, 2008), 470–72; Terry Phillips, 'No Man's Land: Irish Women Writers of the First World War', in *No Country for Old Men: Fresh Perspectives on Irish Literature*, eds. Paddy Lyons and Alison O'Malley Younger (Bern: Peter Lang, 2009), 265–80; and Maud Ellmann, 'The Irish Novel 1914–1940', in *The Oxford History of the Novel in English, vol. 4: The Reinvention of the British and Irish Novel, 1880–1940*, eds. Patrick Parrinder and Andrzej Gasiorek (Oxford: Oxford University Press, 2010), 451–72 (462).
13 On the Battles of the Aisne, see Arthur Banks, *A Military Atlas of the First World War* (London: Heinemann Educational Books, 1975), 58–59 and John Keegan, *The First World War* (London: Hutchinson, 1998), 133 and 136–38.
14 For a brilliant analysis of this novel, see Maud Ellmann, *Elizabeth Bowen: The Shadow across the Page* (Edinburgh: Edinburgh University Press, 2003), 96–112.
15 Elizabeth Bowen, 'Regent's Park and St. John's Wood', in *People, Places, Things*, ed. Allan Hepburn (Edinburgh: Edinburgh University Press, 2008), 100–109. For a history of

the garden suburb, see Mireille Galinou, *Cottages and Villas: The Birth of the Garden Suburb* (New Haven: Yale University Press, 2010).
16 Kathleen Coyle, *Magical Realm: An Irish Childhood* (1943; repr., Dublin Wolfhound Press, 1997), 8. An exhibition of Coyle's work in Derry Central Library, 24 February–7 March 2014, was curated by Susan McWilliam, who also made a creative film about her life and writing: https://vimeo.com/87353881
17 For a brief treatment of this novel, see Foster, 477.
18 Friedrich Nietzsche, *Thus Spoke Zarathustra: A Book for Everybody and Nobody*, trans. Graham Parkes (Oxford: Oxford University Press, 2008), 98–100.
19 James Joyce, *A Portrait of the Artist as a Young Man*, ed. John Paul Riquelme (New York: W. W. Norton, 2007), 179.

Chapter 2

'I KNEW WHAT IT MEANT / NOT TO BE AT ALL': DEATH AND THE (MODERNIST) AFTERLIFE IN THE WORK OF IRISH WOMEN POETS OF THE 1940S

Lucy Collins

The term 'modernist afterlife' brings into sharp relief the complex question of literary temporalities. The difficulty in establishing a chronology of modernist writing inevitably troubles our evaluation of its legacy, our ability to tell its 'life' from its 'afterlife'. In different geographical settings, as well as in different art forms, various patterns of formal development and thematic preoccupation can be traced, yet even within these situations there are multiple modernisms, rather than a single, coherent movement. Tyrus Miller has remarked on the capacity of late modernist texts to express the 'aging and decline' of modernism at the same time as they anticipate future developments.[1] For writers in Ireland, many of whom came belatedly to modernism, the durational aspects of the movement may have seemed less clear. Ireland's cultural development in the early decades of the twentieth century was dominated by the Irish Literary Revival, which has usually been seen as antithetical to modernism.[2] However, as Terence Brown points out, both movements play with the intersection between 'historical time and mythological timelessness'.[3] For revivalists and for modernists the relationship between the individual and the collective is placed within a temporal framework; the influence of both movements meant that both lyric and modernist subjects in Irish poetry tend to be understood through their shifting relationship to time. For Irish women poets of the twenties and thirties, the need to negotiate between traditional and experimental forms shed particular light on the temporalities of the female subject. In particular, the representation of death and afterlife allowed women poets to explore anxieties concerning their formation and endurance as creative artists.

The relationship between women poets and modernism in Ireland is, in turn, a complex one. Broadly speaking, international modernism moved through a period in the first decade of the twentieth century when issues of gender and sexuality were of key importance, to a phase around mid-century when modernist texts tended to be viewed within a gender-neutral frame. This pattern was reflected in approaches to literary criticism, too, as Cristanne Miller has observed: 'Much early feminist criticism on female poets argued for the consideration of a separate women's tradition of poetry, constructed either in parallel or in opposition to men's. Later forms of this argument refer to women's counter-strains, or oppositional discourse, within a single poetic tradition'.[4] In Ireland, however, the situation was much more problematic for women writers, since the high point of modernism occurred at a time when women were becoming increasingly marginalized within Irish literary culture, thereby eliminating the power of choice in the formation of a separate tradition. Though women poets had made a significant contribution to revivalist poetics they did not flourish artistically in post-independence Ireland, where aesthetic debates tended to be polarized around whether the future of Irish literature lay in native or experimental expression.[5] The mid-century period was challenging for all Irish writers, but Anne Fogarty has argued persuasively for the serious effects of what she has called Ireland's 'unremittingly androcentric' modernist scene: 'the lost work of Irish women poets cannot simply be salvaged and added victoriously to the imaginary, capacious and all-embracing museum of national literary tradition'.[6] Instead, women's exclusion from both sides of the aesthetic divide emphasizes the tendency to separate experimental modernism from mid-century realist writing in the male-dominated literary debate of the time.[7]

The early years of the Free State were marked by political, economic and cultural isolationism; this, together with a reduced emphasis on the importance of cultural production to national formation, contributed to the persistent view that the mid-century period in Ireland was one of little lasting artistic value. The moribund, or at least truncated, state of native publishing and printing seemed to confirm this impression. After the collapse of Maunsel, a stalwart of late revivalist publishing, there was no dedicated publisher of poetry until Dolmen Press was founded in 1951. In addition, opportunities to publish in Britain were radically curtailed during World War II.[8] Periodical publication in Ireland offered greater opportunities but, even though some of the most prominent modernist magazines in Britain and America were edited by women, in Ireland they had little direct involvement in printing after the demise of Cuala Press.[9] This meant that male publishers and editors had a disproportionate level of control over what was printed and read in Ireland, leading to reduced opportunities for women to contribute to literary and critical cultures. Although the publications that were most hospitable to work by women were conservative in outlook, such as the long-lived *Dublin Magazine*, women were acutely aware of the value, or even the necessity, of negotiating between a range of creative styles and strategies rather than aligning themselves with one. This meant that compromises between gradual change and radical stylistic innovation were bound to occur.

The women whose work is the focus of this essay – Mary Devenport O'Neill (1879–1967), Rhoda Coghill (1903–2000) and Sheila Wingfield (1906–1992) – combine elements of formal regularity with glimpses of the fragmented subjectivity that we associate with modernism. Importantly, too, they had very different artistic careers, and their relationships to the networks of writing and publishing were also divergent. There is no assumed unity of purpose here but, rather, evidence of individual writers contesting the literary establishment in a range of ways. Yet their concern to interrogate the practice of poetry itself is significant, and their treatment of the individual human subject innovative and challenging. The poems I have chosen to explore here all address, in some way, the issue of afterlife itself: they are concerned with mortality and with its implications for creative process and literary legacy. In the modernist context this theme is an important one: intergenerational artistic relationships draw attention to death and rebirth as cultural tropes; experientially, two world wars confirmed the fragility of both individual human lives and Western civilization itself. Women had a complicated relationship to war during this period: although many occupied medical or administrative roles, they were not directly involved in the fighting and thus bore witness to the events in unique ways. Specifically, women's identification as mourners emphasized the emotional impact of violence on entire communities. Modernist poetry often engages directly with acts of mourning at the same time as it acknowledges the representational challenges this engagement involves. Sarah Cole identifies restlessness as an important dimension of literary depiction of violent death, 'as if the fact of arriving at a representational strategy adequate to the violence of life is itself a step toward accepting it'.[10]

In the Irish context this particular subject is a nuanced one, given the revolutionary origins of the state and the prolonged violence of the civil-war period.[11] Thus, there is a marked difference between the idealism of revivalist work of the late nineteenth century and the anxiety evident in poetry produced during the Anglo–Irish war and the civil war that followed independence. W. B. Yeats's 'Meditations in Time of Civil War' is the most significant example of this representational unease: 'somewhere / a man is killed or a house burned / yet no clear fact to be discerned'.[12] Eva Gore-Booth's poetry also moves away from its revivalist roots as she confronts the moral failings that both militarism and revolution express.[13] Robert Buch's argument that the response to violence and suffering is not only horror and awe but also states of 'transcendence and revelation' especially applies to Gore-Booth's work.[14] For both these poets, though, the physicality of death is an important dimension of their acts of witness. Modernist ambiguity concerning the representation of mortality extends to the disposal of the dead – in the words of David Sherman, the corpse becomes 'a site of ideological recalcitrance and disorientation' not easily made subject to the forces of rationalization or secularization.[15] This figuration of the corpse relates closely to the processes by which the dead are remembered, both privately and publicly. For Irish poets writing in the early decades of the newly independent state the moral obligation to attend to the dead was countered by the need to forget them in the interests of a collective future. Yet the closure that death rituals suggest in fact also facilitates the dead's afterlife among the living.[16] Thus, a concern with mortality became at once the means by which the past could be transcended and acknowledged by these writers.

As well as heeding the specific conditions of recent Irish history, poets writing in 1940s Ireland were acutely aware of the country's neutrality in World War II. The war gave rise to a period of unprecedented loss of life internationally and created a moral dilemma that few Irish poets chose to explore directly. Modernist techniques allowed the widespread destruction of the period, and the challenges to representation that it presented, to be registered in form and language. Thus, the responses to death to be found in the work of Irish modernist women poets diverge significantly from the writing of their revivalist counterparts, for whom a late-Victorian sentimentality attended the subject of mortality, even when writing of World War I. For modernist women the representation of death could also be a means to interrogate the terms of contemporary artistic representation and to explore the difficulties of adopting a fragmented subjectivity when the female writing self – and her artistic legacy – was itself under question.

At both ends of the modernist spectrum, the representation of death and dissolution preoccupied women. Temple Lane, a poet who often seemed entrapped by traditional lyric modes, chose the death ritual as the pivotal emblem of her 1940 collection, *Fisherman's Wake*. The title poem is indicative of aspects of Lane's recognizable style and subject matter: a rural setting with strong emphasis on sensory response, an evocation of a world of tradition and folk practices, a fixed verse form using iambic pentameter and full rhyme. Yet this poem meditates on the suddenness of death, where the bleak seascape – 'I heard more sorrow in the calling sea' – is set against the conviviality of human interaction.[17] The irony of a man, once reckless and loud, rendered saintly by prayer and death ritual becomes part of a larger consideration by Lane of the relationship between folly and wisdom – wisdom that is only possible in the moments before death, when the energies of life have ceased. The liminal states that Lane addresses conventionally here are explored in more innovative ways by Blanaid Salkeld (1880–1959), the most formally experimental of the Irish women working at this time. Her 1937 volume, ... *the engine is left running*, explores the randomness of human meaning – a topic that in Salkeld's poems of the 1940s is specifically linked to the tensions between the abundant energies of creation and the limitations of fixed positions, linguistically and culturally.[18] Often construed in formal terms as an undoing of selfhood in language, this process acknowledges the risk-taking involved in artistic expression: 'I thankfully retreat / Into a gloomy hazard like the tomb's'.[19]

As in the case of Blanaid Salkeld, Mary Devenport O'Neill often contemplated the difficulties of rendering existential states in language and also engaged in a variety of artistic practices throughout her career. Born in 1879, she published just one collection of poetry, *Prometheus and Other Poems*, in 1929, and a relatively small number of single poems after that date. 'Scene-shifter Death' is among those late works and was written when Devenport O'Neill was in her mid-sixties. Since she was a talented painter and a writer of verse plays, it is important to see this late work as reflecting her larger artistic preoccupations and, therefore, as expressive of what poetic form specifically can offer to the meditation on mortality. In its depiction of the subject moving between states, this poem invokes not just the existence of an afterlife, but also a subtle refutation of such fixed ideas of progression and chronology. The poet's approach to mortality is one of waiting – not passively, but rather with a sense of attuned observation. This is less a poem about death, than it is a meditation on the power of the imagination to erase temporal limitations:

> As it is true that I, like all, must die,
> I crave that death may take me unawares
> At the very end of some transcendent day;
> May creep upon me when I least suspect,
> And, with slick fingers light as feather tips,
> Unfasten every little tenuous bolt
> That held me all my years to this illusion
> Of flesh and blood and air and land and sea.
>
> I'd have death work meticulously too –
> Splitting each moment into tenths of tenths,
> Replacing each infinitesimal fragment
> Of old dream-stuff with new.

> So subtly will the old be shed
> That I'll dream on and never know I'm dead.[20]

The poem opens with an acknowledgment of the inevitability of death, yet the speaker in fact seeks to avoid conscious thought, to remain 'unaware' of the experience she is undergoing. This dissociation of thought and action is a particular preoccupation for women poets: by dwelling on the inner life of thought and feeling, women poets created a space for imaginative exploration not afforded them in public life.

In Devenport O'Neill's work the apparent simplicity of language and form is deceptive. Here, the entwined processes of intellect and intuition are both deployed and interrogated. The poem implicitly expresses the desire for the fullest enjoyment of life, postponing death to 'the very end of some transcendent day'. This version of a sonnet plays with our expectations of smoothness and regularity, however. Rhythm and rhyme run counter to one another: the rhythm begins in iambic pentameter, before slipping in lines 12 and 13; conversely, a clear rhyme scheme takes some time to become established. Yet this strategy fittingly expresses the transition the poem seeks to explore – the rhythm of life becoming unsteady as the inevitability of death asserts itself in the final rhyming couplet.

In a shift that recognizes life as the illusion, the poem enacts a significant change in perspective that, since it appears in the first eight lines of the poem, disturbs the normal expectation of the sonnet form. This temporal interference is what the poet explicitly wishes: she imagines personified death breaking down the units of time, while artistically she pre-empts this dismantling of order. This occurs at a formal level, too: the explicit separation of the lines into sections of eight, four and two enacts the diminishing of the self that impending death will bring. This subtle awareness of the dissolution process, and its appearance here as both theme and form, is important in the modernist context because this process emphasizes the links between temporal and subjective states. The notion of life as illusion introduces new representational challenges for which spare modernist language provides an appropriate mode, stripping back the surface texture of the experiential world. For Devenport O'Neill, a minimalist approach to language allows the details of everyday existence to acquire conceptual significance.

Rhoda Coghill's understated work also creates a world that is intensely present to its readers and from which the relationship between space and time can be interrogated. In 'Burren, Co. Clare' the speaker describes herself as 'drift[ing] on a quiet wave / Of happening' that has shaped this unique landscape; in urban environments, too, the sense of movement and stasis is present in both the imagery of the poem and its rhythms.[21] The close links between bodily experience and temporality yield to a concern with mortality. 'To His Ghost, Seen After Delirium' reprises the myth of Orpheus and Eurydice: in recalling Orpheus to the world of the senses, the speaker acknowledges her own position between life and death, where 'wanton thoughts / and not-thoughts, which would steal from me / all memory of being, and at last / steal me from life'.[22] Here, losing the memory of life precedes death itself, so that the process of mental detachment becomes a preparation for her physical demise. Implicitly, too, the relationship between thought and feeling is explored – the dynamics of lyric subjectivity and the intellectual project of modernism contest one another in Coghill's work in ways that draw attention to the subtlety of her formal strategies. For these, the poet-speaker demands recognition: the 'crown of olives' that recognizes her artistic achievement. Yet the nature of this demand suggests her awareness that it will not be fulfilled.[23]

From the dialogic underpinning of 'To His Ghost, Seen After Delirium' comes the singular meditation of 'Dead'. This is Coghill's starkest representation of dissolution and, although it is the least oblique in expression, it is also the work that most distinctly troubles the idea of singular human subjectivity.

> I was the moon.
> A shadow hid me
> and I knew what it meant
> not to be at all.
> The moon in eclipse is sad,
> and sinless.
> There is no passion in her plight.[24]

The first line of the poem contradicts established forms of meaning and identity, suggesting the movement of the speaking self into an imagined space of concealment. The subject position here is defined by otherness and loss, as well as being directly linked to female identity. It offers the perspective of death as a temporal process – a future from which there can be no return for the subject. But it also figures death spatially as a removal from the possibility of human connection, a state of invisibility. This dynamic draws attention to the troubling process of constructing and representing subjectivity for a number of these women. In this, however, they are prescient in their treatment of the subject as one of universal concern.

While visual motion is an important aspect of many of Coghill's poems, here the sense is not one of dynamism but rather of slow, inexorable movement. This suggests, much as Devenport O'Neill's poem indicated, human powerlessness in the face of temporality and change. Neither poet assumes a passive attitude but, rather, an attentive stoicism concerning the passage of time. Again, the relationship between conscious and unconscious states is interrogated here, as the subject is described as 'eyeless behind no eyelids / has neither sleeping nor waking'.²⁵ Yet, in attempting to come to terms with the experience of death and with what the state of nonbeing might entail, Coghill considers a world the opposite of Devenport O'Neill's. While the earlier poem portrayed death and life as overlapping states, this text exaggerates the gulf between them, trying to come to terms with death as a complete absence, or as complete emptiness: 'no body, parts, nor passions, / no loving, perceiving, / having, nor being'.²⁶ In this respect Coghill is attempting something radical, yet the description of existence devoid of its sensory power only serves to emphasize that power in language. This is confirmed in the final image of the ship under water, drifting and sinking toward tangible reality, to the weeds and stones on the seabed. Coghill's grounding in sensory materiality is a return to imaginative bedrock, and an acknowledgement of the strangeness of these elements.

Like Coghill, Sheila Wingfield also works in a combination of lyric and modernist modes, but where Coghill often represents the passage of time in terms of natural cycles, Wingfield is preoccupied by classical worlds and the passing of civilizations – a long view of history that may have been shaped by the uneasy position of ascendancy families within the independent Irish state. Born in England, but later the wife of the Ninth Viscount Powerscourt, Wingfield was doubly marginalized in mid-century Ireland, and the trajectory of her work traces the toll this isolation took on her creative life. 'Odysseus Dying', among the earliest of Wingfield's poems, is quintessential in its uniting of emotional and intellectual ground: here, death is figured as a moment of experiential intensity in which one's earliest memories overtake more prominent life events. Wingfield's first volume, *Poems*, published in 1938, reveals a preoccupation with mortality that would evolve in important ways over the ensuing decades. The three-part structure of 'The Dead' – another early poem – pursues a particular enquiry: the dead are first effaced, they are 'thinned […] to so fine a mist / That, harried in a drove, / They run ahead'.²⁷ The wind, evoked four times here, whips away lingering impressions, yet still the dead remind the living, however fleetingly, of their own final end. In a turn resembling Devenport O'Neill's seamless shift from life to afterlife, Wingfield considers how the dead may be both aloof from the 'childishness' of 'live and woken things' and are even distanced from their own past selves that the living strive to recapture. Despite this, we measure the meaning of our lives against their endurance beyond death, even sacrificing attention to the present moment in order to do so.

Wingfield's second volume, the striking sequence *Beat Drum, Beat Heart* (1946), reveals the significance of the war period as a catalyst for aesthetic change. This long, four-part poem juxtaposes the relationship between public and private versions of selfhood, exploring how the individual relates to the wider world, both in war and in peace. In contrast to the darkness and confusion that shapes the experience of men in the first two sections of the poem, the perspective of women emphasizes both an intellectual and an intuitive engagement. In spite of these signs of promise, however, many of Wingfield's poems after this point would register the inextricable links between philosophical questioning and the confrontation of mortality.

A quarter century later, 'Darkness' is concerned not with lasting memory but with failures of understanding, with the question of how human fault can be balanced in the absence of an afterlife:

> And what will mitigate my life's long fault,
> > I beg you, if authority's black stuffs
> > Should fail to reconcile me
> > To the final blindfold?
> > Cassock and mortar-board
> > Are under the same burden,
> > Suffer the same problem, as ourselves;
> > While conscience comes at night and stings
> > The darkness: much as Carthage, ploughed under,
> > Was then sown with salt.[28]

Neither knowledge nor faith can explain death – religious and scholarly institutions are subject to the same limitations as the individual, both in terms of intuition and intellect. The poet chooses Carthage as her key metaphor in this opening part of the poem. Destroyed by the Romans in 146 BCE it was re-founded to become one of the most important cities of the empire, thus providing apt expression for Wingfield's interest in how civilizations renew themselves, how they find another form. This is linked, in her own case, to the way in which the resources of ancient history can be made her own – a modernist impulse to reuse the materials of the past for new personal and cultural meaning. The poet evokes other modes of understanding, too – 'a conjurors' cloak; the Queen of Spades' – testing the power of magical or occult practices as means of explaining what religion and culture cannot.

Wingfield's construction of meaning remains largely cerebral here, however, and at this stage in the poem the phenomenal world is only useful as a series of signs. When the speaker does 'enter' the world in the fullest sensory way, it is to project a scene in which she is both present and absent:

> Let me predict my funeral weather
> > Biting at black coats,

> With the new box – cave dark and cupboard thick –
> Brought to a lurching halt
> Near brambles and tipped headstones in the family
> Burial ground, and flurryings
> Of shocked and interrupted jackdaws …
>   With so much still unlearned, ignored;
> So many moments of compassion skimped
> By me or lost; this private graveyard seems
> An apt memorial, with its church a ruin,
> And its quiet cracked
> By the quick clatter of black wings
> In crude assault.[29]

The description of the interment relates to the burial ground of the Wingfield family adjacent to the Powerscourt estate. The poet's presence and absence is expressive of her sense of marginality within the family, yet the 'new box' reflects some of the suffocation she felt in her particular personal circumstance and cultural moment. This poem, unlike Wingfield's earlier text, immerses the self fully in this experience, scrutinizing not the larger trappings of reputation but the darker misgivings of the moral self. What she is anxious about are sins of omission, fittingly punished not by retribution but by emptiness, evoked by the ruinous church and its dark birds.

The dissolution of subjectivity is an enduring preoccupation for these modernist Irish women poets and embraces both imaginative power and imaginative failure. All three poets had truncated writing lives: both Coghill and Devenport O'Neill published just one full-length collection, while Wingfield's output dwindled from the 1960s onward. All contemplate the struggle to write and the fear of creative diminishment. Within all these poems the insubstantial nature of unitary subjectivity emerges, and with it a corresponding sense that the afterlife is tied in complex ways to our self-perception in this life. For these women poets, then, the modernist afterlife is not a place they can rest in peace.

Notes

1. Tyrus Miller, *Late Modernism: Politics, Fiction, and the Arts between the World Wars* (Berkeley: University of California Press, 1999), loc. 89, Kindle edition.
2. John Wilson Foster, in his essay 'Irish Modernism', notes 'the coincidence of Irish Revivalism and international Modernism', suggesting that, though the revival was seen as an instance of belated Romanticism, it addressed modernity in significant ways. Foster, *Colonial Consequences: Essays in Irish Literature and Culture* (Dublin: Lilliput Press, 1991), 44–59 (45). Later studies, such as Edwina Keown and Carol Taaffe's *Irish Modernism*,

make a strong case for the interdependence of revivalist and modernist modes. See *Irish Modernism: Origins, Contexts, Publics* (Bern: Peter Lang, 2009).

3 Terence Brown, 'Ireland, Modernism and the 1930s', in *Modernism and Ireland: The Poetry of the 1930s*, eds. Patricia Coughlan and Alex Davis (Cork: Cork University Press, 1995), 32.

4 Cristanne Miller, 'Gender, Sexuality and the Modernist Poem', in *The Cambridge Companion to Modernist Poetry*, eds. Alex Davis and Lee M. Jenkins (Cambridge: Cambridge University Press, 2007), 76.

5 Revivalist women poets such as Katharine Tynan (1858–1931) and Dora Sigerson Shorter (1866–1918) were significant literary figures during their own lifetimes, publishing for a range of different readerships. The printing of poetry by women contracted sharply from the late 1920s onward and did not expand again until the 1960s. See *Women in Modern Irish Culture: A Database of Irish Women's Writing, 1800–2005*, accessed 2 November 2014, http://www2.warwick.ac.uk/fac/arts/history/irishwomenwriters/

6 Anne Fogarty, 'Gender, Irish Modernism and the Poetry of Denis Devlin', in *Modernism and Ireland: The Poetry of the 1930s*, eds. Patricia Coughlan and Alex Davis (Cork: Cork University Press, 1995), 210.

7 For detailed examination of the implications of these gendered debates, see Anne Mulhall, '"The well-known, old, but still unbeaten track": Women Poets and Irish Periodical Culture in the Mid-twentieth Century', *Irish University Review* 42, no. 1 (2012): 32–52.

8 The shortage of appropriate materials reduced the quantity and range of publication in Britain during the war. Though major publishers honoured their long-term relationships with Irish writers, opportunities to publish in journals and newspapers were greatly curtailed. See Clair Wills, *That Neutral Island: A Cultural History of Ireland during the Second World War* (Cambridge, MA: Harvard University Press), 277–98.

9 In the United States Harriet Monroe founded *Poetry* in 1912, while Margaret Anderson and Jane Heap founded the *Little Review* in 1914. Other modernist publishing ventures that featured women were the Hogarth Press in England – which Virginia Woolf ran with her husband, Leonard – and the Dun Emer Press (later the Cuala Press) in Ireland, a collaboration between Evelyn Gleeson and the Yeats sisters. The only poetry publishing enterprise in mid-century Ireland to be run by a woman was Gayfield Press, which poet Blanaid Salkeld founded with her son, the artist Cecil French Salkeld.

10 Sarah Cole, *At the Violet Hour: Modernism and Violence in England and Ireland* (Oxford: Oxford University Press, 2012), 4–5.

11 The execution of the leaders of the 1916 Rising caused a profound shift in support for the republican cause in Ireland. This, together with increasing opposition to Ireland's participation in World War I, helped Sinn Féin to win a large majority of the Irish seats in the 1918 elections. Refusing to sit at Westminster, these members assembled in Dublin to form a separate Irish parliament. After affirming the foundation of an Irish republic the new government found itself in direct opposition to the British military in a war of independence. Following a truce in July 1921 the Anglo-Irish Treaty was signed on 6 December 1921. Disagreement over the terms of the treaty caused civil war in the 26 counties from June 1922 to April 1923, a war that ended in a victory for the pro-Treaty forces.

12 W. B. Yeats, *The Collected Poems of W. B. Yeats*, ed. Richard Finneran (New York: Macmillan, 1983), 205.

13 Eva Gore-Booth's first book, *Poems*, published in 1898, conformed to revivalist expectations in both subject matter and style. The collections that followed in 1904 and 1905 continued to emphasize the sensory potential of the lyric mode. As her engagement

with education and social work deepened, Gore-Booth's poetry evolved to become at once more outspoken and more spiritually inclined. See, in particular, *Broken Glory* (Dublin: Maunsel and Co., 1918).

14 Robert Buch, *The Pathos of the Real: On the Aesthetics of Violence in the Twentieth Century* (Baltimore: Johns Hopkins University Press, 2010), 18.
15 David Sherman, *In a Strange Room: Modernism's Corpses and Mortal Obligation* (Oxford: Oxford University Press, 2014), 5.
16 Robert Pogue Harrison argues that the dead, to be truly dead, must be made to disappear: 'It is only because their bodies have a place to go, that their souls or images or words may attain an afterlife of sorts among the living'. Harrison, *The Dominion of the Dead* (London and Chicago: University of Chicago Press, 2003), 1.
17 Temple Lane, *Fisherman's Wake* (Dublin and Cork: Talbot Press, 1940), 3.
18 Salkeld published no full-length collection between 1937 and 1955, though she produced a number of single poems during the 1940s. This evaluation takes account of her work from the late thirties to the early fifties as indicative of her creative preoccupations during the period.
19 Lucy Collins, ed., *Poetry by Women in Ireland: A Critical Anthology 1870–1970* (Liverpool: Liverpool University Press, 2012), 221.
20 Ibid., 207.
21 Rhoda Coghill, *The Bright Hillside* (Dublin: Hodges Figgis, 1948), 3.
22 Ibid., 20. H. D.'s poem 'Eurydice' similarly moves from passive to assertive modes. H. D. *Collected Poems 1912–1944*, ed. Louis L. Martz (New York: New Directions, 1986), 51–55.
23 Kathy D'Arcy examines Coghill's exploration of the woman artist in this poem and in 'Lamenting a Sterile Muse' in '"Almost Forgotten Names": Irish Women Poets of the 1930s, 1940s and 1950s', in *Irish Literature: Feminist Perspectives*, eds. Patricia Coughlan and Tina O'Toole (Dublin: Carysfort Press, 2008), 118–19.
24 Coghill, 26.
25 Ibid., 26.
26 Ibid., 26.
27 Lucy Collins, ed., *Sheila Wingfield: Poems* (Dublin: Liberties Press, 2013), 44–45.
28 Ibid., 87.
29 Ibid., 87–88.

Chapter 3

'WHATEVER IS GIVEN / CAN ALWAYS BE REIMAGINED': SEAMUS HEANEY'S INDEFINITE MODERNISM

Leah Flack

> Whatever is given
> Can always be reimagined.
> — Seamus Heaney, 'The Settle Bed'[1]

At a moment when theories of postmodernism seemed to offer the most comprehensive assessment of post-war literature and culture, Seamus Heaney argued for the continued relevance of the modernist project. In a 1986 essay, 'The Impact of Translation', Heaney evaluates the legacies of modernism:

> The breach made by the war years did not succeed in dissociating Lowell and his contemporaries living under the roof of English from the enterprise of the great modernists. Pound and Eliot and Joyce may have regarded themselves as demolitionists of sorts but from a later perspective they turned out to be conservationists, keeping open lines to the classical inheritance of European literature. In getting ready for the end of the world, they extended its life expectancy, indefinitely.[2]

Heaney's historical approach to the European literary tradition leads him to view modernism and postmodernism as productive moments in its survival and expansion. He draws attention to modernism as a movement poised between tradition and innovation, the past and the future. He returned to the modernists over the course of his career to determine his own role in continuing their work of cultural conservation. Reading the potential multiple meanings of his final word here – 'indefinitely' – signals an important tension in this ongoing evaluation of modernism. First, the modernists made possible an indefinite, potentially unending lifespan for the European literary tradition, a tradition in which he could participate in the years of the Troubles. However, the outcome of this modernist inheritance may be viewed as indefinite, uncertain or ambiguous.

In recent years, the field of modernist studies has shared Heaney's sense that the inheritance of the modernist project remains indefinite (in both senses). For example, a recent *PMLA* article by David James and Urmila Seshagiri tracks how contemporary novelists such as Tom McCarthy, Ian McEwan and Zadie Smith 'reassess and remobilize narratives of modernism'.[3] Heaney offers a compelling case study that extends this conversation in terms of genre, geography and history. Beginning in the 1960s and continuing into the twenty-first century, his critical and creative engagement with modernism shows him doing precisely what James and Seshagiri identify as the work of twenty-first century metamodernism: 'open[ing] up alternative futures' for his poetry 'through engagements with [his] modernist past'.[4] Heaney's open-ended engagements with his modernist past suggest that modernism was important to him precisely because it was an indefinite movement that demanded an invigorating and continuous reappraisal. Modernism never appeared to be a stable, unified archive in his view: his writings show him reading James Joyce, T. S. Eliot, Osip Mandelstam and other modernists in dynamic, sometimes conflicted relation to one another as distinct models of a modernist past that he would preserve and extend. In this way, Heaney's writings have creatively anticipated more recent critical conversations that have transformed a static sense of modernism into multiple modernisms and have also raised questions about the future of both modernism and modernist studies.

In a 1974 essay, Heaney called for an urgent renewal of the work of Yeats, Joyce, and other early twentieth-century writers to 'define and interpret the present by bringing it into significant relationship with the past'.[5] In the opening decades of his career, he experimented with different ways of bringing the past and present into significant relation as he sought to articulate and defend the value of poetry at a violent moment in Irish history. The modernists were part of his literary past, but they also offered him a set of models for generating useful connections between history, the present and the future.

The poems of *Station Island* and the essays of *Government of the Tongue* suggest that he turned to Osip Mandelstam when he exhausted his readings of Eliot and Joyce as modernist forebears. Although some critics have tended to focus on Heaney's attraction to Mandelstam as a symbolic figure of moral courage in an era of totalitarian oppression, he also saw Mandelstam as a critical alternative to Anglo-Irish modernism, and one who helped him to overcome what he saw as the limits of that project.[6] Mandelstam helped him to cultivate a creative, playful and (borrowing a term Heaney used to describe

Mandelstam) 'exultant' mode of negotiating the demands of history and poetry. In the 1980s, Heaney came to understand Eliot and Pound's approach to the literary past as static, authoritative and entrenched. At the same time, he discovered in Mandelstam a way of reading the past and present as protean and free. Heaney's twenty-year engagement with Mandelstam's bold 'modernist creation of tradition' (in Clare Cavanagh's phrase) helped him to find a path towards psychological liberation and to conclude in 'The Settle Bed' that, 'whatever is given' – which might include one's own past, the literary tradition, contemporary politics and the future – 'Can always be reimagined'.[7]

In Heaney's assessment, an Eliotic model of modernism was sharply limited by its commitment to and embodiment of potentially stultifying ideals of mastery and authority. Early on, Heaney found himself overwhelmed and intimidated by Eliot's poems: in Heaney's school days, Eliot stood as an image of an authoritarian gatekeeper of sorts, whose poems made him feel his 'unfittedness [...] as a reader or writer' and an 'inarticulate ache towards knowing, towards adequacy, towards fitting oneself out as a reader of modern poetry'.[8] Heaney's essays concentrate on Eliot not only as a poet, as a representative of a modernist canon, but also as a reverent reader of the European canon (as Heaney notes, 'If Eliot did not help me to write, he did help me learn what it means to read.').[9] Eliot's Dante, Heaney noted, was 'stern and didactic'.[10] Heaney evaluated Eliot and Pound as readers and concluded that they saw Dante as the 'repository of tradition' and came to him 'early, as students, as young men, they studied him in an academic context; they wore his poem like a magic garment to protect themselves from the contagion of parochial English and American culture; and, finally, they canonized him as the aquiline patron of international modernism'.[11] Heaney's responses to Pound and Eliot reveal his scepticism about the academic and institutional processes of canonization that tended to treat the literary tradition as static, inflexible and authoritative.

Although it might be easy to conclude from Heaney's essays that he was mostly critical in his reading of Eliot, he did turn to Eliot's poetry as one example of how to bring the past and present into significant relation, a task that acquired new weight in the era of the Troubles. The volume *North* (1975) shows him struggling to discover a form and language that would enable him to respond to contemporary Irish history without being paralyzed by it (particularly after he decided to leave Northern Ireland and move to County Wicklow in 1972). As Anthony Cuda shows, the original epigraph to the first section of *North* is a passage from 'Little Gidding', which includes the following:

> This is the use of memory:
> For liberation, not less of love but expanding

Of love beyond desire, and so liberation
From the future as well as the past.
Thus, love of a country
Begins as attachment to our own field of action
And comes to find that action of little importance
Though never indifferent.
History may be servitude,
History may be freedom.[12]

On a typescript edition of *North*, Heaney cancelled this epigraph. Given the epigraph's original position on the page facing 'Antaeus', it seems likely that it highlights the volume's exploration of the 'use of memory', seen not only in its appropriation of myth in 'Antaeus' and 'Hercules and Antaeus', but also in the volume's bog poems (e.g., 'The Tollund Man' and 'Bog Queen'). All of these poems try out different ways of refracting the present through representations of the past to perform an archaeological inquiry into the origins of contemporary violence (by identifying, as most readings tend to, the Irish with Antaeus and the British with Hercules – also using poems such as 'Punishment' and 'Bog Queen' to mediate a response to the tarring of Catholic women in Northern Ireland). Eliot's poem proposes that memory might be an engine of liberation from both the past and future. The poems of *North*, however, veer from this Eliotic agenda by presenting a drama of a thwarted, frustrated desire for liberation: reading these poems, we feel the past as a weight and a challenge to the poet that he cannot fully negotiate.

Station Island (1984) shows Heaney sifting through different modernist legacies to discover an enabling, liberating use of memory. The first section in *Station Island* features direct and indirect references to both Mandelstam and Joyce, among others (in poems such as 'Chekhov on Sakhalin' and 'Shelf Life'); 'Station Island,' the volume's second section, culminates in a memorable encounter with Joyce; and the final section ('Sweeney Redivivus') displays an affinity with Mandelstam's irreverent use of the past. This volume foregrounds images of fleeing, flying and leaping to convey an experience of psychological liberation that is generally absent from *North*. As Heaney noted of 'Station Island', 'The pattern was the simple one of setting out, encountering tests and getting through to a new degree of independence; on such matters, Joyce is our chief consultant.'[13] At the end of this sequence, a figure of Joyce appears to free Heaney from his burdens, telling him, '"let others wear the sackcloth and the ashes / Let go, let fly, forget. / You've listened long enough. Now strike your note".'[14] The poem echoes Joyce's own images of flight – such as Stephen's famous ambition to 'fly by those nets' of 'nationality, language, religion'.¹⁵ However, the poem's phrasing suggests more of a releasing of burdens – to 'let fly' – rather than an active attempt to follow Stephen's example by fleeing. The pilgrim describes his reluctance to move beyond Joyce's influence by citing his allegiance to 'a moment in Stephen's diary for April thirteenth'.¹⁶ The passage to which he refers – a passage written on Heaney's birthday – expresses Stephen's moral indignation about his conversation with the dean of studies regarding the word 'tundish', and concludes in frustration: 'Damn the dean of studies and his funnel! What did he come here for to teach us his own language or learn it from us? Damn him one way or the other!'¹⁷ Heaney identifies with Stephen's sense that he is dispossessed by his knowledge of the language of the colonizer decoupled from the authority to assert that knowledge. In response, the poem envisions that Joyce steps in to free him from this bind:

'Who cares,'
he jeered, 'any more? The English language
belongs to us. You are raking at dead fires,

a waste of time for somebody your age.
That subject people stuff is a cod's game,
Infantile, like your peasant pilgrimage.

You lose more of yourself than you redeem
doing the decent thing. Keep at a tangent [...]'¹⁸

This ending positions itself as a turning point of sorts, one that frees the poem from a Joycean conflict within the English language without dictating what comes next. It is clear that at this turning point in Heaney's career, to borrow a phrase from James and Seshagiri, he 'reassess[ed] and remobilize[d] narratives of modernism' to open a new, undetermined future for his art. Moving from 'Station Island' to 'Sweeney Redivivus' suggests that once Heaney is freed from the conflicts that threatened to paralyze Stephen, he learns to 'keep at a tangent' by turning to an outside context, a foreign language and a distant poet, Osip Mandelstam.

This liberating experience in 'Station Island' paves the way for the 'Sweeney Redivivus' poems, a sequence of poems that Heaney wrote during and after his translation of *Sweeney Astray*. These poems suggest his movement towards an exultant model of modernism that depended on reading Joyce and Eliot in dynamic relation to Mandelstam. I take this term from one of Heaney's interviews with Dennis O'Driscoll, in which he notes:

> There was certainly a liberation in [Mandelstam's] prose. It was metaphorical, impressionistic, exultant even. Without realizing it, I'd been under the sway of T. S. Eliot and his repressive attitude towards 'appreciation' and 'impressionistic' criticism, but Mandelstam changed that. His comparison of the mind in the act of composition to a fugitive escaping across a river jammed with Chinese junks. That gave me permission, as they say, to do a bit of exulting of my own.[19]

'Exult' etymologically implies (from the Latin *ex-* + *salire*) 'to leap up, to leap out'. Heaney read Mandelstam's exultant writings as a joyous gesture of leaping beyond the boundaries of the familiar. His writings about Mandelstam show his sustained interest in the joyful imaginative and psychological liberation he sensed in Mandelstam's way of reading and remaking the European tradition. For example, Heaney compares Mandelstam's reading of Dante to Eliot's academic readings and notes that Mandelstam produced 'the most inspiring, the most delightfully approachable re-creation we could hope for'.[20] He argues:

> What Mandelstam does [in contrast to Eliot and Pound] is to bring [Dante] from the pantheon back to the palate; he makes your mouth water to read him. [...] He transmits a fever of excitement in the actual phonetic reality of the work and shares with us the sensation of his poet's delight turning into a sort of giddy critical wisdom.[21]

Two works that Heaney turns to frequently in his discussions of Mandelstam illustrate this practice of 'giddy critical wisdom': these are an early Homeric poem from the teens and the enigmatic 1934 essay, 'Conversation about Dante', which might be seen as a manifesto of exultant modernism.[22] The fact that Heaney was drawn to these works suggests his interest in Mandelstam's way of negotiating the demands of the literary tradition as he brought the past and present into significant relationship.

Mandelstam wrote 'Conversation about Dante' in 1934, the year he was arrested for speaking a poem mocking Stalin (for which he was sentenced to internal exile) and the year when the All-Union Congress of Soviet Writers declared socialist realism the only form of official art. This historical context helps make manifest the essay's implicit connections between literary and political authority in its promotion of Dante as a figure of unofficial, unorthodox, subversive writing. Mandelstam uses Dante to protest against various intertwined forms of literary, political and social authority and authoritativeness. He begins by attempting to unsettle the various canonical images of Dante that persisted in literary history: 'Dante's fame', Mandelstam notes (part of what attracted Pound and Eliot to Dante, as Heaney argued), 'has been the greatest obstacle to understanding him and to a profound study of his work'.²³ Mandelstam's rejection of Dante's institutional authority in favour of what he called his artistic credibility helped him to articulate a theory of language grounded in semantic instability, musical resonance and untranslatability. On more than one occasion, Heaney quoted Mandelstam's statement from this essay that 'any given word is a bundle, and meaning sticks out in various directions, not aspiring toward any single official point'.²⁴ Mandelstam's encounter with Dante's Italian nurtured this resonant theory of language, which he used to protest against various forms of official meaning.

Although Mandelstam could read and speak Italian, he was well aware that 'foreigners' cannot 'penetrate the ultimate secret of foreign poetry'. He noted, 'we cannot be judges, cannot have the last word'.²⁵ And it seems this was precisely the point. His reverence for the musicality of Dante's Italian was intensified by his perpetual sense of being an outsider to this music, of not being fully able to lay claim to Dante's language. Mandelstam's inability to claim readerly authority over Dante supported his wider argument in this essay against authority of various kinds. Mandelstam's irreverent, joyous reading of Dante offered Heaney a vision of the literary tradition as open, unfinished and anti-authoritarian. This vision proved to be a useful alternative to what he at times viewed as an orthodox, institutionalized, academic Anglo-American modernist canon grounded in the kinds of stern, didactic readings Heaney identified with Eliot and Pound.

Mandelstam's particular way of exploiting his distance from Dante's Italian offers a way to apprehend Heaney's sustained attraction to Eastern European poetry written in languages he did not know. A number of critics have asked, as Magdalena Kay has done, if Heaney could have been interested in any number of poets writing in his own language, then 'why did he venture so far afield?'²⁶ Kim Cheng Boey proposes that Russia serves as a kind of 'negative elsewhere' that allowed Heaney to 'break the insular mould of perception', and Eugene O'Brien agrees, saying that Heaney sought to 'broaden the language of the tribe in order to include the language of alterity'.²⁷ Mandelstam served not only as a means for broadening his perspective beyond the Anglo-Irish tradition but also as a model for thinking across cultural divisions.

Heaney's readings of Mandelstam's poems affirm his interest in Mandelstam's intertextual engagement with the classical past, which may be viewed as an alternative to the different mythic methods employed by Joyce and Eliot.²⁸ Far from viewing the past as a source of mythic order by which to organize what Eliot characterized as the 'anarchy and futility' of contemporary history, Mandelstam argued in an early essay, 'yesterday has not yet been born. It has not yet really existed. I want Ovid, Pushkin, and Catullus to live once more, and I am not satisfied with the historical Ovid, Pushkin, Catullus'.[29] His lyric poems tend to radically reimagine classical literature, and the internal demands of his poems always trump the demand to be faithful to the classical works he appropriates. Heaney appears to have been drawn to Mandelstam's way of reimagining this classical past – for example, he cited his admiration for 'Insomnia. Homer. Taut sails', which features a speaker who is reading the *Iliad*'s catalogue of ships to try to fall asleep:[30]

> Insomnia. Homer. Taut sails.
> I have read through half the catalogue of ships …
> This long list, this train of cranes,
> That once ascended over Hellas.
>
> Like a fleet of cranes to foreign shores
> Godly foam on kings' heads […]
> Where are you sailing? Without Helen
> What would Troy be to you, Achaean men?
>
> Both the sea and Homer: everything is moved by love …
> Where is there for me to turn? Now, Homer is silent …
> And the Black Sea resounds
> And with a terrifying roar approaches my pillow. …[31]

The poem foregrounds the process by which Mandelstam deconstructs and reconstructs Homer's warrior epic to make a lyric poem about love as the moving force for everything. It appropriates Homer's crane similes, which appear at the beginning and end of the catalogue of ships, before addressing the poem's Greek heroes. In the first stanza, the cranes associate the act of reading with flight – here, we see a performance of reading as exultation, of leaping up and out of the *Iliad* to such an extent that Homer falls silent. In so doing, it ignores the *Iliad*'s answer to the poem's questions to the Achaean men and insists on its own answer – that love moves all. The poem's experience of flying away from the speaker's reading culminates in a sonic climax – the Russian lines of the final stanza begin by echoing the Russian words for 'sea' and Homer in the phrase 'i more i Gomer', which then breaks into the hissing, onomatopoetic sound quality of the closing lines: '*I more **Ch**ernoe vitiyst-vuia **sh**umit / I **s** stra**sh**nym gro**kh**otom pod**kh**odit k i**z**golov'iu*' (highlighted letters indicate where the repetition of sounds that endow these lines with a hissing quality). The repetition of 'ch', 'sh', 's' and 'kh' sounds amplifies the 'terrifying roar' which brings the poet sleep. Mandelstam's engagement with Homer has led him to an intense sonic experience with the music of his own language.[32]

After Joyce liberates him from the conflicts of the past at the end of 'Station Island', Heaney embraces Mandelstam's mode of rewriting tradition in the 'Sweeney Redivivus' poems. The word 'redivivus', meaning 'brought back to life', signals an ambition to remake the literary past in a way that recalls Mandelstam's insistence that his poetry would make Pushkin, Ovid and Catullus live once more. Heaney points to the exultant quality of these poems by noting that in them he 'finally got a bit of lift-off'.[33] The 'Sweeney Redivivus' poems foreground the intensive, unfolding experience of poetry as an insistently present-tense experience of reimagining its medieval source text, *Buile Suibhne* (in a way that echoes Mandelstam's recreation of Homer in 'Insomnia. Homer. Taut sails'). 'The First Gloss' launches the series by drawing our attention to the moment that brings these poems into being – the poet's command to himself to 'Take hold of the shaft of the pen. / Subscribe to the first step taken / from a justified line / into the margin'.[34] This poem generates a rich, suspended temporality: it creates a proleptic sense of itself coming into being in the margins of an ancient text that is not directly quoted. The poems that follow continue to foreground poetry as an unfolding psychological, emotional and intellectual experience that engages the past in order to be liberated from its weight. 'Sweeney Redivivus' and 'Unwinding' present an experience of memory that depends on forgetting and a mode of knowledge that arises from unlearning the past. In these poems, the speaker's 'head [is] like a ball of wet twine / dense with soakage, but beginning / to unwind', and he confronts everything that 'will have to be unlearned / even though from there on everything / is going to be learning'.[35]

The 'Sweeney Redivivus' section uses flight as a self-conscious motif expressing its own attempts to leap outside of the boundaries of familiarity and convention. The poem 'The First Flight' notes: 'I was mired in attachment / Until they began to pronounce me / A feeder off battlefields', a statement that repeats the kinds of indictments underlying the paralyzing self-doubt of *North* a decade earlier. However, this speaker finds the means to transcend attachment,

> so I mastered new rungs of the air
> to survey out of reach
> their bonfires on hills, their hosting
>
> and fasting, the levies from Scotland
> as always, and the people of art
> diverting their rhythmical chants
>
> to fend off the onslaught of winds
> I would welcome and climb
> at the top of my bent.[36]

The metaphoric quality of these lines associate the act of creating a poem with Sweeney's climb away from the attachments that threaten to paralyze him. The Sweeney figure and the poet alike master 'new rungs of air' – in voice and in flight – to achieve liberation.

This kind of liberation, Heaney came to discover, was part of the intrinsic value of lyric poetry. An essay Heaney wrote in the same period when he composed the *Station Island* poems describes lyric poetry in a way that contextualizes the self-conscious poetry of that volume:

> In that liberated moment, when the lyric discovers its buoyant completion, and the timeless formal pleasure comes to fullness and exhaustion, something occurs which is equidistant from self-justification and self-obliteration. A plane is – fleetingly – established where the poet is intensified in his being and freed from his predicaments.[37]

As Heaney came to learn in large part from reading Mandelstam and his Eastern European contemporaries, to describe lyric poetry in this way is not an aesthetic retreat from politics. Poetry's experience of freedom can be a political gesture. In the 1980s, Heaney determined that Mandelstam symbolized the 'efficacy of song itself, an emblem of the poet as potent sound-wave; and when one thinks of the note of the soprano which cracks glass, one has yet another image of the way purely artistic utterance can put a crack in the officially moulded shape of truth in totalitarian society'.[38]

Heaney appreciated that Mandelstam's poetry arose from his profound sense of freedom, a freedom that he cultivated through giddy, creative readings of tradition, and that he asserted in a totalitarian society hostile to poetry. By using poetry as a medium in which he could maintain imaginative connections between the past and present, Mandelstam was able to envision the future at a bleak moment in history. In 'Conversation about Dante', he defended the perpetual movement of poetic speech as an engine of spiritual and psychological freedom. He concludes from an inspired reading of Dante that 'it turns out that the word is much longer than we thought, and we remember that to speak means to be forever on the road'.[39] Heaney's poetry hints at a debt to this idea. *Station Island*'s final poem, 'On the Road', presents an expansive sense of geological time. It concludes with an image of one of the Palaeolithic era Lascaux Cave paintings, a 'drinking deer', in language that restores life to it, with its 'expectant muzzle / and a nostril flared'.[40] This image is suggestive of the threads of cultural continuity running through human history. It fulfils Heaney's own call to renew the task of cultural restoration and preservation that he understood to be the urgent work of modernism.

'Crediting Poetry', Heaney's 1995 Nobel Prize acceptance speech, underscores his career-long preoccupation with discovering a way to defend poetry as an essential medium of psychological and political liberation in the late twentieth century. This address and the poem 'M.' from *The Spirit Level* (1996) emphasize the critical role Mandelstam played in helping Heaney to credit poetry. 'M.' reaches across cultural and historical fault lines to re-animate Mandelstam's language in a way that recalls Mandelstam's own inspiring encounters with the barely accessible historic voices of Homer and Dante:

> M.
> When the deaf phonetician spread his hand
> Over the dome of a speaker's skull
> He could tell which diphthong and which vowel
> By the bone vibrating to the sound.
>
> A globe stops spinning. I set my palm
> On a contour cold as permafrost
> And imagine axle-hum and the steadfast
> Russian of Osip Mandelstam.

This poem operates via a structural and conceptual analogy between Mandelstam and Heaney as poets. This is Mandelstam, the deaf phonetician, as a figure of self-imposed limitations apprehending the tactile and sonic experience of Dante and Homer without primary concern for translating their semantic meaning. This poem generates tension between intimacy and distance: Heaney remains distant from the geographic specificity of Mandelstam's language, but this distance itself is a kind of tribute to Mandelstam's own use of semantic and sonic barriers. The sound of 'M.' generates intimacy: the second stanza rhymes the poet's 'palm' with 'Mandelstam' (reproducing and specifying the first stanza's rhyme between 'hand' and 'sound'). Mandelstam's commitment to sound in his particular way of bringing the literary past back to life helped Heaney to negotiate the pressures of poetry and history. Discovering in Mandelstam's modernism a way to reimagine the past, present, and future, Heaney extended its 'life expectancy, indefinitely'.

Notes

1 Seamus Heaney, 'The Settle Bed', in *Seeing Things* (New York: Farrar, Straus and Giroux, 1991), 29.
2 Seamus Heaney, 'The Impact of Translation', in *The Government of the Tongue: Selected Prose, 1978–1987* (New York: Farrar, Straus and Giroux, 1990), 42–43.

3   David James and Urmila Seshagiri, 'Metamodernism: Narratives of Continuity and Revolution', *PMLA* 129, no. 1 (January 2014): 87–100. Also see David James, ed., *The Legacies of Modernism: Historicising Postwar and Contemporary Fiction* (Cambridge: Cambridge University Press, 2011); David James, *Modernist Futures: Innovation and Inheritance in the Contemporary Novel* (Cambridge: Cambridge University Press, 2012); and Marjorie Perloff, *Twenty-First Century Modernism: The 'New' Poetics* (Oxford: Wiley-Blackwell, 2002).
4   James and Seshagiri, 'Metamodernism', 88.
5   Seamus Heaney, *Preoccupations: Selected Prose, 1968–1978* (New York: Faber and Faber, 1980), 60.
6   In this, I agree with the following readings of Heaney's complex engagement with Mandelstam: Stephanie Schwerter, *Northern Irish Poetry and the Russian Turn: Intertextuality in the Work of Seamus Heaney, Tom Paulin, and Medbh McGuckian* (New York: Palgrave Macmillan, 2013); Magdalena Kay, *In Gratitude for All the Gifts: Seamus Heaney and Eastern Europe* (Toronto: University of Toronto Press, 2012); and Kim Cheng Boey, 'The Dublin-Moscow Line: Russia and the Poetics of Home in Contemporary Irish Poetry', *Irish University Review* 36, no. 2 (Autumn–Winter 2006): 353–73.
7   Clare Cavanagh, *Osip Mandelstam and the Modernist Creation of Tradition* (Princeton: Princeton University Press, 1995).
8   Seamus Heaney, *Finders Keepers: Selected Prose, 1971–2001* (Farrar, Straus and Giroux, 2002), 29
9   Ibid., 40.
10 Ibid., 191.
11 Ibid., 194.
12 As Cuda explains, Heaney returned to this passage throughout his career, including in a private memorial for Robert Lowell. See 'The Use of Memory: Seamus Heaney, T. S. Eliot, and the Unpublished Epigraph to '"North"', *Journal of Modern Literature* 28, no. 4, (Summer 2005): 152–75.
13 Dennis O'Driscoll, *Stepping Stones: Interviews with Seamus Heaney* (Farrar, Straus and Giroux, 2008), 249.
14 Seamus Heaney, *Station Island* (London: Faber and Faber, 1985), 93.
15 James Joyce, *A Portrait of the Artist as a Young Man* (New York: Norton and Company, 2007), 199.
16 Heaney, *Station Island*, 93.
17 Joyce, *Portrait*, 252.
18 Ibid., 93–94.
19 O'Driscoll, *Stepping Stones*, 175.
20 Heaney, *Finders Keepers*, 191.
21 Ibid., 194.
22 For example, see O'Driscoll, *Stepping Stones*, 174. Heaney frequently cited 'Conversation about Dante', including in his Nobel Prize address, 'Crediting Poetry'.
23 Osip Mandelstam, *The Complete Critical Prose*, ed. and trans. Jane Gary Harris and Constance Link (Ann Arbor: Ardis Publishers, 1997), 258.
24 Ibid., 259. See, for example, O'Driscoll, *Stepping Stones*, 175, for Heaney's reference to this line.
25 Ibid., 269.
26 Kay, *In Gratitude*, 11.
27 Boey, 'The Dublin-Moscow Line', 365; Eugene O'Brien, *Seamus Heaney: Creating Irelands of the Mind* (Dublin: The Liffey Press, 2002), 70.

28 In his review of Robert Tracy's bilingual edition of Mandelstam's poems, Heaney concluded from Tracy's prefatory remarks on Mandelstam's citational strategies that his poems were 'as firmly rooted in both an historical and cultural context and in physical reality as Joyce's *Ulysses* and Eliot's *Waste Land*'. *Government of the Tongue*, 79.
29 T. S. Eliot, '*Ulysses*, Order, and Myth', *The Dial* 75 (1923), 483; Mandelstam, *Complete Critical Prose*, 70.
30 O'Driscoll, *Stepping Stones*, 174.
31 My translation. I analyze this poem more fully in the second chapter of my book, *Modernism and Homer: The Odysseys of H.D., James Joyce, Osip Mandelstam, and Ezra Pound* (Cambridge: Cambridge University Press, 2015).
32 See Heaney, *Government of the Tongue*, 174. Although Heaney did not read Russian, he did read Tracy's annotations in the dual language version of Mandelstam's first book of poetry. He also had extensive discussions with Joseph Brodsky about translations of Mandelstam's poetry, which raises the possibility (about which I can only speculate) that he may have discussed the sound quality of one of his favorite Mandelstam poems with Brodsky.
33 O'Driscoll, *Stepping Stones*, 240.
34 Heaney, *Station Island*, 97.
35 Ibid., 98–99.
36 Ibid., 102–3.
37 Heaney, *Government of the Tongue*, xxii.
38 Ibid., xx.
39 Mandelstam, *Complete Critical Prose*, 259.
40 Heaney, *Station Island*, 121.

Chapter 4

JAMES JOYCE AND THE LIVES OF EDNA O'BRIEN

Ellen McWilliams

In Edna O'Brien's 2012 memoir, *Country Girl*, she recalls observing the Dublin literati of the 1950s, the Dublin of Patrick Kavanagh, Flann O'Brien and Austin Clarke, and she appears in one scene as a fascinated recorder of male anxieties of influence:

> Joyce was constantly spoken of in these circles, and not always favourably. […] [Flann O'Brien], when asked if he resembled Joyce, would say "that nothing could be further from Detroit", and that *Finnegans Wake* was a "wallet of literary underwear". […] His harshest jibes, however, were for the Prairie Professors, Americans, talking through their "caubs" and descending on Dublin to write their theses on Herr Joyce. […][1]

This essay examines the politics of Joyce biography, the different anxieties of influence to be found in the history of writing Joyce's life, and explores why these matter to reading Edna O'Brien. The profound influence of the relationship of O'Brien and Joyce, between one of Ireland's most important contemporary writers and the dominant architect of Irish modernism, can be observed in her fiction. It appears, for instance, in the style and form of novels such as *A Pagan Place* (1970), in which O'Brien adopts Joycean techniques in translating the interior life of the novel's protagonist, and *Night* (1972), which can be read as an adaptation of Molly Bloom's soliloquy. But the affinities between these two writers are most dramatically played out in O'Brien's life writing, in her biography of Joyce and in *Country Girl*. In O'Brien's non-fiction, we can most readily observe her fascination with the life of Joyce and her critically alert interventions in the history of writing Joyce's life.

As O'Brien writes the life of Joyce, she engages with the different accounts of Joyce's life as generated by his family, colleagues and critics – accounts that constitute the multifaceted, and sometimes conflicting, corpus of Joyce biography. She navigates that history as a woman writer who shares a well-documented affinity with Joyce's work but, at the same time, she keeps a careful distance between her own creative life and Joyce's achievements. O'Brien takes up different subject positions in imagining his life and in casting Joyce as a character in her own life. In particular, her life writing offers a range of self-conscious and knowing processes of fictionalization that extend from the passionate celebration of an all-important modernist predecessor to the assertion of her own position as a contemporary Irish woman writer expanding the boundaries of the Irish literary canon. These strategies found in O'Brien's life writing provide the Irish woman writer a means of coming to terms with the legacies and achievements of Irish literary modernism.

In engaging with Joyce's life and work, O'Brien shows a vivid awareness of the politics of the canon of Joyce biography, a familiarity that she shares with other scholars, and one that is sensitive to the challenge of writing Joyce's life. In particular, she invokes as an influence Richard Ellmann's magisterial 1959 biography, *James Joyce* – which remains the most lauded of the many accounts of the author's life – by way of pledging her allegiance to the greatest of Joyce's biographers. Yet to do so is also to acknowledge the scholarly anxieties generated by Joyce. Even Richard Ellmann was not immune to such anxieties. In the introduction to the Festschrift for Ellmann published after his death, the editors describe how, at one point, the American-born Ellmann feared he had become an object of resentment in Irish literary circles – one of the 'prairie professors' pilloried by the gathered company in scenes captured by O'Brien in *Country Girl*.[2] This anecdote offers one reminder of some of the tensions in the politics of Joyce biography and calls attention to the obstacles that O'Brien faced in taking on the life of Joyce in the form of a literary biography.

Richard Ellmann's work offers further insights into the complexities of self-representation vis-à-vis Joyce. Ellmann edited Stanislaus Joyce's memoir, *My Brother's Keeper: James Joyce's Early Years*, published in 1958, just a year before the first edition of Ellmann's biography. *My Brother's Keeper* surveys the first 22 years of Joyce's life from the perspective of Stanislaus, although Ellmann offers an illuminating introduction and footnotes that jog Stanislaus along as he tells his brother's story. As editor, Ellmann contributes directly to the material production of the text. He defers to Stanislaus Joyce in his introduction and footnotes, always referring to him as 'Professor Joyce'; at times, however, he expresses his authority and expertise by pausing to expand on Stanislaus's text or to place certain references for the reader. His introduction tempers the image of Stanislaus as a mere servant to his brother's genius by gallantly drawing attention to how Stanislaus made an active contribution to his brother's writing life and suggesting that they shared an intellectual companionship that was important to the development of the young James. And Ellmann ultimately brings the narrative to a close by announcing the death of Stanislaus Joyce; the reader arrives at the final page and receives a note that reads: 'The manuscript ends here'.[3] This text offers rich examples of how the biographer can and does position himself as a central 'character' in the story of his subject's life.

The vexed nature of authorial positioning in the literary biographies of Joyce is evident elsewhere and further foregrounds the contests that O'Brien was all too conscious of in taking on the challenge of writing Joyce's life. Ira B. Nadel confronted the conundrum faced by the Joyce biographer writing after Ellmann by addressing the proliferation of James Joyce's 'many lives':

> Yet how does one write such a life? Brenda Maddox's *Nora* (1988), Peter Costello's *James Joyce: The Years of Growth* (1992), and Morris Beja's *James Joyce* (1992), are three recent attempts to tell or retell the Joyce story; along with critical essays by Bernard McGinley and Ron Bush, they suggest conflicting but convincing visions and alternate readings of Joyce. Collectively, their visions of the life – rather than a life – set the stage for a new narrative: just as there are now many texts of *Ulysses*, there are many lives of Joyce. The challenge, however, is to present these contradictory selves in a persuasive but documented biographical account.[4]

It is with an awareness of this complex, sometimes fraught, self-reflexive history that O'Brien takes a studied attitude to Joyce and to the canon of Joyce biography. She moves across a spectrum of subject positions, from the deeply reverential to the playfully irreverent, from veneration to casual intimacy, and does so in ways that are set by the terms of her own writing interests and commitments.

Joyce is, of course, not the only writer to emerge in O'Brien's canon of life stories. O'Brien has also written a biography of Byron, the nineteenth-century English poet whom Stephen Dedalus chooses to defend in *A Portrait of the Artist as a Young Man* (1916). Byron is initially given a small walk-on part in O'Brien's work: in the epilogue to *The Country Girls*, published in the 1987 edition of the trilogy, in which Baba describes Kate's psychological breakdown as 'all that kind of Lord Byron lunacy'.[5] Later, O'Brien grants Byron a significantly more conventional biographical treatment.[6] *Byron in Love* (2009) is written with a studied detachment that maintains a careful distance between O'Brien, the biographer, and her subject, and the prose style of the work is restrained in ways that are markedly different from her more personal treatment of Joyce.

O'Brien's biography of Joyce is not her only engagement with modernist narratives. T. S. Eliot appears as an important player in her account of her first encounter with Joyce in *Country Girl*, where she recalls her discovery of Joyce via Eliot's *Introducing Joyce* (1942). And in her play about Virginia Woolf, *Virginia* (1981), O'Brien offers a different kind of exercise in life writing that attempts to encompass the author's life and adapt it for the stage. Of these modernist influences, Joyce remains the most important fixation in O'Brien's life and work. In the novel *The Country Girls* (1960), Caithleen Brady develops a preoccupation with Joyce's *Dubliners*. She has to defend the life of Joyce in the face of dismissive retorts from her friend and nemesis, Baba:

> "Will you for Chrissake, stop asking fellas if they've read James Joyce's *Dubliners*? They're not interested. They're out for a night. Eat and drink all you can and leave James Joyce to blow his own trumpet."
> "He's dead."
> "Well, for God's sake, then, what are you worrying about?"[7]

This early scene lays down an important template for O'Brien's own literary relationship with Joyce. She moves between the reverence of Caithleen and the exuberant irreverence of Baba, who represent two different possible modes for living – as well as for reading Joyce.

Caithleen and Baba also, I would argue, represent two different roles taken up by O'Brien as she fashioned her own public responses to Joyce. In an interview published in 2000, O'Brien appears as an earnest supplicant when asked about Joyce's importance to her writing life:

> Oh yes, I thank James Joyce. I fold my hands and say, "God bless you James Joyce," every day. I was working in a chemist shop in the Cabra Road here in Dublin and obsessed about writing. I came across a little book called *Introducing James Joyce*, by T. S. Eliot. […] I learnt from it about the dazzlement, audacity, and fluidity of language.[8]

Later, in her memoir, *Country Girl*, she returns to this all-important formative encounter with Eliot's *Introducing Joyce*:

> I bought it for fourpence and carried it with me everywhere, including to pharmacy lectures, so that I could read it at will and copy out the sentences, luminous and labyrinthine as they were. It was when I copied them that I began to realise how great they were, the short, flawless snatches of dialogue, lush descriptions of corpses and steers and pigs and kine, of sea and sea stones, and then the ordinary ascensions, in which worlds within worlds unfolded.[9]

In scenes such as this, O'Brien seems to embrace fully the role of earnest apprentice, but such scenes are matched by encounters with Joyce in which she identifies him as an equal, a literary companion and compatriot.

O'Brien's *James Joyce*, first published in 1999, is ambitious in its attempt to tell the complete story of Joyce's life, although it gravitates towards the shared history of Joyce and Nora Barnacle. The opening of the biography includes a carefully executed homage to what she calls the fluidity of Joyce's language:

> James Joyce, poor joist, "a funnominal man, supporting a gay house in a slum of despond". His name derived from the Latin and meant joy but at times he thought himself otherwise – a jejeune Jesuit spurning Christ's terrene body, a lecher, a Christian brother in luxuriousness, a Joyce of all trades, a bullock befriending bard, a peerless mummer, a priestified kinchite, a quill-frocked friar, a timoneer, a pool-beg flasher and a man with the gift of the Irish majacule script.[10]

This companionable familiarity with Joyce calls into view a very different relationship with her patron saint. It suggests an intimacy that has a levelling effect in her relationship with her subject. As a means of setting the tone of the biography this opening serves two important functions. First, it playfully evens the field, drawing Joyce into an intimate conversation on O'Brien's terms; second, it establishes a clearly defined relationship, based on equality and mutuality, not just with Joyce, but with the formidable canon of Joyce biography. In her memoir, she recounts one of her first meetings with Ernest Gébler, whom she would later marry: 'He was so cosmopolitan and so cultured. He spoke of James Joyce with a familiarity and referred to Leopold Bloom as Poldy'.[11] The power and literary authority conferred by being on such casual and intimate terms with Joyce is fully appropriated by O'Brien in the early pages of her *James Joyce*.

O'Brien's biography of Joyce was first published in the United States as part of the Penguin Lives series. This series brings its biographers into contact with great authors with whom they have a special affinity. For example, the Canadian author Carol Shields wrote the life of Jane Austen for the series. Austen looms large in Shields's work, both in her explicit referencing of Austen's work as well as in these authors' shared reception. Like Austen, Shields has at times found herself regarded as a miniaturist in ways that problematically risk limiting the importance and value of her work. Shields's prologue establishes a personal and intimate history between the author and her subject and opens with an anecdote about how she and her daughter co-presented a paper at the 1996 meeting of the Jane Austen Society of North America.[12] The Penguin Lives series, then, unapologetically gives the biographer free rein to write the biographical equivalent of a fan letter, one guided by the biographer's primary interests and instincts.

The poetic license allowed by the Penguin Lives series is most apparent in the parts of Joyce's life that O'Brien chooses to amplify in her biography. It is also evident in the book's material presentation. In the bibliography of O'Brien's *James Joyce*, for example, sources appear not in alphabetical order, but in order of 'author preference'. The bibliography is very clearly a version of O'Brien's own private canon, which is not in any way concerned with scholarly convention – not even with the bibliographical conventions of including details of date and place of publication. Richard Ellmann and Stanislaus Joyce are, unsurprisingly, given special billing on O'Brien's list. This format recapitulates the intimacy, not only with Joyce, but also with Joycean scholarship that confers, in O'Brien's opinion, authority over her subject.

Because of the anxiety generated by Joyce as a prized but challenging biographical subject and O'Brien's assertive move to strike a position in critical conversations about the writer, early reviews of the book expressed a good deal of unease on the part of literary scholars. In *World Literature Today* (2001), a review by William Pratt opens on a particularly sceptical note: 'What Edna O'Brien and James Joyce have in common is that they are both Irish writers, which may be justification enough for readers of Edna O'Brien, but may leave readers of Joyce wondering if the book is justified. Is a feminist perspective on Joyce worth having? Well, here it is, like it or not[…]'.[13] Pratt goes on to express particular concern at how '[s]he is rather condescending to most of the critics of Joyce's work[…]'.[14] In dramatic contrast, and in an unusual case of two reviews of the same book appearing in a single issue of a journal – the *James Joyce Quarterly* – Michael Gillespie offers separate responses to two different editions of the biography: a review of the Weidenfeld and Nicolson edition, published in the United Kingdom, and a second review of the version published by Penguin in the United States. Gillespie's reviews are thoughtful and self-questioning contemplations of the scholarly anxieties that arise when the life and work of Joyce are taken up outside of the academy. In the first review, he concludes that '"a *little learning* is a dang'rous thing," but I'm not sure if the phrase should apply to O'Brien or to me',[15] while the second review of the corrected American edition is a good deal less ambivalent about endorsing the work, as the author is reassured that the necessary amendments have been made to more accurately represent a number of the details of Joyce's history.[16]

As noted by a number of her critics, O'Brien is most interested in this biography in the women in Joyce's life. O'Brien also takes special care over what she calls 'Writers and their mothers – the uncharted deep',[17] which reflects the importance of mother-daughter relationships in all of her work, most strikingly in *The Country Girls Trilogy* (1960–64), her earlier memoir, *Mother Ireland*

(1976), and the more recent novel, *The Light of Evening* (2006). She describes how, in writing her first novel, 'I wanted to be a good girl, particularly to my mother, and not to offend her. On the other side of that coin, what they call the dark side, I wanted to kill her, indeed I did kill her – she dies in the first fifty pages of *The Country Girls*'.[18] In keeping with this, much of O'Brien's writing history is shot through with what Anne Fogarty identifies as a recurring matrophobia in one strand of Irish women's writing.[19] Fogarty argues that O'Brien's fiction is not alone in its matrophobic tendencies, which she sees as part of a larger anxiety in Irish women's fiction about being subject to the same oppressive regimes that determine and limit the life of the mother figure in contemporary novels about Irish women's lives.

However, O'Brien's treatment of Joyce's mother in the biography runs contra to the evidence of matrophobia found elsewhere in her work. She offers an extended and sympathetic defence of Joyce's mother, May Joyce, describing her correspondence with her son in the following terms:

> Her letters to him in Paris are a cry for reconciliation and her own strangled longing for recognition. She was not, she wished him to know, as stupid as he thought her to be and her ignorance was not for want of a longing desire to better herself. Here was a woman over forty, ten children living, five dead, a husband who invariably drank his pay-packet, writing to her gifted son of his ambitions and the prospects which lay ahead for him. Her solicitude is heartbreaking, he is not to touch the drinking water unless it is filtered or boiled.[20]

Such moments of recognition are suggestive of some of the concerns that drive O'Brien's worries over the reception of her own reading of, and relationship with, Joyce. She goes on to make a case for his mother's influence on his work: 'Her letters are amazing testaments to her love for him and they are as well the first glimpse of the galloping unpunctuated style which would become Molly Bloom's distinctive trademark'.[21] Here, O'Brien reads Joyce's mother, and more particularly May's epistolary writing, as an influence on the male author who would one day influence her own work.

O'Brien's biography is also especially keen to attend to the story of Nora Barnacle and in many ways can be read as a biography of the Joyces, the story of their life together.

Nora Barnacle is introduced as 'a Galway girl who had run away from her family after a brutal beating by a jealous uncle because of her seeing a local Protestant boy'.[22] This history of rebellion, jealousy and family feuding resembles, of course, the plot of O'Brien's own early life as it unfolds in her memoir, *Country Girl*. With that in mind, it is also clear that O'Brien writes the life of Joyce with a particular alertness to the role Nora Barnacle has been cast in his life. O'Brien writes about Nora with a full and, at times, wry awareness that they share a common West of Ireland ancestry, a shared history that risks casting O'Brien, too, in the role of Joyce's handmaiden: 'He was a Dubliner, she was from Galway; she was to bring in her jingles, her stories, her pisreogs the echoes of her ancestry, the other half of Ireland – soil, gloom, moon grey nettles, the warring clans and the mutinous Shannon waters'.[23] With such commonalities in mind, O'Brien often comes to Nora's defence. For example, she reframes the Joyces' erotic epistolary history:

> These letters are about more than smut. First and foremost they are a measure of the inordinate trust that he had in Nora to allow him to be all things, the child-man, the man-child, the peeping Tom, and the grand seducer. But there is also her own sexual prowess, no small thing for a convent girl from Galway and a radical thing in defiance of that male collusion whereby women are expected to maintain a mystique and conceal their deepest sexual impulses.[24]

From that point on the detail in O'Brien's biography is almost as concerned with Nora as it is with James. By offering a full account of Nora's exasperation, tolerance and constancy, O'Brien pushes readers beyond the more familiar myths of Nora. Also, by attending to the letter writing of both May Joyce and Nora Barnacle, she foregrounds the importance of the letter as a non-canonical but significant form for the woman writer, an idea that is explored in detail in her 2006 novel, *The Light of Evening*, which is made up in part of letters between an Irish woman writer in England and her mother at home in the West of Ireland.

In her own life, Nora Barnacle sought to put the record straight on a number of counts and at times actively resisted endeavours by her husband's critics to misrepresent her by reading her through his fiction. In an interview published in *Harper's Bazaar* in 1952, she directly refuted the notion that she was Molly Bloom: 'I have heard people think I am Molly Bloom in *Ulysses*, but I'm not; Molly Bloom was much fatter. Anyway I know who was Molly Bloom; she was from Zurich. And I know who Anna Livia Plurabelle was too; she was from Trieste where we lived too'.[25] Nora emerges as sceptical of Joyce's critical following and offers a playful take on her husband's legacy: '"Joyce loved to read too", said Mrs Joyce. "What authors did he like?" I asked. "Well, as a matter of fact", she said and smiled, "he spent a good deal of time reading himself"'.[26] O'Brien shares with Nora a playful sense of Joyce, his work and his reputation. O'Brien, too, has been mistaken for Molly Bloom, a recurring motif explored in detail by Rebecca Pelan, who offers a revealing account of the fetishization of O'Brien as author. Pelan identifies how a crude fixation with O'Brien's physical appearance, the supposed sexual content of her work, and her apparent West of Ireland authenticity has too often distracted from serious critical attention to her work.[27] Such caricaturing of O'Brien persists even in ostensibly sympathetic responses to her life and work. In a 2000 review of *Wild Decembers*, Jonathan Yardley described O'Brien as 'a force of nature, a wild Irish rose whose prose aches with the music and the passion of her native land',[28] while an article on O'Brien by E. Jane Dickson, published in *The Times* in 2003, titled 'In the Court of Queen Edna', figures her as 'a minxy Mother Ireland, the kind of woman who might, if she chose, pluck a harp with one hand and milk a cow with the other'.[29] O'Brien herself calmly reflects on these problematic representations of her person and work in the prologue to *Country Girl*, in which she describes how in her later years she has too often been imagined as 'a bargain basement Molly Bloom'.[30]

There are echoes of Joyce's life and work throughout O'Brien's *Country Girl*. A more developed reading of these interactions in *Country Girl* might examine the episodic structure of the autobiography, her careful attention to domestic detail, the echoing of childhood dramas and traumas, the suffering of family life, the fascinations and persecutions of Catholic ritual and the final call to her mother's deathbed. Most strikingly, O'Brien's description of the visceral world of her novels resonates powerfully with the Joycean world of 'ashpits and old weeds and offal', evoked so powerfully in one of his best known letters, dated 23 June 1906: 'It is not my fault that the odour of ashpits and old weeds and offal hangs round my stories. I seriously believe that you will retard the course of civilisation in Ireland by preventing the Irish people from having one good look at themselves in my nicely polished looking-glass'.[31] The world of O'Brien's home place as it is described in her memoir conjures up similarly visceral associations: she figures herself as imaginatively tethered '*to the world of stirabout and bowel movements, to the cold dark rooms reeking of vomited drink, to the cold dark rooms waiting for their next hideous commission of sin*'.[32] Joyce is, then, a constant if discreet companion in *Country Girl*. But for all of this sympathy there is a marked change of tone when it comes to, for example, Joyce's mythical women. At one point, O'Brien in her memoir addresses Anna Livia, the female character central to *Finnegans Wake*, very directly: ' "Soft morning, I am leafy speaking", Anna Livia said, except that my mornings were neither soft nor leafy as I set out for work on a crock of a bicycle, trying to negotiate my way between the other cyclists, the buses and people late for work'.[33] And so, like Nora Barnacle before her, O'Brien the country girl turned working girl goes out of her way, where required, to put the record straight, by setting the realities of women's experience into conversation with powerful mythologies.

O'Brien stays one step ahead of the assumptions of her critics in a number of ways: by contesting the fashioning of Nora Barnacle and, indeed, herself as a 'Wild Irish Rose' or a 'Minxy Mother Ireland', by writing Joyce's life on her exclusive (and at times irreverent) terms and by casting him as one of the male friends and companions who move in and out of the story of her life in *Country Girl*. Of her friendship with Richard Burton, O'Brien recalls in her memoir: 'Men for me were either lovers or brothers[; ...] Richard Burton was a brother, and a bard brother at that'.[34] Joyce is O'Brien's most important bard brother, one who offers inspiration and companionship, but one she holds at a distance when required, and so her biography of Joyce and her memoir find ways of refusing any fixity in how her work and her life might be linked to his. In her biography of Joyce, she concludes: 'In *The Book as World* the author Marilyn French says that "it seems certain that Joyce had a contempt for women". It doesn't; in his thoughts just as in his works, everything about him was both complex and paradoxical'.[35] O'Brien, too, the Irish woman writer charged with the formidable project of writing the life of Joyce, insists on being both complex and paradoxical, and her life writing, in its different forms, maintains a careful balance of power with her most important modernist sibling.

Notes

1. Edna O'Brien, *Country Girl* (London: Faber, 2012), 107.
2. Susan Dick, Declan Kiberd, Dougald McMillan and Joseph Ronsley, eds., *Omnium Gatherum: Essays for Richard Ellmann* (Montreal: McGill-Queen's University Press, 1989), xvi.
3. Stanislaus Joyce, *My Brother's Keeper: James Joyce's Early Years*. (Cambridge, MA: Da Capo, 2003), 259.
4. Ira B. Nadel, 'Joyce and Blackmail', *Journal of Modern Literature* 22, no. 2 (1998–99): 215.
5. Edna O'Brien, *The Country Girls Trilogy* (London: Penguin, 1988), 527.
6. Edna O'Brien, *Byron in Love* (London: Weidenfeld and Nicolson, 2009).
7. Edna O'Brien, *The Country Girls Trilogy* (London: Penguin, 1988), 150.
8. 'Interview with Edna O'Brien', in *Reading the Future: Irish Writers in Conversation*. (Dublin: Lilliput Press, 2000), 216.
9. Edna O'Brien, *Country Girl* (London: Faber, 2012), 96.
10. Edna O'Brien, *James Joyce* (London: Phoenix, 2000), 1.
11. Edna O'Brien, *Country Girl* (London: Faber, 2012), 111.
12. Carol Shields, *Jane Austen* (London: Phoenix, 2001), 1.
13. William Pratt, 'Review of *James Joyce* by Edna O'Brien', *World Literature Today* 75, no. 1 (2001): 126.
14. Ibid.
15. Michael Patrick Gillespie, Review of *James Joyce* by Edna O'Brien, *James Joyce Quarterly* 36, no. 1 (1999): 699.
16. Michael Patrick Gillespie, 'Review of *James Joyce*' by Edna O'Brien. *James Joyce Quarterly* 36, no. 1 (1999): 699–701.
17. Edna O'Brien, *James Joyce* (London: Phoenix, 2000), 22.
18. 'Interview with Edna O'Brien', in *Reading the Future: Irish Writers in Conversation* (Dublin: Lilliput Press, 2000), 211.
19. Anne Fogarty, 'The Horror of the Unlived Life: Mother-Daughter Relationships in Contemporary Irish Women's Fiction', in *Writing Mothers and Daughters: Renegotiating the*

Mother in Western European Narratives by Women, ed. Adalgisa Giorgio (New York: Berghahn, 2002), 85–118.
20 Edna O'Brien, *James Joyce*. (London: Phoenix, 2000), 17.
21 Ibid., 19.
22 Ibid., 35.
23 Ibid., 37.
24 Ibid., 74–75.
25 Sandy Campbell, 'Mrs. Joyce of Zurich', *Harper's Bazaar*, October 1952, 171.
26 Ibid., 254.
27 Rebecca Pelan, 'Reflections on a Connemara Dietrich', in *Edna O'Brien: New Critical Perspectives*, eds. Kathryn Laing, Sinéad Mooney and Maureen O'Connor (Dublin: Carysfort Press, 2006), 12–37.
28 Jonathan Yardley, 'Ireland's Feud Chain', *The Washington Post*, 6 April 2000. UCD/SC, O'Brien Papers, OB/201.
29 E. Jane Dickson, 'In the Court of Queen Edna', *The Times*, 1 February 2003. UCD/SC, O'Brien Papers, OB/572.
30 Edna O'Brien, *Country Girl* (London: Faber, 2012), xi.
31 Stuart Gilbert, ed., *Letters of James Joyce* (London: Faber, 1957), 63–64.
32 Edna O'Brien, *Country Girl* (London: Faber, 2012), 148
33 Ibid., 83.
34 Ibid., 185–86.
35 Edna O'Brien, *James Joyce* (London: Phoenix, 2000), 89.

Chapter 5

MODERNIST TOPOI AND LATE MODERNIST PRAXIS IN RECENT IRISH POETRY (WITH SPECIAL REFERENCE TO THE WORK OF DAVID LLOYD)

Alex Davis

'There are the Alps', wrote Basil Bunting of Pound's *Cantos*: 'you will have to go a long way round / if you want to avoid them'.[1] For Irish poets at mid-century, no less than for the Northumbrian Bunting, modernism proved an unavoidable massif – even, or perhaps especially, when they wrote out of a sceptical or even antagonistic response to it, as in the cases of Padraic Fallon and Austin Clarke. More recently, certain Irish poets one would scarcely identify with a Poundian 'Other Tradition' have engaged more profitably with modernism than Fallon and Clarke, as in Seamus Heaney's ventriloquism of Joyce in the closing section of 'Station Island', and Derek Mahon's recurrent return to the scene of the modern by means of his evocation of 'the Men of 1914' in 'A Kensington Notebook', *The Golden Bough* in 'The Last of the Fire Kings', an avant-garde precursor in 'An Image from Beckett' and, more generally, the exilic preoccupations of 'Ovid in Tomis'.[2] Such 'citation' of modernism, however, stands in marked contrast to the late modernist practice one finds in the work of certain contemporary Irish poets who, in various ways, have chosen to position their work in the slipstream of the stylistic experimentation of high modernism, including Trevor Joyce, Geoffrey Squires, Maurice Scully, Billy Mills and Catherine Walsh.[3] In this chapter, I read the poetry of David Lloyd as illustrating a similarly productive appropriation of earlier modernist praxes, as distinct from the thematically significant deployment of modernist topoi one witnesses in, for example, Mahon and Heaney.

In the early 1950s, Padraic Fallon contributed a 'Journal' to *The Bell*: a series of candid and, on occasion, caustic commentaries on recent and contemporary poetry. In an entry dated 8 December 1951, he writes:

> Pound's *Cantos* were built to express the whole vision of the poet by using all his material. In that they were successful. He uses an art-form in which he can be mythic and moronic in the same space of a line. He can be stately and slummy, cryptic, gnomic and diffusive on the one page. Pound found an art-form for the whole man by chucking his early love of the stanzaic form for a medium that gave him any freedom he required in dealing with any kind of material. *Il miglior fabbro*? I think so.[4]

Self-communing, Fallon asks: 'What then about yourself? [...] Will you chuck the stanza-trunks and walk naked?' The sly closing allusion to Yeats's 'A Coat' circles back to Fallon's critique, slightly earlier in this piece, of Yeats's '[over-]elaborate stanza-making'.[5] The poetic nudity entertained by Yeats, of course, is the discarding of 'a coat / Covered with embroideries / Out of old mythologies', not the shedding of traditional verse forms.[6] Fallon's quip redeploys Yeats's image to posit an opposition between the constraints on poetic movement imposed by 'stanza-trunks' and the 'freedom' granted Pound by the adoption of free verse in *The Cantos* and elsewhere. However, Fallon is very far from advocating that one follow Pound's lead; Pound, he maintains, is *sui generis*, *The Cantos* testimony to his gargantuan intellectual appetite, 'a way to disgorge his giant eating, something so formless that it must be a form in itself, a book that has eaten up all the books'.[7] 'You're not a book', warns Fallon.

> And when you write free verse it slows up your feet, you cannot take those little flying dives on a rhythm that the finch takes when he nips from one tree to another, shutting and opening his wings, wayward but keeping the direction. That's why you dislike Eliot, the cumbersome, the lumbersome, trundling his portentous yeas and nays from one heap of garden rubbish to another. Eagle, indeed. He had never a feather to fly or moult.[8]

Fallon concludes his journal-entry by championing neither Yeats nor Eliot (nor, one presumes, Pound) as an example for the contemporary Irish poet: 'You have read them, you have absorbed them, they are part of your bloodstream. Go thou and do not likewise'.[9]

Fallon's remarks are representative of the often tense dialogue with modernist poetic practice in Irish poetry from the first decade of the twentieth century on, *pace* Edna Longley's strategic claim, made in the mid-1970s, that the publication in 1973 of Thomas Kinsella's 'The Divided Mind' and John Montague's 'The Impact of International Modern Poetry on Irish Writing' 'perhaps mark the point at which the revolution of Pound and Eliot became relevant to Ireland'.[10] The 'relevance' of Pound, if not Eliot, to Irish poetry might be more accurately dated to 1909, and Joseph Campbell's and T. D. FitzGerald's presence in the group of poets associated with the Tour Eiffel meetings in London.[11] The Irish Imagism of Campbell and FitzGerald is an instance of a productive engagement with (in this case, early) modernist *poiesis*, one which we find repeated – in diverse modes – in the poetic praxis of a number of subsequent Irish poets, such as Thomas MacGreevy, Brian Coffey, Samuel Beckett, Denis Devlin and Sheila Wingfield.

Fallon's 'absor[ption]' of modernism is rather different, I think; equally part of the 'bloodstream' of twentieth- and twenty-first century Irish poetry, it is an instance of what one might term *ideational modernism*: the appropriation of modernist topoi rather than the adoption and development of avant-garde devices.[12] Seamus Heaney perceptively comments that, for all Pound's importance to Fallon, 'it would be a mistake to enlist Fallon's work in general into the Poundian line. His sense of form remained too intimate with traditional conceptions of harmony and logical structure, and his ear too responsive to the old tunes of verse-writing for Pound's kind of modernism to take him over.'[13] In this regard, Fallon's reductive identification of modernism with the abandonment of 'stanza-trunks' in favour of the (questionable) freedom of free verse is indicative of an absorption of modernism largely indifferent to issues of form.

Pound's appearance in Derek Mahon's lyric-sequence 'A Kensington Notebook' (1983) is an instance of ideational modernism:

The operantics of
Provence and Languedoc
Shook the Gaudier marbles
At No. 10 Church Walk

Where 'Ezra Pound, M.A.,
Author of *Personae*',
Sniffed out the image with
Whiskery antennae;

Rihaku, nursed Osiris'
Torn limbs; came to know
Holland St. stone by stone
As he knew San Zeno [...]

> The Spirit of Romance
> Flowered briefly there
> Among jade animals[14]

Mahon's poem references both Poundian subject matter and Poundian form: the poetry collection *Personae* (1909), the critical works *The Spirit of Romance* (1910), 'I Gather the Limbs of Osiris' (1911–12) and the polemics on behalf of Imagism (1913), all conjoin the poem's formal allusion – by way of its quatrains – to the 'stanza-trunks' donned by *Hugh Selwyn Mauberley* in 1920. *Mauberley* was Pound's valediction to the London that Mahon succinctly evokes – its form driven by Pound's growing disaffection with the avant-garde poetic milieu his earlier work had done so much to create. Hence his 'decision' (with Eliot) 'that the dilution of *vers libre*, Amygism, Lee Masterism, general floppiness had gone too far and that some counter-current must be set going. [...] Remedy prescribed [Théophile Gautier's] "Émaux et Camées" (or the Bay State Hymn Book). Rhyme and regular strophes'.[15] Hugh Haughton's adroit description of 'A Kensington Notebook' as 'a formal pastiche of and homage to [...] a pastiche sequence' nevertheless suggests too close a homology between the formal similarities of the two sequences. Mahon's urbane *imitatio* of the quatrains and telegraphese style of sections of *Mauberley* constitutes a 'quotation' of a modernist 'counter-current' of the late teens that is now quite empty of the formal imperatives that had driven Pound to the example of Gautier in the first place. Rather, Mahon's choice of form serves deftly to underline certain key thematics in the poem: that of the marginal role of the modern artist, exemplified in Pound and, elsewhere in the sequence, Ford Madox Ford and Wyndham Lewis. In this respect, Mahon's Pound in London is the exact contemporary of his 'Ovid in Tomis', in which the Roman poet's exile by the Black Sea from AD 8 becomes the basis for a bleakly humorous 'portrait', in Haughton's commentary, of 'an intellectual coming to terms with the exilic nature of modernity'.[16]

In a not-unrelated fashion, the advice offered by Joyce to the pilgrim-persona in the final section of Seamus Heaney's 'Station Island' (1984) signals an engagement with modernism conducted primarily on the level of ideas:

> You lose more of yourself than you redeem
> doing the decent thing. Keep at a tangent.
> When they make the circle wide, it's time to swim
>
> out on your own and fill the element
> with signatures on your own frequency,
> echo soundings, searches, probes, allurements,
>
> elver-gleams in the dark of the whole sea.[17]

These lines are 'Joycean' only in their insistence on Stephen Dedalus's notion of the artist's *non serviam*.[18] Modelled, clearly enough, on Eliot's encounter in 'Little Gidding' with 'a familiar compound ghost', the passage draws on modernist precedents in order to further the sequence's interrogation and, finally, rejection of what an earlier poem had called '[o]ur tribe's complicity'.[19] Heaney's *terza rima* brings to mind Eliot's unrhymed approximation of the same verse form in the second movement of 'Little Gidding'; but, like the *Mauberley*-esque quatrains of 'A Kensington Notebook', the shared form has the primary function of reinforcing the conceptual level of the poem, as articulated in the admonitory words of Heaney's Dantean interlocutor.

I am not suggesting that these examples from Mahon and Heaney constitute some variety of 'modernism lite', but simply that their relationship to modernism needs to be parsed with due care to modernism's many afterlives in Irish poetry.[20] The strongly historicist dimension to modernist scholarship since the 1990s often prompts the extension of the temporal boundaries of modernism to embrace cultural productivity throughout the twentieth century and beyond. Laura O'Connor's chapter on 'W. B. Yeats and Modernist Poetry' in *The Cambridge Companion to Irish Modernism*, for example, '[s]anctioned by the expansionist trend of new modernist studies', concludes with the examples of Medbh McGuckian and Nuala Ní Dhomhnaill. While recognising the extent to which the stylistic features of certain women's poetry of the 1930s to the 1950s (Blanaid Salkeld's, for example) bear 'the [formal] hallmarks of modernism', O'Connor's overriding preoccupation with the (post-)Yeatsian 'neo-bardic role of poet as public intellectual' – which she describes as '*the* distinctively Irish-modernist achievement' – effectively confines McGuckian's and Ní Dhomhnaill's 'modernism' to 'feminist revisions of the bardic poem', along similar lines to that made by Eavan Boland in 'Mise Eire' and related prose.[21]

One weakness with this argument is that it does not do justice to Irish poets whose work is written out of a deeply felt kinship to various modernist praxes and to whom the issue of the 'neo-bardic role of [the] poet' seems largely irrelevant. A strand of recent modernist scholarship has questioned the interpretative efficacy of speaking of modernist style(s) at all – as Mark Wollaeger usefully summarizes, 'if modernism is simply, as some have argued, the expressive dimension to modernity, and if modernity itself is defined very broadly, the utility of the term "modernist", as opposed to "modern", begins to fade.' It is true that certain poetic and narrative techniques (verbal collage, so-called stream of consciousness, etc.) no longer seem definitive of modernism. Nevertheless, as Wollaeger continues, formal criteria surely remain an important 'subset' to any adequate 'sense of [the] decentered resemblance' of the artworks in this period.[22] That this is the case finds indirect confirmation from the Shklovskian baring of the device in the contemporary poetic practice of David Lloyd, as in his poem 'Fade' from *Arc & Sill* (2012):

> The tears in things
>   Smoke threads the tissue
>
> the fading linen frayed
>   to the shoulders
>
> (the truth of him, his
>   faith to the object
>
> ash slips from the ring
>
> the persistence of the dream
>   in the jacket's frayed shoulders
>
> lingers a smile, a smoke-net
>   fraying from the lips
>
> smoke marbles the air
>
> hand to the brow a precise
>   space for the other
>
> loyalty to things
>   in their vanishing[23]

An elegy for the political scientist Michael Rogin, the poem references Virgil's *sunt lacrimae rerum*, Pound's Canto LXXIV and, most significantly perhaps, the exactness of the cigar-smoker in Mallarmé's oblique *ars poetica* 'Toute l'âme résumée', whose presence here gives to Rogin (and Lloyd) an almost Objectivist 'loyalty to things / in their vanishing' reminiscent of George Oppen's punctilious discriminations. The allusion to Pound's elegiac defiance at the collapse of fascist Italy, and the deaths of 'Ben and la Clara *a Milano*' appears initially incongruous. Yet it has the effect of a *détournement* or 'derailment' of its source, forcing a jarringly ironic subject rhyme between the efforts of the left-wing Rogin and '[t]he enormous tragedy of the dream in the peasant's bent shoulders' Pound laments at the beginning of *The Pisan Cantos*.[24]

Of course, the self-reflexive irony of 'Fade' is that which those modernist bedfellows, the New Critics, taught us is the signature of *any* achieved poem – it is present in abundance in Mahon's best lyrics. Elsewhere in Lloyd's oeuvre, however, we find work that accords more strongly with the mistrust voiced at the close of his well-known essay, '"Pap for the Dispossessed": Seamus Heaney and the Poetics of Identity', regarding the contemporary relevance of a prevalent variety of Post-Romantic lyricism. Like the proverbial conjuror producing the rabbit from a hat, Heaney, Mahon et al., argues Lloyd, invariably 'crystallise specific emotions out of an experience' by means of an aesthetic governed by an expressive mimeticism subtended by a self-identical poetic self.[25]

Lloyd's antipathy in this regard is shared by a number of the poets published by Michael Smith and Trevor Joyce's New Writers' Press (copublishers of *Arc & Sill*), especially in the period from 1970 on. Joyce's own rejection of 'the poetry of expression' as trivially inadequate to the actualities of our information-saturated lived experience has led him in certain works to experiment with procedural composition.[26] *Syzygy* (1998), for instance, powerfully uses the rigorous formal dictates of its adopted 'method' both to reflect and critique forms of social and philosophical systematization of the individual and his or her environment.[27] In a related abjuration of lyric expressiveness, Lloyd's *Coupures* (1987) concludes with a procedural text comprised of five pages of jagged prose 'cuttings', each individual line strip-mined from preexistent material and juxtaposed with that which precedes and follows in a manner that flouts not only syntactic continuity but even the integrity of the individual word:

> til they slammed the brakes on, & we rode straight on through
> licking through the pages like a card index, duckrabbitduckra
> ving, washing, going out for a coffee; and how in almost unbr[28]

As so often in procedural works, the underlying method can only be glimpsed as through a glass, darkly: if, on the one hand, the text declares 'the order is quite arbitrary', such arbitrariness is clearly enough the product of procedural rules governed by the reiterated page layout (the identical number of lines per page and characters and spaces per line).[29] One of the pleasures of reading the most thought-provoking proceduralist works is not dissimilar to that which can be derived from the traditional scansion of verse: the recognition of rules governing apparent diversity. But the chosen procedural method – no more than the iambic pentameter – is devoid of significance in isolation from the semantic content it marshals: a proceduralist work of any conceptual interest is not a *roman-à-clef*, to which knowledge of the method used will provide the key to its exhaustive understanding. In Lloyd's text, the (possibly 'quite arbitrary') choice of procedure of construction produces a rebarbative mashup of narrative pieces, among which an insistent motif of erotic desire is reiterated plangently but emptily, the disjunctive form depriving it of cumulative resonance, frustrating both sexual and narrative closure. Such voided narrative compulsion recalls that of *The Unnamable*, the slivers of text like Beckett's 'vice-existers' reiterating disjointed, insistent feelings of non-fulfilment. One of the cut-up source texts is Yeats's play *The Cat and the Moon*, the existential antinomies of which, in their new context, assume the disorientating instability of the gestalt figure of the duckrabbit, rather than suggesting any possibility of unity of being.

Lloyd's deconstruction of narrative in *Coupures* is signalled by an epigraph from Denis Roche's *Dépôts de savoir et de technique*, a work that Marjorie Perloff argues 'makes language the arena of production rather than representation'.[30] Lloyd's *Taropatch* (1985) had earlier experimented with this kind of productive 'arena', although its procedural premise, no more than *Coupures*, does not thereby eschew the referential axis of language. Alluding in its title to Dana Hilliot's musings on the near homonym of the musical instrument and 'Tarot Pack' in Malcolm Lowry's *Ultramarine*, *Taropatch* is a patchwork of 15 texts, approximating the example of Aleister Crowley's 15-card Thoth Tarot spread. As in *Coupures*, the procedure can be viewed as a formalist motivation of the device – an enabling *technique* à la Roche – that, in this case, produces a spread of texts demanding, as in Tarot, a reading attentive not only to each 'card' but to their possible interactions. One interpretation might focus on the interplay of myths, both classical and biblical, between the poem-cards. In one, Zeus' seduction of Danae ('He melts from the seat of his power / Into the nervous gold shower') wittily merges with that of Bath-sheba by King David ('O how her suddy & delicate limbs / Shimmer & fuzz his valued standards'); in another, as Phaeton's 'reins jerk from a long desired command', the plummeting Icarus 'is dashed into breakers'.[31]

The mythic parallels bring to mind the title of Lloyd's chapbook *Change of State* (1993), a sequence equally concerned with moments of abrupt metamorphosis. The catastrophe theory of René Thom lies in the background of this latter work (in its first publication the poem was accompanied by diagrams illustrating Thom's theory[32]): states of equilibrium succumbing to unpredictable change, like 'fabric shearing' or 'the bulk of the world cascading / Over the selvedge'. As in Yeats's 'Easter, 1916', such moments have a seemingly unmappable quality in their dislocation of what struck consciousness before as mere reiteration:

> All changed –
> By mere citation – we hesitate on the step
> Of what we were. Is it in their words?[33]

Change of State concludes with a poignant evocation of mutability, as the smell of basil brings to the speaker's mind 'that moment, the one / in the overshaded garden', prior to an irrevocable loss of another's intimacy. Unlike the olfactory revelation granted Blake by the wild thyme in his Garden at Felpham or the restorative power of 'mint, thyme and basilicum' for the imprisoned Pound in *The Pisan Cantos*,[34] the basil's sharp aroma here imparts a keen sense of utter loss:

> Can you recall
> the pungency of basil, it rises from the spray,
> from the brown bag, and here I am
> thinking to make you dishes of white pasta
> reeking of this green herb. But you're gone now
> and can't be at my table.[35]

Personal deprivation, reinforced by a rigorously unsentimental proceduralism, is pursued in *Vega* (2009), which takes its epigraph from Eugenio Montale's *Mottetti*: '*Lo sai: debbo riperderti e non posso*' ('You know: I must lose you again and cannot'). Throughout the work the pathos of intolerable private loss rubs shoulders with intolerance at the privations of those politically 'disappeared' or incarcerated. The latter theme chimes with recurrent preoccupations of Lloyd's cultural criticism; its insistent presence in *Vega* powerfully conjoins the politics of form exemplified by this text. As a sonnet sequence, *Vega* might seem distinct from the procedural works, *Coupures* and *Taropatch*, and more in the stream of a 'lyric' tradition including (let us say) Heaney's 'Glanmore Sonnets'. Firstly, however, the adoption of the sonnet form is itself to choose a 'constraint' on the production of a text that differs from those of procedural texts, narrowly defined, only in its literary pedigree, as a consequence of which a sonnet's 'meaning' is, arguably, simply less unpredictable than those generated by other, more *outré*, operations. Indeed, *Vega*'s interpenetration of private and public – the veritable DNA of the sonnet – is, after all, very much in the Sidnean tradition, the poems' stellar imagery inescapably acknowledging *Astrophil and Stella*. Secondly, and more significantly, Lloyd's upbraiding of the 'Glanmore Sonnets' for their pastoral 'complacencies',[36] their gingerly keeping political violence at arm's length, signals an impatience with a lyricism that shrinks from the *Vabanquespiel*: the 'high-stakes game', that is played by a poet like Vallejo, in whose work Lloyd has shown a deep interest. Vallejo's avant-garde deformations of lyric register suffering, both his and others', but the poetry remains faithful to the irreducible *specificity* of others' privation precisely by means of its articulation in the most intensely personal of poetic modes. Crucially, a concomitant of the proceduralist dimension to Lloyd's poetics is not the abandonment of the lyric; and in this respect his work thus differs sharply from that of certain influential North American neoconceptualist writers, including Kenneth Goldsmith and Vanessa Place. In the latter, a lambasting of the lyric 'I' is revealingly complicit with a procedural method that, in its appropriation of pre-existing materials to produce a 'new' text, almost callously disregards the congealed labour of the original producer, as Andrea Brady has cogently argued.[37]

Among *Vega*'s sources is Freud's 1907 essay, 'Delusion and Dream in Jensen's *Gradiva*'. In Wilhelm Jensen's tale a young archaeologist, Norbert Hanold, becomes obsessed with a bas-relief of a young Roman woman and dreams he encounters her in Pompeii during the eruption of Mt Vesuvius. Subsequently, having travelled to the site of the ancient town, he meets the living double of his 'Gradiva', and comes gradually to the realization that she is a childhood friend, his love for whom he had repressed and displaced onto the bas-relief. Whereas for Freud the narrative illustrates dreaming's potential for wish fulfilment, in *Vega* there is no redemptive recuperation of the lost object, neither in fantasy nor in fact, the cruelly oxymoronic epigraph from Montale underscored by the stellar imagery of the sequence. In the opening sonnet, 'Lyre', the hopeful claim that 'Your late star tracks back' is shadowed by the knowledge that Vega is the brightest star in Lyra, a constellation in which the Greeks discerned Orpheus' lyre. This is a presentiment of the disjunction between the conclusion to the sequence and that of Jensen's novella: whereas Hanold happily finds his Eurydice through the delusion surrounding Gradiva, *Vega*'s katabasis ends in Orphic loss and dismemberment:

> You who were constellation,
>   clearing, beat
> play this in dismembrance of me
>
> in pieces
>   for my unforgetting[38]

The figure of Gradiva, 'she who walks', was a favourite among the surrealists, a fact to which *Vega* possibly alludes ('whatever door passed through you').[39] Be that as it may, images of liminality – thresholds, edges, membranes – pepper Lloyd's poems, especially those in *Sill* (2006). In this collection, the 'drums in the ear, tympanum / stretched to attention'[40] suggest not only *The Unnamable* – 'I'm the tympanum, on the one hand the mind, on the other the world'[41] – but also Derrida's reflections on the permeability of the apparent boundaries set to interiority in 'Tympan' and *The Ear of the Other*. In Lloyd such sills are always cusps: those inexorable experiential 'changes of state' constitutive of subjectivity and its engagement with the other.

Notes

1 Basil Bunting, 'On the Fly-leaf of Pound's Cantos', in *Complete Poems*, ed. Richard Caddel (Oxford: Oxford University Press, 1994), 114.
2 On the 'Other Tradition', see Marjorie Perloff's influential *The Poetics of Indeterminacy: Rimbaud to Cage* (Princeton: Princeton University Press, 1981).
3 On these poets see, e.g., Niamh O'Mahony, ed., *Essays on the Poetry of Trevor Joyce* (Bristol: Shearsman, 2014); Harry Gilonis, 'The Spider, the Fly and Philosophy: Following a Clew through Maurice Scully's *Livelihood*', in *The Fly on the Page: The Gig Documents # 3*, ed. Nate Dorward (Willowdale, ON: The Gig, 2004), 29–43; Claire Bracken, '"Each nebulous atom in between": Reading Liminality – Irish Studies, Postmodern Feminism and the Poetry of Catherine Walsh', in *New Voices in Irish Criticism 5*, eds. Ruth Connolly and Ann Coughlan (Dublin: Four Courts, 2005), 97–109; Eric Falci, *Continuity and Change in Irish Poetry, 1966–2010* (Cambridge: Cambridge University Press, 2012), 186–204; and Alex Davis, *A Broken Line: Denis Devlin and Irish Poetic Modernism* (Dublin: University College Dublin Press, 2000), 135–76.
4 Padraic Fallon, *A Poet's Journal and Other Writings 1934–1974*, ed. Brian Fallon (Dublin: Lilliput, 2005), 12.
5 Ibid.
6 *The Variorum Edition of the Poems of W. B. Yeats*, eds. Peter Allt and Russell K. Alspach, 3rd imp. (London: Macmillan, 1966), 320.
7 Fallon, *A Poet's Journal*, 12; cf. the interest shown by Fallon's contemporary, Austin Clarke, in the formless giantism he believed characterized *The Cantos*: 'into this gigantic scrapbook of free verse and fragmentary prose Mr Pound pastes his quotations, jottings, and ironic comments upon human history'. *Reviews and Essays of Austin Clarke*, ed. Gregory A. Schirmer (Gerrards Cross: Colin Smythe, 1995), 188.
8 Fallon, *A Poet's Journal*, 12–13.
9 Ibid., 15.
10 Edna Longley, 'Searching the Darkness: The Poetry of Richard Murphy, Thomas Kinsella, John Montague and James Simmons', in *Two Decades of Irish Writing: A Critical Survey*, ed. Douglas Dunn (Manchester: Carcanet, 1975), 118–53 (121). Longley's recent reflections on modernism and Ireland can be found in her *Yeats and Modern Poetry* (Cambridge: Cambridge University Press, 2013), *passim*.
11 See Helen Carr, *The Verse Revolutionaries: Ezra Pound, H.D. and the Imagists* (London: Jonathan Cape, 2009), 165–75, 180–85; and Alex Davis, 'Whoops from the Peat-Bog? Joseph Campbell and the London Avant-Garde', in *The Irish Revival Reappraised*, eds. Betsey Taylor FitzSimon and James H. Murphy (Dublin: Four Courts, 2004), 145–53.
12 *Conceptual* modernism suggests itself as less inelegant; however, owing to the importance of conceptualism to various avant-garde practices, the adjective is potentially misleading.
13 Seamus Heaney, introduction to *The Collected Poems of Padraic Fallon*, ed. Brian Fallon (Oldcastle: Gallery, 1990), 16; cf. John Goodby, *Irish Poetry Since 1950: From Stillness into History* (Manchester: Manchester University Press, 2000), 30.
14 Derek Mahon, *Collected Poems* (Oldcastle: Gallery, 1999), 144–45; this is a slightly revised version of the poem collected in *Antarctica* (1985).
15 Quoted in John J. Espey, *Ezra Pound's 'Mauberley': A Study in Composition* (Berkeley: University of California Press, 1955), 25; and see Espey's discussion at ibid., 25–48.
16 Hugh Haughton, *The Poetry of Derek Mahon* (Oxford: Oxford University Press, 2007), 196, 170.

17 Seamus Heaney, *Station Island* (London: Faber and Faber, 1984), 93–94.
18 As Neil Corcoran observes, the lines contain 'some of Heaney's own most characteristic signatures: the nouns of the passage carry a distinctly Heaney-like, not Joycean, notation'. Neil Corcoran, 'Heaney's Joyce, Eliot's Yeats', *Agenda* 27, no. 1 (1989): 37–47 (41).
19 *The Complete Poems and Plays of T. S. Eliot* (London: Faber and Faber, 1969), 193; Seamus Heaney, 'Casualty', in *Field Work* (London: Faber and Faber, 1979), 23.
20 For an example of such discrimination, see David Wheatley, 'Picking At It', review of *New Collected Poems*, by Derek Mahon, *Dublin Review of Books* 20 (2011), http://www.drb.ie/essays/picking-at-it.
21 Laura O'Connor, 'W. B. Yeats and Modernist Poetry', in *The Cambridge Companion to Irish Modernism*, ed. Joe Cleary (Cambridge: Cambridge University Press, 2014), 77–94 (77, 90, 91); emphasis added. Significantly, O'Connor's thesis leads her to describe Heaney's 'Station Island' as 'a self-canonizing poetic autobiography in the Irish-modernist mode'. Ibid., 86.
22 Mark Wollaeger, introduction to *The Oxford Handbook of Global Modernisms*, eds. Mark Wollaeger with Matt Eatough (Oxford: Oxford University Press, 2012), 11, 12.
23 David Lloyd, *Arc & Sill: Poems 1979–2009* (Bristol: Shearsman Books; Dublin: New Writers' Press, 2012), 38. Lloyd's cultural and literary criticism has been at the centre of debates within Irish Studies since the publication of his study of Mangan, *Nationalism and Minor Literature*, in 1987. During this same period, Lloyd has produced a series of poetry chapbooks with small presses, from *Taropatch* (1985) to *Kodalith* (2014). With the exception of the last, *Arc & Sill* collects these and other work of the past three decades; *Kodalith* is available as an online chapbook from Smithereens Press: http://smithereenspress.com/publications/sp9.html.
24 *The Cantos of Ezra Pound*, 13th printing (New York: New Directions, 1995), 445.
25 David Lloyd, '"Pap for the Dispossessed": Seamus Heaney and the Poetics of Identity', in *Anomalous States: Irish Writing and the Post-Colonial Moment* (Dublin: Lilliput, 1993), 13–40 (35). Lloyd's much-cited critique questions the political and ethical adequacy of Heaney's assumption of an umbilical relationship between bourgeois poetic subject and Irish national identity – the romantic nationalist ideology informing such 'representativeness' on the poet's behalf, eliding and obfuscating the complex realities of a postcolonial social formation.
26 Trevor Joyce, 'The Point of Innovation in Poetry', in *For the Birds: Proceedings of the First Cork Conference on New and Experimental Irish Poetry*, ed. Harry Gilonis (Sutton: Mainstream Poetry Press, 1998), 18–26 (19); Joyce quotes Mahon's 'A Disused Shed in Co. Wexford' as an example of 'the poetry of expression'.
27 For a discussion of Joyce's text, see Davis, *Broken Line*, 161–63.
28 Lloyd, *Arc & Sill*, 144.
29 The page dictating the procedure is from *Finnegans Wake*.
30 Marjorie Perloff, *Poetic License: Essays on Modernist and Postmodernist Lyric* (Evanston: Northwestern University Press, 1990), 68.
31 Lloyd, *Arc & Sill*, 101, 96.
32 David Lloyd, *Change of State* (Berkeley: Cusp Books, 1993).
33 Lloyd, *Arc & Sill*, 85.
34 See Blake's *Milton*; Pound, Canto LXXIX, in *Cantos*, 507.
35 Lloyd, *Arc & Sill*, 91.
36 Lloyd, 'Pap for the Dispossessed', 34.

37 '[T]he conceptualist writer exists in a parodic relation to both freedom and labour. [...] [T]he poet is free of the labour of producing language; the reader is free of the labour of reading and constitutes a "thinkership". (Conceptual writing, Goldsmith has argued, should not be read; it's too boring to be read.) As for labour: in his 800-page retyping of an edition of the *New York Times*, Goldsmith duplicates the labour of journalists, copyists, editors, typesetters, printers and distributors who are responsible for the generation and publication of the text. Free from the wage relation, his labour – retyping hundreds of pages of stock abbreviations and numbers, for example – constitutes art as parody. The foresworn possibility of replicating the entirety of the newspaper with just a mouse click makes Goldsmith's decision to subject himself to the painful arduity of retyping a kind of nostalgic tribute to craft models of art. Or, it is self-punishment, a saintly asceticism or schizoid obsession. It is the fetter of labour turned into ornament'. Andrea Brady, 'Conceptualism, Poetry and Bondage' (unpublished manuscript). My thanks to Prof. Brady for furnishing me with a copy of her paper.
38 Lloyd, *Arc & Sill*, 9, 26.
39 Ibid., 13.
40 Ibid., 62.
41 Samuel Beckett, *'Molloy', 'Malone Dies', 'The Unnamable'* (London: Calder, 1994), 386.

Chapter 6

'AMACH LEIS!' (OUT WITH IT!): MODERNIST INHERITANCES IN MICHEÁL Ó CONGHAILE'S 'ATHAIR' ('FATHER')

Sarah McKibben

Since its popularization after World War I, the term *modernism* has come to have both a broad and an enduring application within Anglophone as well as European cultural analysis. Until recently, it was far less commonly employed in discussions of Irish-language (Gaelic) literature and culture, however. Signifying 'the tendency of experimental literature of the early twentieth century to break away from traditional verse forms, narrative techniques, and generic conventions in order to seek new methods of representation appropriate to life in an urban, industrial, mass-oriented age', modernism – like its generative cognate, modernity – was more often seen as something reacted to than enacted in Irish, with its enduring associations with rural life, tradition and cultural revival.[1] Yet, as recent interventions have underscored, not only did prose writers of the Gaelic Revival share, or anticipate, key preoccupations of modernism, they also prompted late-modernist, counter-Revival challenges. A key aspect of the afterlife of Irish(-language) modernism inheres in an ongoing revision of terms set at the turn of the twentieth century (as this chapter explores), concluding with a discussion of a compelling coming-out story – 'Athair' ('Father'), winner of the 1997 Hennessy Literary Award, by prominent contemporary writer, publisher and member of Aosdána, Micheál Ó Conghaile (b. 1962).

Not only forcibly and recently confronted by the ruptures of modernity – including mass political movements, rapid economic and demographic change, and what Kevin Whelan has called 'the hollowing-out of indigenous Irish culture' after the Great Hunger – Irish writers, like other modernist pathbreakers, were also positioned at a remove from the English literary inheritance, energized by a persistent oral tradition, motivated by cultural nationalism to challenge literary and social conventions and, perhaps, inspired by having less to lose.[2] Accordingly, a broad swathe of mostly Anglo-Irish, Protestant Irish writers partook enthusiastically of this modernist 'culture of experiment'[3] with its literary qualities of interiority, perspectivalism, radical juxtapositions, elevation of style and form, parody, self-conscious artistry and allusiveness,[4] as well as its broader queering of social and sexual mores. Indeed, some of modernism's most famous figures are Irish writers in English, such as James Joyce (1882–1941) and Samuel Beckett (1906–1989), each of whom radically departed – though in sharply different ways – from the stylistic, philosophical and ideological norms that preceded him.

By contrast, Irish-language writing of the late nineteenth and early twentieth century was long associated with Revival, not modernism, the two assumed to be incompatible. Often portrayed as a retreat from failed political campaigning for Home Rule, the Gaelic Revival of 1881–1921 was a broad, trans-Atlantic, cultural nationalist movement of writing, scholarly recovery, activism and psychological and economic uplift that emerged alongside the de-feudalizing Land Acts.[5] The Gaelic Revival sought to recover and revitalize native Irish language, culture and self-esteem following its precipitous post-Famine decline after generations of subalternization and derision. While the contemporaneous Irish Literary Revival produced its works in English, thinking Irish essentially 'lost', thereby incurring the distrust and even hostility of contemporaneous Gaelic revivalists, it similarly drew on (suitably sanitized) medieval and contemporaneous Irish-language sources to recover a precious cultural inheritance expressing a distinct national character. The (dual-language) Revival thus reiterates the longstanding preoccupation with nationalism in Irish society.

The Revival's underscored continuities with the past and later recruitment to conservative ends by the newly independent state made it appear opposed to modernist imagining – and usefully so for modernist writers who sought to differentiate themselves from their forebears.[6] Yet there is no doubt that the initial energies of the Revival were profoundly inspirational both within and beyond Ireland. It was more complex than received wisdom has it, and the movements had numerous points of overlap, from ideology to praxis. Revival works – especially in Irish – do look far less formally inventive than do avowedly modernist works, for reasons I outline below, but the key question of language also connects the movements. In Ireland, a Continental 'avant-garde sense of language as exhausted and enervated' with its 'concomitant longing for spiritual renewal through new languages of art, coincided with the Irish nationalist search for an autonomous mode of cultural expression'.[7] Revivalist thinking thus helps to generate one of the most avant-garde aspects of modernism. Rather than being opposed to modernism, the Revival appears to be 'an incubatory moment of it'.[8] Indeed, we do well to recognize the audacity of the Gaelic Revival's fundamental premise: that they could bring a profoundly marginalized and disadvantaged vernacular back to common usage, reversing a widespread sociolinguistic effect of modernity itself.[9] As Louis de Paor suggests, 'those arguing for a resuscitation of native models might even be presented as more radical than their cosmopolitan counterparts'.[10] The anticolonial challenge they mounted was both real and sustained, notwithstanding many Victorian traces in their work.

Writing modern literature in Irish was hardly straightforward. Writers who chose to compose in Irish had to revitalize the very language itself in the face of a massive and ongoing decline in the number of native speakers, and widespread illiteracy among them, such that writers themselves were not always masters of their medium. Writers could draw upon neither reference works nor editions of earlier literary achievements, nor an established publishing tradition, nor a comprehensive contemporary vocabulary in the language, but had at once to recover, renovate and invent needed resources, from dictionaries to words. 'Many of the leading writers of the Gaelic Revival never read a book in the Irish language in their formative years', Philip O'Leary explains.[11] Highly developed in its literary and scholarly register up to the seventeenth century, the largely spoken language that emerged from the nineteenth century in three distinct dialects retained rich, living practices of verbal performance but lacked a settled orthography, agreed-upon stylistic norms, or an official standard form, debates over which provoking considerable contention. Perhaps the largest controversy, which raged for decades, was stirred by the question of a prose literary standard, or 'whether the new prose of the Revival should attempt to pick up where the tradition had been ruptured in the seventeenth century or [...] accept the fact of discontinuity and root itself in the spoken language as it had evolved for two hundred years'.[12] That the question was *which standard* to apply, not whether the language could be revived, testifies to the confidence of the movement despite Anglophone writers' exaggerated laments for the 'lost' native tongue.

Another major difference in the situation of writers in Irish was that of audience. Writers in English could legitimately – if ambitiously – dream of accessing a broad potential readership both within Ireland and far beyond it. By contrast, writers who chose to write in Irish addressed a tiny, proximate and highly opinionated audience disproportionately composed, like them, of non-native speakers of varying degrees of proficiency. Many readers were far from fluent and thus, unwilling or unable to grasp complex syntax, were more interested in grammar books than literary productions. While textbooks or folk tales might sell four or five thousand copies or more, original literary works could sell in the low double digits. Revival-era writers in Irish also wrote for diverse, rural, *Gaeltacht* audiences fluent in Irish, though often minimally literate in the language, and who were more familiar with folk tales than urban forms: in fact, many writers expected their works to be read aloud rather than read well into the twentieth century.[13] All of these audiences were liable to be offended by representations perceived as negative or derogatory, given the legacy of colonialist denigration emblematized by the simian caricatures of *Punch*. And these audiences, and their very real limitations, had to be taken into account by those who wrote for them.

Given the state of the language and the relatively small number of writers, the resulting quality of published work varied greatly in quality. 'The content deemed most likely to interest and inspire native speakers was that contained in existing folktales already in oral circulation', and the consequent 'regurgitation and circularity of this approach failed to encourage, or reward, literary innovation or artistic experimentation'.[14] With prominent exceptions, 'the aesthetic was to be consistently subordinated to the mundane and ideological throughout (and, indeed, well past) the early years of the Revival'.[15] The most prominent Revival critic – activist, writer and educationalist Patrick Pearse (Pádraig Mac Piarais) (1879–1916), an almost exact contemporary of James Joyce – was, however, an indefatigable progressive champion of openness and artistic freedom. Such progressives, as Philip O'Leary terms them, believed that 'historic Ireland was not a misty if magnificent realm of saints, scholars, and heroes, but a vibrant culture fully in the European mainstream'.[16] For, as Pearse declared, 'in Ireland, "cosmopolitanism" [...] is only another word for Anglicisation'.[17] As another progressive put it, rather than being 'a suburb of a suburb' (that is, of England), Ireland should find its own connection with contemporary European thinking.[18]

Repeatedly and clearly, progressive revivalists championed the modern in revivalist writing. Pearse advocated finding models among contemporary European writers, especially those of France, Belgium, Russia and Norway, ideally in 'the characteristic literary type of the present day': that is, 'the short story', which he argued was best suited to the condition of the Irish language.[19] Irish writers, according to Pádraic Ó Conaire (1882–1928), should 'put the new literature on a level with every other modern literature throughout Europe'.[20] While acknowledging the appeal of language made authentically 'sinewy', 'idiomatic', 'virile and racy' (of the soil), Pearse insisted that language alone 'does not constitute literature. Style and form are essential'.[21] Writers must put themselves in their work and not simply cleave to folk models: '[I]t is time for our Irish writers to make a brave effort to express *themselves* – to tell us what they feel' and thus to create their own 'distinctive "styles"'.[22] Pádraic Ó Conaire agreed that 'an duine féin' (the person himself) was the focus of 'an nualitríocht úd' (that modern literature).[23] Yet, unlike modernists who obscured their debts to the past, Pearse saw knowledge of an occluded Irish tradition as a prerequisite. 'Central to his poetics is the idea that modernization of literary form and style in Irish requires a deeper engagement with precedents in the native tradition and a realignment of the relationship with contemporary Europe that had been disrupted by English colonialism', not one or the other, but both in tandem.[24]

The most modernist of the Revivalists, however, was not Pearse but fellow progressive Pádraic Ó Conaire. Like Pearse, Ó Conaire helped to pioneer the short story genre in Irish from as early as 1904, before it was fully assimilated into Anglophone writing.[25] Whether set in urban locales, or within a Gaeltacht stripped of the usual pieties, Ó Conaire's stories delve into the exactions of modernity on a community suffering its dislocating effects, particularly soul-crushing poverty that leads to endemic emigration.[26] Ó Conaire's novella, *Deoraíocht* (Exile, 1910), written in London, demands particular attention as 'the earliest example of modernist fiction in Irish'.[27] Like its author, the narrator came to London to find work; unlike Ó Conaire, narrator Micil Ó Maoláin is hit by a car soon afterwards, losing his arm and a leg, winning compensation, and then working in a travelling sideshow as a freak paid to roar rather than speak. At two climactic moments in the unpolished yet compelling text, however, Micil bursts forth in Irish to protest the injustice of his and others' treatment, before dying alone and broken back in London. Depicting 'urban life in spare, descriptive language with many neologisms', Ó Conaire demonstrates the capacity of the Irish language to tackle novel subjects while conveying the profound scepticism about urban life felt by most Revivalists.[28] Though the structure is clumsy, 'the novel's interrogation of dislocation and despair, of marginalisation and isolation' shares the central concerns of European modernism.[29] *Deoraíocht*'s eminently modernist 'preoccupation with the effects of industrial technology and a centralized economy on the individual brought up in a traditional society', forced by circumstance to emigrate to do the hardest work, often resulting in crippling injury, captures the stigma 'experienced by the colonized Irish seeking work in London in the early twentieth century'.[30] Modernity is revealed as a machine *producing* stigma, as its new technologies relentlessly crush and enfreak the workers whose communities it has earlier subalternized.[31] Micil's explosive and powerful demand for 'cead cainte' (permission to speak) dramatizes the need for political awakening among modernity's victims and, as Bourke notes, for concomitant artistic speech acts in their own language by those subjected to stigma.[32] This is modernism from a very different vantage point. Ó Conaire's acute and uncompromising work, eagerly read but also vilified and censored,[33] anticipates the more fully developed (late) modernism of mid-century, which in turn cites that very phrase demanding voice (in Máirtín Ó Cadhain's *Cré na Cille*).

By contrast, though novel in an Irish-language context and instantly canonized in school and university curricula, Pearse's literary work does not appear to enact the modernist principles he embraced in his criticism, nor to address 'cúrsaí an fichiú haois' (twentieth-century matters) at all.[34] In their determinedly idealized, often didactic portraits of the Gaeltacht and its people – as in 'Íosagán' (Jesukin), about an old man fallen from Catholic practice who is recovered to faith by the intercession of the eponymous holy child right before his death – Pearse's stories remain 'stubbornly conventional in their validation of traditional community values, and morally conservative despite their technical innovation'.[35] In so doing, however, Pearse arguably enacted 'a fully conscious aesthetic strategy' that offered an 'interpretation of life in the Gaeltacht, not as it was, but as it should and, to some extent, could be'.[36] In place of the stigma 'of a place notorious for poverty, danger and dirt', Pearse replaced 'that stigmatised and stigmatising image with an idea of community designed to revitalise and invigorate the Irish-speaking west, encouraging like-minded tourists to visit and helping to stem emigration while kindling the imagination of the metropolis' in a notion of 'imagined community'.[37] Whereas Ó Conaire dramatized stigma, Pearse countered it, each in the derided language of the community itself.

Yet such idealized representations came to be seen not as critical interventions opposing stigma, but as constraining, hegemonic nationalist pieties that were recycled by conservative state rhetoric and bombastic language activists alike. Despite taking concrete steps to enact its Revivalist principles, the new state's efforts fell far short, often seeming minimalist and tokenistic – as they continue to do.[38] Latter-day revivalists were seen as colluding in the deployment of a heteronormative, heavily moralized vision of Gaelic authenticity and purity that authorized the overwhelmingly conservative state's regulatory power even as the Gaeltacht itself was marginalized and fetishized. This context is inseparable from the afterlives of Revival modernism, since the idealized image of the Gaeltacht functioned as state dogma and language-movement creed: a profoundly dehumanizing, hegemonic, constraining misrepresentation for speakers and writers of Irish. Thus it is that late modernism in Irish[39] – epitomized in prose by Myles na gCopaleen/Flann O'Brien and Máirtín Ó Cadhain – is also termed Counter-Revivalist for its grimly acerbic savaging of stereotypes of the Gaeltacht derived from Revival writing, which underpinned 'the calcified discourse of national identity'.[40]

Stylistically, Micheál Ó Conghaile's realist 1997 tale of a young man anxiously coming out to his father is not especially edgy or experimental.[41] Nor does 'Athair' ('Father') parade its modernist artifice, craft or literariness. It centres neither on modern anomie, nor on the leitmotifs of the atomized cityscape. Yet, upon closer examination the story discloses a multivalent engagement with international modernist thematics and with the specifically Irish modernist heritage of Revival and Counter-Revival, showing how persistent those afterlives continue to be. Like key works of English and Irish modernism, 'Athair' concerns itself with secrets and queer disclosures, difficulty of speaking/communication, and ambiguity, while invoking a modernist coming of age in relation to traditional communities. But like Revival modernist texts, the story revisits the stigmatization experienced by marginalized communities, their exclusion from received narratives of national identity and literary tradition, and concomitant misapprehensions about Irish and its speakers (including misapprehensions by those speakers themselves). Like late modernist Counter-Revival texts, the story employs meta-literary humour to flaunt the flexibility, acuteness and wit of Irish, its speakers and literature. In so doing, the story transforms its inheritance toward its own ends – at once rewriting and recovering a radical Revival legacy of and for queer writers. If modernism was always queer – as Heather Love rhetorically asks, 'Is *queer modernism* simply another name for modernism?'[42] – then Ó Conghaile ultimately brings us full circle.

From the beginning, 'Athair' deploys modernist thematics to evoke the possibility that the father will reject his son and cast him out of their community. For all its queerness, modernism often taught that some secrets were better kept. After all, neither E. M. Forster's gay romance, *Maurice*, nor his grimly karmic, colonialist gay revenge fantasy, 'The Life to Come', were published in his lifetime, while the homoerotics remained occluded in his published works.[43] Even if not overtly self-destructive, pathetic or doomed, gay characters were often closeted, their messages legible only to the initiated. 'Athair' evokes this heritage as it offers a genre-appropriate moment of crisis compressed into a short story readable 'in a single sitting', in Poe's famous dictum – in which the narrator, appropriately enough, remains seated for the duration.[44] Although set in the kitchen alongside the stove, symbolic heart of the house and of the Irish storytelling tradition, Ó Conghaile's story foregrounds modernist tropes of communicative difficulty, linguistic limits and failures of connection through the limited perspective of the 22-year-old narrator. The youngest child, last of three to live at home on the farm, has evidently just told his aged, recently widowed father that he is gay – and it has gone very badly, as the first line records: 'Cén chaoi a mbeadh a fhios agamsa céard a dhéanfainn – th'éis dom é a inseacht dó – mar nach bhfaca mé m'athair ag caoineadh cheana ariamh. Ariamh!' (147) ('How could I know what to do – after I had told it to him – when I'd never seen my father crying before. Ever!'). An exact counterpart to the father's presumed shock is that of the son at the extraordinary, 'halting' and 'evasive' display of emotion that he similarly struggles both to name and to process. In the pages that follow, words seem unsayable, and attempts at speech are interrupted with a series of broken-off statements and half-questions festooned with ellipses and interspersed with painful silences. Even once the pair succeeds in speaking more – although still not using the crucial word, 'gay' – agonizingly ambiguous phrases at crucial junctures deny narrator and reader alike certainty about the ultimate outcome.

The son's descriptions expose his fear of a painful dénouement. As he awaits some words from his 'hesitating' father in response to the extradiegetic disclosure that precedes – and thus generates – the story, son like father is unable to meet the other's glance. He is immobilized by anxiety: 'Shuigh mise ansin i mo dhealbh – gan fanta ionam ach teas mo choirp' (148) ('I sat there like a statue – nothing left of me but body heat'), dramatizing how much depends upon his father's response. While the parental lamentation was bad, he reflects, the silence was far worse: 'Ach bhí an tost marfach éiginnte, dúshlánach: chomh mall fadálach pianmhar le breith' (148) ('But the silence was deadly, uncertain, challenging: as slow, tedious and painful as a judgment'). As shown by the Silence=Death Project founded in 1987 by gay activists in New York, this is a killing silence, as the son potentially faces the end of life as he knows it, social death, or even homophobic violence should his father reject him. In coming out, the son has chosen to subject himself to his father's response and to regulation.[45] But the modernist embrace of 'silence, exile, and cunning' was never as romantic for those forced to it as a means of (closeted) survival rather than a flight by nets.[46]

Once recovered, language seems tellingly inadequate: a further failure. When the father's words finally come, a full page and a half in, he stops after just three words, saying 'Agus tá tú ...' (148) ('And you are ...'). He seems, ironically and wittily, to resist the 'teacht amach' ('coming out') of the word 'gay' as if he cannot bear to repeat the son's action using 'focal nach móide a múnlaíodh as a scornach tuaithe féin ariamh' (148) ('a word his country throat had hardly have ever formed before'). Even the word itself troubles things: 'Focal stráinséartha ... Focal nach raibh fiú nath measúil Gaeilge ann dó nó má bhí, ní in aice láimhe ...' (148) ('A strange word ... a word there wasn't even a respectable Irish term for, or if there was, not near at hand ...'). By implication, if Irish *does not* have a word for gay, can the narrator ever be accepted, or fully inhabit his varied identities? He feels compelled to interrupt his father when he repeats, 'Agus deir tú liom go bhfuil tú ...' (148) ('And you tell me that you're ...'), by answering quickly, 'Tá' ('Yes'), himself, becoming, in a pointed neologism, 'chomh focalsparálach céanna' ('just as word-sparing') as his father, repeating 'Táim' ('I am') to fill the gap, to which the father ominously responds, 'Go sábhála Dia sinn' (148) ('May god save us').

Seemingly familiar stereotypes accumulate as the father questions who knew, and how the son had a girlfriend if he was gay (the father hoping the son is mistaken). The father's response to the son's sad query of 'Céard eile a d'fhéadfainn a dhéanamh?' (151) ('What else could I do?') is the most potentially cutting yet, as he throws the son's words back at him: ' "Cá bhfios domsa céard a d'fhéadfá a dhéanamh. Nach bhféadfá bheith ar nós chuile dhuine eile ... sin, sin, nó fanacht sa mbaile". Bhí cling ina ghuth nuair a dúirt sé an focal *baile*'. ("How do I know what you should've done. Couldn't you be like everyone else ... that, that, or stay at home?" There was a ring in his voice when he said the word *home*'). The rejection of his son's question and seeming inability to imagine himself in the son's place may mean the failure of empathy, the ring in his voice signalling regret at the son's failure to repress himself – unless 'home' turns out still to be home, after all. The son replies 'Ní fhéadfainn' ('I couldn't'), 'Ní fhéadfainn go deo ... Ní hé nár thriail mé ...' (151) ('I couldn't forever ... It's not that I didn't try ...'), trailing off sadly rather than explaining further, 'Faitíos nach dtuigfeadh sé' (151) ('Afraid that he wouldn't understand'), confident neither in his newly claimed identity nor in his parent's capacity to understand him. The father suddenly grasps why the son travelled so often to Dublin, that 'aisteach agus contúirteach' (152) ('quare and dangerous') place.[47] Unlike the Gaeltacht, the city is where you can be gay, and the city is itself 'queer/quare, odd', a perception at the heart of modernism, and of this story. The father having made his declaration about the city – legible either as alarming pronouncement and anticipation of the son's expulsion, or merely homespun rural truth – he begins to prepare for evening milking, emptying the cooler, scalding the pail with the water from the singing kettle, as the son sits awkwardly watching him perform the son's own accustomed tasks, unsure where he stands.

As the father prepares to exit and thus to terminate the narrative encounter and perhaps the relationship, the son's emotions heighten. Time begins to slow masterfully in conclusion, opposing meanings still proliferating. Further stereotypical questions follow, evoking exclusion and judgment – or parental insight and concern – as the father suddenly queries his son about his health, meaning AIDS. Is this a sign of reinscribed stigma: just as gayness is urban, it is disease? Or can genuine concern be detected in the father's subsequent relief? In a further exchange, the father exclaims at the thought of neighbours knowing, 'cineál múisce ina ghlór' (154) ('a sort of disgust in his voice'). In turn, the son's acknowledgment that they probably *do* know prompts his father's most searing question: '"Agus an bhuil tú ag ceapadh go bhfuil tú ag fanacht thart anseo?" ar sé de léim, noda imníoch scanrúil in a ghlór, dar liom' (154) ('"And are you thinking that you're staying around here?" he burst out, an anxious, terrified sound in his voice, I thought'). Wounded, the son cannot determine whether this is 'ceist' ('a question') or 'ráiteas' ('a statement'), though he internally reaffirms his desire to stay and care for his father. The progression of the narrative is interrupted as the son thinks of gay young men he has known in Dublin (that supposedly enlightened metropolis) who have been kicked out, beaten, locked up, hounded out of jobs and even driven to suicide. Social opprobrium outlasted the decriminalization of homosexuality in Ireland in 1993, after decades of political activism and countless individual acts of what this story depicts – coming out – which would be the fundamental basis for the overwhelmingly approved 2015 same-sex marriage referendum, something the characters in this story could hardly imagine.[48] The father prepares to go do the milking, pausing to bless himself with holy water, then turns on the threshold and looks beneficently 'díreach orm' (156) ('straight at me') at last, finally 'ag baint an rásáil as mo chuid smaointe uile, is á ruaigeadh ar ais i gcúinní dorcha mo chinn' ('stopping the racing of all my thoughts, and sending them back to the dark corners of my mind'), and thereby signalling the end of ambiguity. He asks, with a final pair of ellipses, '"An seasfaidh tú roimh an mbó bhradach dom?" ar sé, "fad a bheas mé á bleán … tá sine thinn i gcónaí aici …"' (156) ('"Will you stand by the braddy cow for me?" he asked, "while I'm milking … she still has a sore teat …"'). Though not a straight declaration, this last question nonetheless tells the son that he is wanted and needed, that he should stay, and that the father will *stand by* his son as well.

The build-up to the understated yet powerful ending is expert and earned, as the father's fear and revulsion yield to implicit support. A potentially resistant audience lives through the father's stages of grief and denial alongside the anxiety of the hitherto unrepresented persona of the narrator, enacting a multifaceted literary, experiential and narrative coming out in Irish. Presumably, the imperative to normalize gay experience determines the story's accessibly 'straight' narration. But, for those who can discern it, the story also provides an ironic linguistic and meta-literary commentary, particularly in its original language, making its challenge to assumptions about sexuality, language and culture at once more witty, political and assured. For even as the story relates and enacts a coming out, it never actually uses the contemporary word for the 'love that dare not speak its name' (the famous phrase from 'Two Loves' [1894] by Oscar Wilde's young lover, Lord Alfred Douglas, reiterated in Wilde's 1895 trials). Although evidently said to momentous effect just prior to the story's start, every time 'gay' is to be used again, an ellipsis intervenes, as the father tries and fails to say it, the son interrupts him, and so forth. The word is even described – as having 'fuaim ghlugarnach' (148) ('a gurgling sound'), the initial *g* confirming which word it is but, again, not repeating it. The inexperienced, ideologically constrained narrator also frets over the lack of a corresponding 'respectable' word in Irish, airing commonly held perceptions of Gaelic heteronormativity, linguistic archaism, and cultural backwardness alongside facile linguistic determinism. Evidently, you cannot even say 'gay' in an Irish story about coming out – so the story *about* coming out itself never quite *does* – although it *does* winkingly employ the words 'amach' ('out') and 'díreach' ('straight') at crucial junctures. It thereby enacts a coded yet playful ambiguity that revisits an earlier modernism's secretive tropes of male homosexuality, suggestively declines fixed identity categories and pregiven scripts – *and simultaneously* tropes on tired assumptions about what Irish is and can do.

This last message is underscored by the text's characteristic linguistic hybridity, as it uses English loanwords reflecting the living, local dialect, most amusingly when the father says that fathers have to have 'chuile fhocal *spelláilte* amach dóibh' (149) ('every single word is *spell*ed out for them'): the English word 'spell' fluently incorporated into Irish syntax, providing yet another joke about (literary) fathers who need retraining, and concepts that supposedly cannot be 'spelled out' in Irish (hence, the loanword, as if the Irish verb *litrigh* did not exist). But of course the reader must grasp the concept (and the sociolinguistic context) in order to make sense of the story and the in-joke, which is, after all, made *in* Irish – that supposedly limited medium. Refining the metaliterary joke still further, Ó Conghaile's text includes several words that can denote 'gay' used otherwise, 'aisteach' (152) ('odd, strange, queer') Dublin, a 'cam' (147) (bent, crooked) tear-track on the father's face and, especially, 'aerach' (152) (gay), this last an adjective modifying the 'merrily' bursting whistle of the kettle that insistently reasserts and promises a return to happy domesticity. For, of course, there is 'gay' in Gaelic and Gaeltacht – and not just homophonically – even if the narrator himself doubts it – he himself and, indeed, the story in which he appears testify to that.

Perhaps most profoundly, the text insists that the inheritance a writer receives is not fixed but subject to challenge, that the possibilities to be extracted are not finite but unbound, and that her or his contribution *and* medium matter. One final example illustrates Ó Conghaile's playful reckoning with the modernist past. Among the many literary forebears summoned up, including Ó Cadhain and Myles na gCopaleen's earlier satiric revisioning of the Gaeltacht, a particularly suggestive figure is Revival activist, revolutionary and short-story pioneer, Patrick Pearse. At once conventional and liberatory, Pearse helped create the idealized, heteronormative, piously policed image of the Gaeltacht that so bedevils the narrator of 'Athair' – becoming one of those troublesome literary 'fathers' who need to have new things spelled out – in so doing helping to create modern literature in Irish. Yet Pearse himself seems to have been gay but deeply closeted, probably even to himself, notwithstanding the sublimated homoeroticism of work that friends urged the oblivious author to temper. Accordingly, Ó Conghaile revisits Pearse's canonical story, 'Íosagán', as the narrator awaits his father's first words, when he describes himself as anxiously sitting 'i mo dhealbh' (148) ('like a statue'). Similarly, the mysteriously socially excluded protagonist of 'Íosagán' sits silently observant by his door, such that 'An té ghabhfadh an bóthar, shílfeadh sé gur dealbh chloiche nó mharmair a bhí ann – sin nó duine marbh [...]' (43) ('A person passing by would think that he was a statue of stone or marble, that or a dead person [...]').[49] Alluding in passing to the tale of sean-Mhaitias, said in the original narrative to have perhaps committed 'peaca uafásach éigin' (13) ('some terrible sin') (12), Ó Conghaile poses it as an occluded gay ancestral story, as he would later make more explicit in his gay Bildungsroman, *Sna Fir* (1999), in which the protagonist imagines flippantly rectifying the enraging lack of gay literary antecedents in his Irish literature exam by declaring 'Bhí sean-Mhaitias aerach' ('Old Matthias was gay'), and reflecting that he did not spend his youth 'ina shuí ina dhealbh le hais a dhorais' ('sitting like a statue beside the door'), but flirting.[50] Pearse was, of course, not only a repressed – and repressive – figure but an expressive and empowering one who envisioned a different, more inclusive, and tolerant world, and whose recuperated afterlife in Ó Conghaile's oeuvre seems highly fitting. It was he, after all, who in 1901 urged young writers: 'Má tá rud ar bith agat le rádh, amach leis!' ('If you have anything at all to say, out with it!'), an exhortation this story brilliantly embraces.[51]

Notes

1 Pericles Lewis, *The Cambridge Introduction to Modernism* (Cambridge: Cambridge University Press, 2007), xvii.
2 Kevin Whelan, 'The Cultural Effects of the Famine', *The Cambridge Companion to Modern Irish Culture*, eds. Joe Cleary and Claire Connolly (Cambridge: Cambridge University Press, 2005), 137–54 (138). On modernism and uneven development, see Perry Anderson, 'Modernity and Revolution', *Marxism and the Interpretation of Culture*, eds. Cary Nelson and Lawrence Grossberg (Urbana: University of Illinois Press, 1988), 317–38. On modernism and the peripheries, see Joe Cleary, 'European, American, and Imperial Conjunctures', *The Cambridge Companion to Irish Modernism*, ed. Joe Cleary (Cambridge: Cambridge University Press, 2014), 35–62 (38).
3 Lewis, *Introduction*, xx.
4 Adrian Frazier, 'Irish Modernisms, 1880–1930', *The Cambridge Companion to the Irish Novel*, ed. John Wilson Foster (Cambridge: Cambridge University Press, 2006), 113–32 (113).
5 Essential reading is Philip O'Leary, *The Prose Literature of the Gaelic Revival, 1881–1921: Ideology and Innovation* (University Park: The Pennsylvania State University Press, 1994), on which I have drawn heavily here.

6 See, for instance, Emer Nolan, 'Modernism and the Irish Revival', *The Cambridge Companion to Modern Irish Culture*, eds. Joe Cleary and Claire Connolly (Cambridge: Cambridge University Press, 2005), 157–72 (164); and Paige Reynolds, *Modernism, Drama, and the Audience for Irish Spectacle* (Cambridge: Cambridge University Press, 2007), 1–16.
7 Barry McCrea, 'Style and Idiom', *The Cambridge Companion to Irish Modernism*, ed. Joe Cleary (Cambridge: Cambridge University Press, 2014), 63–74 (63). On the modernist literary afterlives of minor (or 'peasant') vernaculars as tropes and as experimental, private languages for modernist expressionism, see Barry McCrea, *Languages of the Night: Minor Languages and the Literary Imagination in Twentieth-Century Ireland and Europe* (New Haven: Yale University Press, 2015).
8 Rónán McDonald, 'The Irish Revival and Modernism', *The Cambridge Companion to Irish Modernism*, ed. Joe Cleary (Cambridge: Cambridge University Press, 2014), 51–62 (51).
9 As recently as the nineteenth century Irish had its largest number of speakers, who were generally confident and persistent; see Nicholas M. Wolf, *An Irish-Speaking Island: State, Religion, Community, and the Linguistic Landscape in Ireland, 1770–1870* (Madison: University of Wisconsin Press, 2014).
10 Louis de Paor, 'Irish Language Modernisms', *The Cambridge Companion to Irish Modernism*, ed. Joe Cleary (Cambridge: Cambridge University Press, 2014), 161–73 (163).
11 O'Leary, *Prose Literature*, 1.
12 O'Leary, *Prose Literature*, 9.
13 O'Leary, *Prose Literature*, 13.
14 Brian Ó Conchubhair, 'The Twisting of Tradition: The Postmodern Irish-Language Short Story', *Twisted Truths: Stories from the Irish*, selected by Brian Ó Conchubhair (Indreabhán: Cló Iar-Chonnacht, 2011), 16–23 (16).
15 O'Leary, *Prose Literature*, 32.
16 O'Leary, *Prose Literature*, 55.
17 O'Leary, *Prose Literature*, 56.
18 Qtd., O'Leary, *Prose Literature*, 58.
19 Qtd., O'Leary, *Prose Literature*, 74.
20 Qtd., O'Leary, *Prose Literature*, 108.
21 Aisling Ní Dhonnchadha, *An Gearrscéal sa Ghaeilge, 1898–1940* (Baile Átha Cliath: An Clóchomhar, 1981), 51.
22 Ní Dhonnchadha, *Gearrscéal*, 51.
23 Ní Dhonnchadha, *Gearrscéal*, 9.
24 de Paor, 'Irish Language Modernisms', 162.
25 Ní Dhonnchadha terms him the earliest writer to grasp the power and resources of the modernist short story (*Gearrscéal*, 71; for acute analysis, see 71–113).
26 See O'Leary's fine discussion of Ó Conaire, *Prose Literature*, 421; 130–36, 421–30.
27 Angela Bourke, 'Legless in London: Pádraic Ó Conaire and Éamon a Búrc', *Éire-Ireland* 38, 3–4 (2003), 54–67, (54). See Pádraic Ó Conaire, *Deoraíocht* (Baile Átha Cliath: An Comhlacht Oideachais, 1994). For translation, see Pádraic Ó Conaire, *Exile*, trans. Gearailt Mac Eoin (Indreabhán: Cló Iar-Chonnachta, 1994).
28 Bourke, 'Legless in London', 55.
29 de Paor, 'Irish Language Modernisms', 164.
30 Bourke, 'Legless in London', 57, 65–66.
31 On enfreakment, see Rebecca Stern, 'Our Bear Women, Ourselves: Affiliating with Julia Pastrana', *Victorian Freaks: The Social Context of Freakery in Britain*, ed. Marlene Tromp (Columbus: Ohio State University Press, 2008), 200–33; and Rosemarie Garland Thompson, 'Introduction', *Freakery: Cultural Spectacles of the Extraordinary*

Body, ed. Rosemarie Garland Thompson (New York: New York University Press, 1996), 1–19.
32 Bourke, 'Legless in London', 67.
33 Father Ua Laoghaire successfully campaigned to have *Deoraíocht* removed from the National University syllabus (O'Leary, *Prose Literature*, 35, 141).
34 Ní Dhonnchadha, *Gearrscéal*, 60, 51.
35 Pádraic Mac Piarais, *Gearrscéalta an Phiarsaigh*, ed. Cathal Ó Háinle (Baile Átha Cliath: Helicon, 1979), 43–51 (43); de Paor, 'Irish Language Modernisms', 163.
36 O'Leary, *Prose Literature*, 122, 123.
37 Angela Bourke, 'The Imagined Community of Pearse's Short Stories', *The Life and After-Life of P.H. Pearse = Pádraic Mac Piarais: Saol agus Oidhreacht*, eds. Roisin Higgins and Regina Uí Chollatáin (Dublin: Irish Academic Press, 2009), 141–55 (146, 141).
38 See Gearóid Ó Tuathaigh, 'Language, Ideology and National Identity', *The Cambridge Companion to Modern Irish Culture*, eds. Joe Cleary and Claire Connolly (Cambridge: Cambridge University Press, 2005), 42–58 (49–50).
39 Dating modernism in Irish from 1940 through the 1960s is 'useful but imprecise' (de Paor, 'Irish Language Modernisms', 165). Here 'late modernist' captures the satiric and meta-literary bent of key prose works of the 1940s. Mark Quigley also troubles conventional chronology in reading Blasket Islands autobiographies of the 1920s and 1930s as 'late-modernist' challenges to elitism and bourgeois nationalism (*Empire's Wake: Postcolonial Irish Writing and the Politics of Modern Literary Form* (New York: Fordham University Press, 2013), 25).
40 Sarah E. McKibben, '*An Béal Bocht*: Mouthing Off at National Identity'. *Éire-Ireland* 38, 1 & 2 (2003): 37–53 (38). See Philip O'Leary, *Irish Interior: Keeping Faith with the Past in Gaelic Prose, 1940–1951* (Dublin: University College Dublin Press, 2010).
41 'Athair' ('Father') was published in the collection *An Fear a Phléasc* (Indreabhán: Cló Iar-Chonnachta, 1997), from which subsequent quotations will be taken. A translation by Frank Sewell, to which I occasionally refer, is found in *Forefront: Contemporary Stories Translated from the Irish*, introduced by Declan Kiberd (Indreabhán: Cló Iar-Chonnachta, 1998), 20–27. Note that the press is now known as Cló Iar-Chonnacht, not Cló Iar-Chonnachta, as founded in 1985.
42 Heather Love, 'Introduction: Modernism at Night', *PMLA* 124, 3 (May 2009): 744–48.
43 E. M. Forster, *Maurice* (New York: W. W. Norton & Co., 1971); E. M. Forster, *The Life To Come and Other Short Stories* (New York: W. W. Norton & Co., 1972), 65–82.
44 On Poe and generic assumptions, see Dominic Head, *The Modernist Short Story: A Study in Theory and Practice* (Cambridge: Cambridge University Press, 1992), 9.
45 Judith Butler, 'Imitation and Gender Insubordination', *Inside/Out: Lesbian Theories, Gay Theories*, ed. Diana Fuss (New York: Routledge, 1991), 13–31 (15).
46 The phrase is Stephen Dedalus's of course; see discussion of this question in Jodie Medd, '"Patterns of the Possible": National Imaginings and Queer Historical (Meta) Fictions in Jamie O'Neill's *At Swim, Two Boys*', *GLQ: A Journal of Lesbian and Gay Studies* 13, 1 (2007): 1–31 (2–3).
47 Phrase translated by Sewell.
48 'I'm sure over the next few years there will be countless insightful theses and international studies and analysis projects done on why Ireland passed marriage equality. [...]

But there is one very simple building block to all of this, and that is the act of coming out. It is visibility that changes attitudes. You cannot hate what you know.' Una Mullally, 'Your world will change when you come out as the person you are'. *Irish Times*, 25 May 2015 <http://www.irishtimes.com/opinion/una-mullally-your-world-will-change-when-you-come-out-as-the-person-you-are-1.2224047>

49 Pádraic Mac Piarais, *Gearrscéalta an Phiarsaigh*, ed. Cathal Ó Háinle (Baile Átha Cliath: Helicon, 1979), 43–51 (43).

50 Discussed in Bríona Nic Dhiarmada, 'Putting the Gay in Gaelic: Queer Sexualities in Contemporary Irish Writing', unpublished MS, (5); Micheál Ó Conghaile, *Sna Fir* (Indreabhán: Cló Iar-Chonnachta, 1999), 83.

51 Qtd., Ní Dhonnchadha, *Gearrscéal*, 49.

Section Two
INSTITUTIONS, ART AND PERFORMANCE

Chapter 7

'MAKE A LETTER LIKE A MONUMENT': REMNANTS OF MODERNIST LITERARY INSTITUTIONS IN IRELAND

Andrew A. Kuhn

Much like literary forms, the institutions that create and sustain literature have significant afterlives. The efforts of editors, publishers and booksellers resonate beyond their time, and their successors inherit the traditions, structures and technologies of the trade. Modernism's publishing legacy lives in the little magazines, manifestos and private presses that embodied the movement, and later publishers and authors have reappropriated and translated these artefacts and institutions to meet the specific conditions of their moment. Increasingly, narratives of modernism have recognized the publishers, booksellers and patrons responsible for producing the books, periodicals and ephemera of the era.[1] These institutions and actors shaped modernist literature by providing its material manifestation, and the format of these works fashioned the reading experiences of subsequent writers. If modernism began in the magazines, as Robert Scholes and Clifford Wulfman have argued, succeeding generations monumentalized and repurposed the publishing tactics that commenced the era.[2]

Mid-century literary publishing in Ireland gathered together the remnants of collapsed modernist experiments, most notably the Cuala Press (1902–46). A leading publisher of the Irish Revival, the Cuala Press printed much of W. B. Yeats's oeuvre and raised the standards for Irish book production through a reinvention of print tradition and a focus on contemporary economic and cultural needs. Later the Dolmen Press (1951–87) revived its logics to rejuvenate a barren literary environment in mid-twentieth-century Ireland. Beginning as an intimate collaboration between printer and poet, the Dolmen Press grew to be the preeminent poetry press of its time and was internationally renowned for its craftsmanship and support of Irish writing. Like the Cuala before it, the Dolmen utilized the private-press model to create book-shaped monuments to modernism. In a time when many writers were openly hostile to influences of this earlier movement, the institutions of literary publishing more fully embraced modernist strategies and the international reputations of their writers. The Dolmen adopted and revised the fine-press tradition and aesthetic aims of the Cuala, and it united the beautiful book with literary content that celebrated the work of contemporary Irish writers alongside the titans of high modernism. In doing so, the Dolmen resumed the modernist tendency to conceptualize Irishness within a cosmopolitan framework.

The Cuala Press, Revivalism and Modernism

In Ireland, questions of modernist institutions are bound up with the Literary Revival and the cultural and political organizations of the early twentieth century. The Gaelic League, Feis Ceoil, the Irish Literary Theatre and Dun Emer Industries, in one way or another, had ties to the practices and ideologies of modernism. In the most obvious sense, they figure prominently in the development and writings of modernists such as W. B. Yeats, James Joyce and Samuel Beckett. In more complex ways, Irish revivalism and modernist aesthetic practices shared specific influences and ideologies. We can understand these institutions in ways akin to the recent critical tendency to read the Revival's literature in modernist terms, which stems from a renewed attention to shared traditions, historical contexts and actors. As Rónán McDonald observes:

> Both the Irish Revival and European modernism have aesthetic roots in French Symbolism and in the work of Darwin and Nietzsche; both reject empiricism, realism, and linear temporality; both seek alternatives to modern epistemologies; both are attracted to primitivism, and mythology and the occult, often as alternatives to conventional religion. And straddling both movements, fitting all these descriptors, stands Yeats, a dominating figure in both the Irish Revival and European modernism, though also, ironically, responsible for some of the later fixed ideas about the Revival that would allow for its tenacious caricature.[3]

Similar comparisons can be made to the origins and aims of the publishing branches of both movements. More than any other Irish publisher of the time, the Cuala Press embodied the shared concerns of the Revival and European modernism.

The Cuala developed from a desire to challenge the primacy of the London book trade. The press began its life as the Dun Emer Press in 1902 and was part of a larger collaborative dedicated to Irish handicraft and the education and employment of women. Elizabeth Yeats, an accomplished painter and art instructor, oversaw the printing department of the Dun Emer, and her brother William Butler acted as literary advisor. Their innovation stemmed from a reworking and synthesis of traditional printing practices, modern book design and Irish nationalism. The medievalism of William Morris's Arts and Crafts movement combined with the modern typography of the Bodley Head formed the distinct feel of the Dun Emer book. In 1908, the printing department broke away from the Dun Emer, and Elizabeth and her sister Lily named their new venture the Cuala Industries, which specialized in printing and textiles. The press produced 77 books over 43 years along with a large number of broadsheets, prints, greeting cards, booklets and other ephemera.[4] In addition to being W. B. Yeats's Irish publisher, the press worked with other prominent Irish literary figures, including many who would become associated with modernism, such as Jack Yeats, Ezra Pound and Elizabeth Bowen.

The politics and ideologies that drove the press were complex and often contradictory. For instance, its progressive stance on women's labour and education was tempered by the Yeatses' more conservative views on gender equality. The staunch, and sometimes violent, nationalist views held by a number of the women who worked at the press conflicted with Elizabeth's more cautious cultural nationalism and the Unionist sentiment of many patrons of the press. Its connections with the Arts and Crafts movement suggested certain affinities with socialism and the resistance to capitalist production; yet, the books, embroidery and weaving it produced became luxury items for bourgeois consumers. Its struggles with issues of gender and labour, nationalism and colonial resistance, materialism and commodification, high and low cultural production and the reworking of tradition reveal the deep affinities between the Cuala and the concerns of modernism.

Furthermore, the private press industry, like the little magazine, was one of the defining institutions of modernist literature. Fine-press printing provided a physical presence for the movement because of the economic and aesthetic autonomy that it offered. 'From Yeats and Pound to Stein and Williams and the writers of the Harlem Renaissance', as Jerome McGann argues, 'fine-printing works, the small press, and the decorated book fashioned the bibliographic face of the modernist world'.[5] In Ireland specifically, private-press production drove much of the literary innovation throughout the twentieth century and into the twenty-first.[6] Viewing this industry within the context of international modernism, the Cuala's opposition to the London-centric book market, the mass-produced book and male-dominated trades defines a legacy that would be repurposed by later generations of Irish publishers and authors.

The Dolmen Press and Monuments to Modernism

Many of the political and aesthetic crises that gave rise to the Cuala once again plagued Irish writing in the mid-twentieth century. The closing of the Cuala in 1945 was part of a larger cultural malaise brought about by censorship, neutrality and economic stagnation. Throughout the 1930s and 1940s, small magazines and presses came and went; however, a defining voice in publishing was conspicuously absent. Although Irish trade publishers, such as M. H. Gill, Browne and Nolan, and the Talbot Press, continued to issue popular fiction and religious and educational texts throughout this period, as Dillon Johnston observed, 'For a serious publisher of literature, writers would have to wait for the founding of the Dolmen Press in 1951'.[7]

Unsure and untrained, Liam Miller in 1951 offered Irish writers a place to publish new works. This enterprise served to fill a void created by the disappearance of literary journals such as *Envoy* (1949–51) and *The Bell* (1940–54) and the shuttering of literary presses such as Maunsel (1905–25) and Cuala. Miller strove to create books whose quality was commensurate with their literary content. As Maurice Harmon states:

> Miller believed in the idea of a sustained, mutually satisfying relationship between the writer and the publisher. The kind of co-operation that had characterized the making of plays in the early years of the Abbey Theatre was replicated in the way that he and the poets worked together. Many who published a book with Dolmen had the rare experience of collaborating with a skilled and imaginative craftsman seeking to match design, materials and literary content.[8]

The results of this artistic approach to publishing were material texts that served as extensions of the literary works, and the collaborative nature of the Dolmen has precedent in the cooperative aesthetic movements of the early twentieth century. A number of critics have observed that Miller's Dolmen Press succeeded the Cuala Press as the premier literary publisher in Ireland, and furthermore, the accomplishments of Miller and his stable of writers constituted a second Revival.[9] The press solidified the reputations of modernists such as Yeats, Joyce and Beckett while supporting the new dispensation for Irish literature represented by Patrick Kavanagh, Thomas Kinsella and John Montague.

In 1956 the Dolmen Press published a book of new poems by Padraic Colum entitled *Ten Poems*, which is a point of continuity between the writers of the Revival and high modernism and a new group of writers that would emerge from the Dolmen. His vision of an epic Ireland places him with Yeats, AE and Douglas Hyde, and like those authors, he was published by the Cuala

Press. Many of his ballads appeared in Cuala's *A Broadsheet* (1908–15). Colum's interests, however, were more broadly modernist. He was an early admirer and reviewer of the works of Joyce and assisted in the compilation of Joyce's modernist masterpiece, *Finnegans Wake* (1939). He traversed those overlapping worlds of revivalism and modernism, and in the early 1950s offered a new collection of his poetry to the emerging Dolmen Press.

Ten Poems ends with a verse on the cultural status of the poem and a commentary on Irish bookmaking. It takes a renowned Irish book for its title, 'The Book of Kells'. The first stanza speaks of the way in which literature is monumentalized in the book:

> First, make a letter like a monument –
> An upright like the fast-held hewn stone
> Immovable, and half-rimming it
> The strength of Behemoth his neck-bone,
> And underneath that yoke, a staff, a rood
> Of no less hardness than the cedar wood.
> Then, on a page made golden as the crown[10]

In these lines, Colum creates an ekphrastic view of the manuscript with its large-stroked letters, fantastical creatures and the symbolic imagery of Christianity.

These bibliographic details speak to the craftsmanship and labour of manuscript production and poetic composition. Under the skilled hand of the scribe, alphabetic characters become stone-hewn monuments, and the image of a staff on the page assumes the tangibility and strength of timber. Colum recognizes 'the quickened skill / Lessoned by famous masters in our school' in the scribal act as well as in the feat of versification. The first stanza displays his 'nether web of endless effort' in textured sounds and themes. He builds the first six lines around the simple end-rhymes that backbone the stanza, and the hyphenated words rib the figure. The Behemoth that sits in the centre of the stanza comes out of the Book of Job, where the God-made creature 'moveth his tail like a cedar: the sinews of his stones are wrapped together'.[11] The 'hewn stone' and 'cedar wood' mirror one another at the ends of the second and sixth lines, suggesting that the poem and book can stand as majestically as any monument of wood and stone.

Colum echoes the careful construction and intricate interlacing of the medieval manuscript. The monumental book needs a similarly wrought poem to memorialize it, and literary works deserve to be enshrined within books that fit their purpose. If modernist Irish authors have been memorialized in statues, bridges and even a class of naval ship, as is the case with the *Samuel Beckett*-class offshore patrol vessel, the object of an impressive book seems the proper place to commemorate their literary works. The Revival appropriated the Book of Kells and other Irish manuscripts as a touchstone for a national visual and craft culture. Artists recreated its uncial letters, delicate interlacing and fantastical creatures for books, periodicals and advertisements. Colum pays tribute to the scribal culture that produced such a book-formed monument.

In the second half of the twentieth century, the Dolmen Press was the primary publisher of the monumental book for Irish literature. In many ways *Ten Poems* echoes the bibliographic features of Irish books fifty years earlier. Printed in the distinctive black and red ink, the majuscule title runs the length of the upper page with a simple publisher name at the foot of the text block (Figure 7.1a–c). Its limited edition, Caslon typeface, Irish rag paper and hand-pulled impressions echo those used in the Cuala editions in which W. B. Yeats developed his modernist voice. Even the equipment used by Miller for the press had its own modernist provenance. Cecil ffrench Salkeld gave Miller a 12-point Bodoni font and wooden hand press that were used by him and his mother, Blanaid Salkeld, at the Gayfield Press, which published Salkeld's experimental verse and her son's illustrations.[12]

The Dolmen's Modernist Revival

The claim that the Dolmen's resurrection of Cuala's publishing strategies constitutes a second Revival depends upon continuities in book design and literary content. The similarities in design are quickly apparent upon a cursory comparison of the books printed by each press. In the later productions, Miller consciously adopts a Cuala-like layout and typography for his studies of Yeats (Figure 7.1d). Miller, like W. B. and Elizabeth Yeats, was inspired by the work of William Morris and the example of the Arts and Crafts Movement. Although Miller preferred humanist, Post-Reformation typefaces for most of his volumes, his work with Michael Biggs on a modern cutting of the medieval Irish uncial script appearing in *A Gaelic Alphabet* (1960) and the Gaelic adaptation of Times Roman used in *An Beal Bocht* (1964) most closely approximate the antiquarian typography that gives Morris's Kelmscott books their distinctive, and largely illegible, style. The Dolmen never imagined itself as a guild, as in Morris's socialist, or the Cuala's more practical, organizations, yet it did retain the movement's aim of fostering artisanal production and aesthetic value over commercial concerns.

In creating the book beautiful, both the Cuala and Dolmen shared a common hardship. Solvency vexed both. Their mode of production was at odds

TEN POEMS
BY PADRAIC COLUM

DUBLIN
THE DOLMEN PRESS
MCMLVII

Figure 7.1a Title page, Padraic Colum, *Ten Poems* (Dublin: Dolmen, 1957). Image courtesy of John J. Burns Library, Boston College.

IN THE SEVEN WOODS : BEING POEMS
CHIEFLY OF THE IRISH HEROIC AGE
BY WILLIAM BUTLER YEATS

THE DUN EMER PRESS
DUNDRUM
MCMIII

Figure 7.1b Title page, W. B. Yeats, *In the Seven Woods* (Dundrum: Dun Emer, 1903). Image courtesy of John J. Burns Library, Boston College.

THE CAT AND THE MOON AND
CERTAIN POEMS: BY WILLIAM
BUTLER YEATS.

THE CUALA PRESS
MERRION SQUARE
DUBLIN IRELAND
MCMXXIV

Figure 7.1c Title page, W. B. Yeats, *The Cat and the Moon and Certain Poems* (Dublin: Cuala, 1924). Image courtesy of John J. Burns Library, Boston College.

THE DOLMEN PRESS YEATS
CENTENARY PAPERS MCMLXV
EDITED BY LIAM MILLER WITH A
PREFACE BY JON STALLWORTHY

DUBLIN: THE DOLMEN PRESS
LONDON: OXFORD UNIVERSITY PRESS
CHESTER SPRINGS, PENNSYLVANIA: DUFOUR EDITIONS

Figure 7.1d Title page, Liam Miller, ed., *The Dolmen Press Yeats Centenary Papers MCMLXV* (Dublin: Dolmen, 1968). Image courtesy of John J. Burns Library, Boston College.

with the profit-seeking sectors of their industry. This is not to overly romanticize the respective presses as completely indifferent to the commercial aspects in the service of art. However, the aesthetic qualities of the books and their contents did often seem to supersede the realities of the ledger. This tendency arises from equal parts disgust at poorly executed trade books, rejection of the dominance of English books and a quixotic attempt to elevate art over the marketplace.

In their concerns for the aesthetics of the book, the Cuala and Dolmen fit into a legacy of modernist book production and typographic experimentation that begins with Stéphane Mallarmé. Dolmen's most famous book, Thomas Kinsella's translation of *The Táin* (1969) illustrated by Louis le Brocquy, has been described as 'an Irish equivalent of the *livre d'artiste*'[13] (Figure 7.2). This collaboration between author and the bookmakers highlights the ways in which the material and visual features of the book complement the linguistic text. These forms of poetic experimentation originate with Mallarmé and continue in the works of poets such as Ezra Pound, William Carlos Williams and Marianne Moore. In 1965, the Dolmen built upon this modernist legacy in Brian Coffey's translation of Mallarmé's *Un coup de dés jamais n'abolira le hasard* (Figure 7.3). The collaboration between Miller and Coffey resulted in an English translation of the poem that took into account Mallarmé's eclectic page layout. Within the poem, the page cannot be an indifferent medium. As the poet suggests, the '"whites," as a matter of fact, take on importance, strike one first of all; verse requires white, like silence around it'.[14] In many of the Dolmen productions this sense of the *livre d'artiste* is present. Aside from *The Táin*, the Dolmen's grandest undertakings were often reserved for modernist masters. The Dolmen edition of James Joyce's *Dubliners* (1986), which includes images of Dublin brushed in printer's ink by le Brocquy in the same mythic style he used for the *Táin*, gives the stories a similar epic tone. The lavish *de luxe* editions of both *The Táin* and *Dubliners* utilize methods and materials that suggest the aura and significance of the Book of Kells as opposed to the mass-produced paperback where most readers encounter these works.

The second point of continuity from Cuala to Dolmen can be found in their shared literary approaches. The modernist legacies of both presses are tied to the works of Yeats. As editor of the Cuala, W. B. Yeats dominated the publishing list, and the press explicitly sought to support Irish writers and revivalist themes. These broad interests anchored the Dolmen Press as well. Miller's devotion to Yeats is present throughout the history of the press. In discussing the *The Yeats Centenary Papers* (1968), Thomas Dillon Redshaw argues that 'by reasserting Yeats's world and the Yeatsian worldview, these and other titles from the Dolmen Press constitute a monument more lasting than bronze'.[15] The press's commitment to a vibrant scholarly discussion of Yeats in works

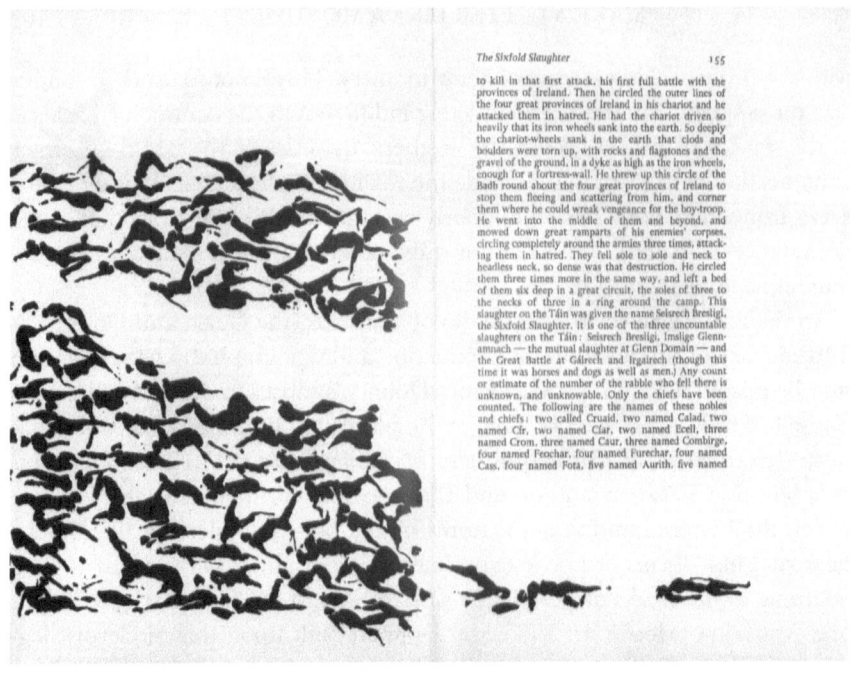

Figure 7.2 Thomas Kinsella, trans., *The Táin*, illus. Louis le Brocquy (Dublin: Dolmen, 1969). Image courtesy of John J. Burns Library, Boston College.

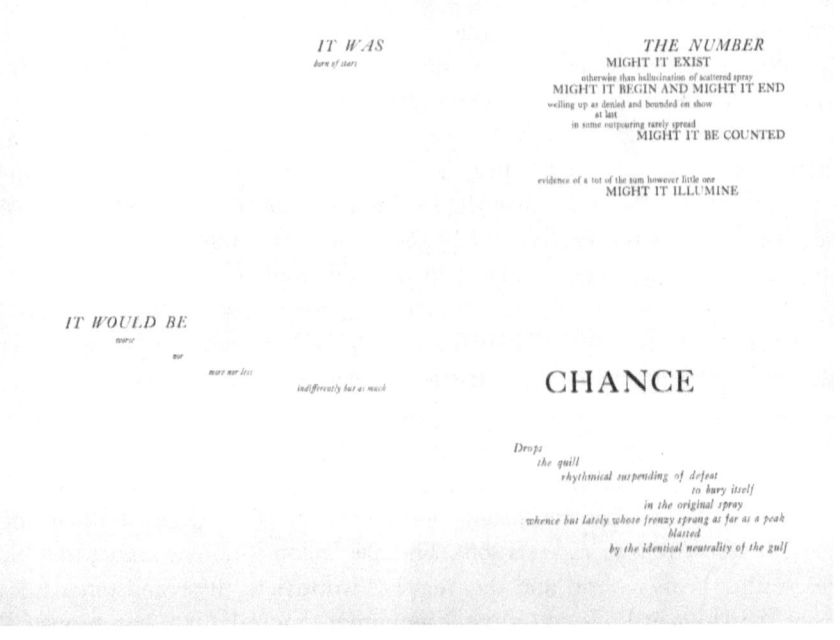

Figure 7.3 Stéphane Mallarmé, *Dice Thrown Never Will Annul Chance*, trans., Brian Coffey (Dublin: Dolmen, 1965). Image courtesy of John J. Burns Library, Boston College.

such as Miller's study, *The Noble Drama of W. B. Yeats* (1977), and the critical series, *The New Yeats Papers* (1977), helped cement Yeats as an Irish writer and a significant voice in modernist literature. Miller also issued some of Yeats's unpublished manuscript material, as was the case with *A Tower of Polished Black Stones* (1971), an early version of *The Shadowy Waters* originally planned for Leonard Baskin's Gehenna Press. The Dolmen was also at the centre of a burgeoning network of organizations dedicated to the poet's legacy. Most of the essays included in the *Yeats Centenary Papers* originated in the Yeats International Summer School in Sligo. Miller chaired the Dublin Yeats Society and was involved in many of the centenary events in 1965.

Literary Institutions, the Local and the Global

Irish literary institutions looked abroad even in the most parochial historical moments. The Cuala sought an international audience and cultivated a cosmopolitan vision of Irish literature that the Dolmen refined for the increasingly globalized literary scene of the later twentieth century. Again, W. B. Yeats looms large in this process. He gathered literary figures and influences from the United States, India, Japan and elsewhere to enrich the resources of Irish literary tradition. He promoted Rabindranath Tagore through a Cuala edition of the *The Post Office* (1914). Again looking east, the Cuala published Ernest Fenollosa's *Certain Noble Plays of Japan* (1916), edited by Ezra Pound. In this volume, Yeats expounds upon the role of international models in the creation of a national literature. He articulated his editorial role by emphasizing the need to absorb the lessons of other literary cultures: 'In the series of books I edit for my sister I confine myself to those that have I believe some special value to Ireland, now or in the future. I have asked Mr. Pound for these beautiful plays because I think they will help me to explain a certain possibility of the Irish dramatic movement'.[16] The introduction further justifies Yeats's dramatic experiments in his recently staged *At the Hawk's Well*, but it also demonstrates the outward-looking nature of Yeats's project and a preoccupation with myth and ethnography that would become hallmarks of modernist literature. Here, Yeats challenges the limits of realism and the unimaginative educational, journalistic and commercial spheres that feed a desire for it.[17] The formal abstraction of Noh offered a corrective to forms of Western art and entertainment that, in Yeats's estimation, had ceased to provide proper emotional depth. He concludes with his desire to reach an international audience with his Celtic adaptations of Japanese forms in saying, 'Are not the fairy-stories of Oscar Wilde, which were written for Mr. Ricketts and Mr. Shannon and for a few ladies, very popular in Arabia?'[18] To my knowledge, no editions of the Cuala book were dispatched to Asia, but Yeats's call for an international literature is present. While volumes by non-European writers are relatively scarce in the Cuala catalogue, the contributions that do appear signify the early stirrings of a cosmopolitan identity that opposes an insular and provincial notion of Irish literary production.

The Dolmen exhibits similar modernist negotiations between the local and the global, which in the case of Ireland often involves the working through of colonial legacies. 'I commenced publishing with the idea that I would issue the work of the young writers and so establish an outlet in their own land for a group who were aware of Ireland's twentieth century emergence as a free nation', Miller wrote. 'The outward projection of a country's culture is weakened and the value of the writer's contribution to the nation's power diminished, if that country's writers must look to a capital other than their own for first publication of their work'.[19] However, this is not to say that the press was not outward looking. In an interview on RTÉ, Miller clarified his view on the Dolmen's role in publishing Irish works in a global world:

> The Ireland I chose to publish in is Anglo-Ireland[; ...] publishing in Irish is a totally separate thing, it[']s subsidized and insular, it's bounded, surrounded by water, confine[d] to our island. But to see what impact writing in English from Ireland could make, I realized quite early on that one had to form friendships or liaisons in the bigger English-speaking world because in my experience [...] the publisher of creative literature in English from an Irish base must export sixty to seventy per cent of his sales.[20]

The realities of the publishing world in the second half of the twentieth century necessitated a global perspective as Ireland increasingly made steps toward modernization and opened itself to international markets.[21]

The most commented-upon study in the Dolmen's *Yeats Centenary Papers* is Hiro Ishibashi's *Yeats and the Noh* (1966). The essay further details Yeats's connection to Noh drama, and Zen more widely, perhaps representing the popularity that Yeats had desired in the Asian world. In terms of the Dolmen's extension of the Cuala's modernist strategies, a commitment to embracing global literature and reconciling specific texts to aspects of Irish identity and literary form continues in a greatly expanded form. For instance, the translations of Jorge Louis Borges found in *Irish Strategies* (1975) highlight the complexities and joys in the translations of language and culture. The volume contains two short stories by Borges translated into both Irish and English. Anthony Kerrigan, the English translator of the book, gives a dream account of a conversation with Borges in which the Spanish author remarks, 'Don't you think, now, that the matter of putting me into English is really a matter of putting me first into Anglo-Saxon, or, even better, now that I think of it, into

Irish?'[22] Kerrigan notes that the book is an attempt to answer this question and, in facing Irish/English translations, the volume achieves a strong sense of cultural fusion on the page. Yet, *Irish Strategies* also suggests rootlessness and dislocation in the form of fantastical histories of Ireland. At the centre of the volume, Borges celebrates the achievements of Joyce in verse. *Irish Strategies* places Borges within a larger Celtic context, as his stories demand, and it challenges insular notions of Irishness as it points to these pan-Celtic connections.

In terms of Irish book production, a similar international character can be found in the work of the Dolmen Press. In addition to the international attention that award-winning art books such as Kinsella's *Táin* garnered, Miller conceived of the Dolmen and the tradition of Irish printing as transcending the boundaries of a national context. In a speech entitled 'Fresh Images Beget: Art Nouveau & Irish Books', Miller draws connections between the aesthetic values of the Art Nouveau movement, which was popular both on the continent and in the United States, to Celtic artwork and Irish book production. In speaking about the Celtic world of *The Táin*, Miller remarks: 'It was a world of artefacts, many of which might have been the product of the new age of skills in gold and silver which accompanied the art of the new book decorators – old skills which in the 1967 Rosc Exhibition in Dublin were re-discovered for us in all their Art Nouveau richness'.[23] While the Celtic Revival imagined the works of Celtic oral culture to be intimately a part of the Irish birthright and a key to forming a nation, Miller wishes to extend this Celtic tradition to the world by noting similar aims in artistic production. His mention of the 1967 Rosc exhibition is also significant because of the way it heralded the arrival of Irish art in the international art scene.

Miller worked to further strengthen ties to an international book market. In 1972 *Clé*, the Irish publishers' association, hosted a conference in Dublin for UNESCO's 'International Book Year', which strove to make books available to all people around the globe. Miller addressed the conference, arguing, in part, that nation-states should keep import duties on books low to allow their citizens to have inexpensive access to writers around the world. Miller and the Dolmen sought to promote the spread of Irish writers not just to the Irish, but desired a cosmopolitan atmosphere for literary interaction, one consistent with the globalization of Ireland in the last half of the twentieth century. As the Dolmen matured, Miller began associations with larger presses, such as the Oxford University Press and other international private presses like the Swallow Press in Chicago, as a means of making his books available to a wider reading public.

In literary Ireland, modernism is king. For better or worse, the legacies of Yeats, Joyce and Beckett dominate the landscape. As national symbols and artists, they generate tourism dollars, launch global conferences and inspire monographs at a tremendous rate. Their success and notoriety have led many to draw upon these literary reputations, especially in times of crisis. After the collapse of the Celtic Tiger, the modernist favourites were trotted out as signs of accomplishment, reinvention and national pride in a world of existential doubt. The publishing world is one set of institutions among many that recognized the value of Irish modernist contributions and strove to memorialize and build upon these achievements to remake the literary world of its own day.

Notes

1. Lawrence Rainey's *Institutions of Modernism: Literary Elites and Public Cultures* (1998) and Mark Morrisson's *The Public Face of Modernism: Little Magazines, Audiences, and Reception, 1905–1920* (2001) exemplify this trend, and studies such as Clare Hutton's 'Joyce and the Institutions of Revivalism', *Irish University Review* 33, 1 (2003): 117–32, have explored these modernist institutions within Irish literary history.
2. Robert Scholes and Clifford Wulfman, *Modernism in the Magazines: An Introduction* (New Haven: Yale University Press, 2010).
3. Rónán McDonald, 'The Irish Revival and Modernism', in *The Cambridge Companion to Irish Modernism*, ed. Joe Cleary (Cambridge: Cambridge University Press, 2014), 52.
4. For an extended history see Liam Miller, *The Dun Emer Press, Later the Cuala Press* (Dublin: Dolmen, 1973).
5. Jerome McGann, *Black Riders: The Visible Language of Modernism* (Princeton: Princeton University Press, 1993), 7. George Bornstein makes a similar argument in *Material Modernism: The Politics of the Page* (2001).
6. Robin Skelton, 'Twentieth-Century Irish Literature and the Private Press Tradition: *Dun Emer, Cuala, & Dolmen Presses* 1902–1963', *The Massachusetts Review* 5, 2 (1964): 368.
7. Dillon Johnston, *Irish Poetry after Joyce* (Notre Dame, IN: University of Notre Dame Press, 1985), 6.
8. Maurice Harmon, 'Introduction', *The Dolmen Press: A Celebration*, ed. Maurice Harmon (Dublin: Lilliput, 2001), 11.
9. Robin Skelton, 'Twentieth-Century Irish Literature and the Private Press Tradition: *Dun Emer, Cuala, & Dolmen Presses* 1902–1963', *The Massachusetts Review* 5, 2 (1964); Thomas Dillon Redshaw, 'Printing a Second Revival: Liam Miller's Dolmen Editions, 1966', *The South Carolina Review* 34, 2 (Spring 2002): 91–107; David Gardiner, 'Reading the Renaissance: John Derricke's *Image of Irelande* (c. 1579) and the Dolmen Press (1966–72)', *Nua: Studies in Contemporary Irish Writing* 1, 2 (Fall 1998): 47–63.
10. Padraic Colum, *Ten Poems* (Dublin: Dolmen, 1957), 22.
11. Job 40:15.
12. Liam Miller, *Dolmen XXV: An Illustrated Bibliography of the Dolmen Press: 1951–1976* (Dublin: Dolmen, 1976), 7–8.
13. Ailbhe Ní Bhriain, 'Le Livre d'Artiste: Louis le Brocquy and *The Táin* (1969)', *New Hibernia Review* 5, 1 (2001): 68.
14. Stéphane Mallarmé, 'Preface', in *Dice Thrown Never Will Annul Chance*, trans. Brian Coffey (Dublin: Dolmen, 1967), n.p.
15. Redshaw, 'Printing a Second Revival', 94.

16 W. B. Yeats, 'Introduction', in *Certain Noble Plays of Japan: From the Manuscripts of Ernest Fenollosa, Chosen and Finished by Ezra Pound* (Dundrum: Cuala, 1916), i.
17 Ibid., viii.
18 Ibid., xix.
19 Liam Miller, 'Poetry in Ireland', qtd. in Derval Turbidy, ' "A Hazardous Venture": The Dolmen Press', in *Oxford History of the Irish Book, vol. 5: The Irish Book in English 1891–2000*, eds. Clare Hutton and Patrick Walsh (Oxford: Oxford University Press, 2011), 576.
20 Liam Miller, 'Two Interviews with Liam Miller', in *The Dolmen Press: A Celebration*, ed. Maurice Harmon (Dublin: Lilliput, 2001), 29.
21 R. F. Foster, *Modern Ireland: 1600–1972* (London: Allen Lane, 1988), 581.
22 Anthony Kerrigan, 'Mnemonic Note to These Histories', in *Irish Strategies* (Dublin: Dolmen, 1975), 9.
23 Liam Miller, 'Fresh Images Beget: Art Nouveau & Irish Books', Dolmen Press Collection ts.127.9, Z. Smith Reynolds Library, Wake Forest University.

Chapter 8

STORM IN A TEACUP: IRISH MODERNIST ART

Róisín Kennedy

A currach struggles through the Atlantic waves off the Aran Islands in Dorothy Cross's 1997 three-minute video, *Teacup* (Figure 8.1). Taken from Robert Flaherty's fictional documentary *Man of Aran* (1934), the grainy black and white footage is contained within the static confines of an ornate china cup, sitting on its saucer.[1] *Teacup* pays homage to the most famous teacup in modernist art, Meret Oppenheim's *Object (Breakfast in Fur)*, (1936, MoMA).[2] *Teacup* deploys many of the strategies of its celebrated antecedent by playing on the relationship between masculinity – by depicting fishermen straining their way through the high seas – and femininity – by placing these images within the delicacy and domesticity of the best china. *Teacup* also mocks the fetishization of the West in Irish culture. Cross's video cleverly subverts the dominant construction of the myth of heroic masculine spectacle located in untamed nature by containing and controlling it within the feminine boundaries of the man-made teacup found in domestic interiors. It thus imparts a sense of the incongruity surrounding the myths of Irish identity.

Nevan Lahart's installation, *A Monument to Sub Minimum Wage: A Whiter than White Social GAMA Steak Slave Sandwich* (2005), centred on a reconstruction of Vladimir Tatlin's iconic *Monument of the Third International*.[3] Lahart was inspired by several public disputes concerning the mistreatment of migrant workers in Ireland, including one case in which workers were paid two euros a day and fed on bread and brown sauce. The installation consisted of a wooden tower at the apex of which was a rotating sculpture of a slice of bread. A spiral of slices of toast spelled out the name of the work, with lanterns made from empty bread packets adorning it. It reworked the confrontational strategies of constructivism and Dada in its use of disparate materials and its provocative references to contemporary social and political controversy. When shown at

Figure 8.1 Dorothy Cross, *Teacup*, 1997, DVD PAL, 3-minute loop. Image courtesy of the artist and Kerlin Gallery, Dublin.

the Eurojet Futures 2005 exhibition at the Royal Hibernian Academy (RHA), the piece caused a mini storm in the Irish media. A prominent Irish bakery threatened legal action due to the publicity generated by the exhibition and fear that it would be mistakenly implicated in the underpayment of workers.

Neither Cross nor Lahart looked first to Irish modernist art in the production of their work, preferring to evoke more subversive practices found in European art. Cross has repeatedly turned to the West of Ireland as a subject using strategies that are ultimately drawn from avant-garde modernism, most notably surrealism. Her practice makes extensive use of the found object, the readymade and the uncanny. Similarly, Lahart's work harnesses several key strategies of the European avant-garde in a playfully provocative manner. The decision of these artists to evoke international rather than Irish modernist art is not the result of ignorance of the history of Irish art. Lahart has parodied the debates and stereotypes associated with the RHA in his work, and Cross's recent exhibition, *Trove*, in the Irish Museum of Modern Art (IMMA) contained many references to the preoccupations and concerns of the art world in modern Ireland.[4]

But contemporary Irish artists tend to see Irish modernist art, like Cross's irreverent framing of Flaherty's *Man of Aran*, as a storm in a teacup. This ambivalent attitude to Irish modernist art needs to be further explored. It comes partly from the perception that much of the modernist art produced in Ireland has had a rather tentative relationship with international modernism, especially the avant-garde, and an equally hands-off attitude to the realities of modern Ireland. This view is closely connected to how Irish modernist art is valued and interpreted more generally by the media and by the major art institutions of the state. In particular, there has been a long-standing tradition of linking Irish modernism to the Celticism of the past rather than the radical questioning of the present that lies at the heart of more critical forms of modernism. The disregard of Irish modernist art evident in the work of Cross and Lahart is even more pronounced in that of earlier artists such as Michael Farrell, whose practice began within the era of modernism. Farrell eventually rejected abstraction, the dominant form of Irish modernist art, choosing to produce more starkly representational work, most notably the *Madonna Irlanda* series of 1977 (Figure 8.2). This centred on an image of the artist contemplating an erotically displayed female nude. It was intended to present a true image of Ireland in contradistinction to the stereotype of the nation as a chaste and devoted mother. Erroneously, but tellingly, Farrell described the main painting as 'The Very First Real Irish Political Painting'.[5] In this statement he acknowledged what he regarded as the failure of Irish modernist art to produce anything that critiqued or challenged the status quo.

The difficulty that contemporary artists have with the legacy of Irish modernist art can be contrasted by its institutional embrace in recent decades. In the era of the Celtic Tiger (ca. 1997–2008) there was a frantic desire amongst dealers, collectors and art institutions in Ireland to promote Irish modernist art and enlist new artists to solidify the reputation of Irish visual art as being as central to modernism as Irish literature. Record-breaking prices for the works of twentieth-century Irish artists such as Jack B. Yeats and Louis le Brocquy dominated not just tales in the media, but the agenda of national cultural institutions and public museums. Much of the rhetoric surrounding these artists has been based on their work's apparent evocation of an Irish, or more specifically, a 'Celtic' sensibility.

The National Gallery of Ireland showcased the cultural authority of Jack B. Yeats when it acquired the contents of the artist's studio in 1997 and in 1999 established an exhibition space dedicated specifically to his paintings and his family.[6] With Yeats being presented by his major biographers, Hilary Pyle and Bruce Arnold, as an essentially apolitical artist, the nature of his contribution to Irish modernism has been much debated.[7] Recent studies have focused on his later painting, which is not easily categorized in terms of

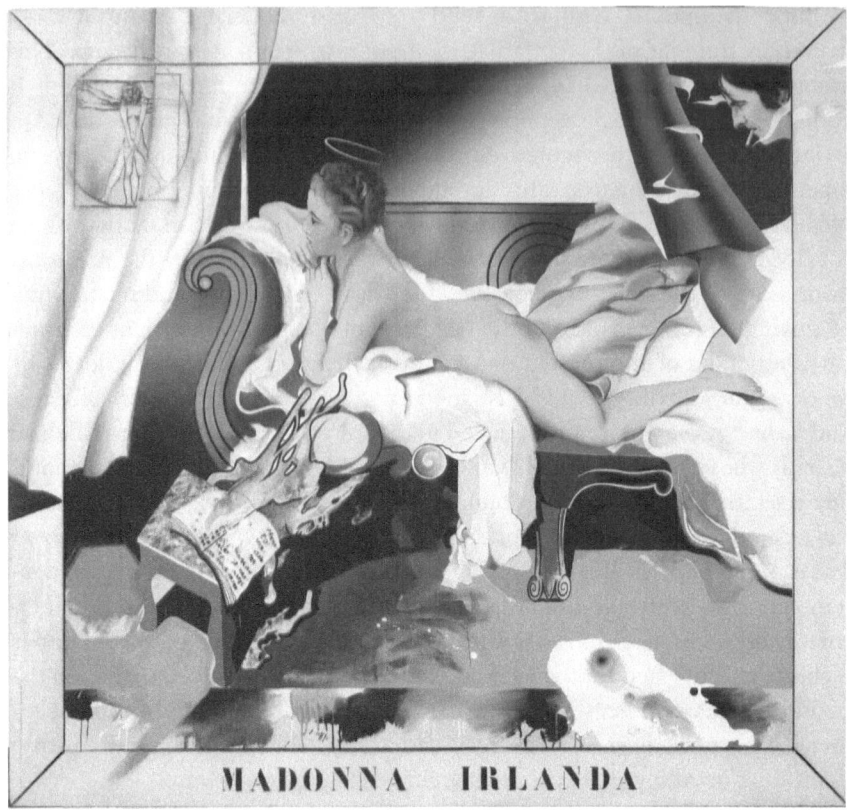

Figure 8.2 Michael Farrell, *Madonna Irlanda*, 1977, lithograph, 45 x 61.88 cm. (17.7 x 24.4 in.). Courtesy of Dublin City Gallery The Hugh Lane.

conventional classifications of modernist art. This work combines elements of expressionism, with an almost surreal distortion of space. At the same time, it refers to a romantic use of narrative that is a legacy of nineteenth-century painting, and a wider awareness of literature and popular theatre. The richly constructed surfaces of these paintings, made between 1928 and 1955, challenge the viewer to unravel their forms and to make sense of the dichotomy between representation and construction. The breaking up of the image has been read as subversive and directly connected to the fragmentation of the Irish psyche in the decades after independence.[8] Such an interpretation was formulated in Yeats's lifetime by two of his most astute critics, Ernie O'Malley and Thomas MacGreevy.[9] Samuel Beckett recognized the achievement, but refused to connect it to Irish identity.[10] However, Yeats's own reticence, the

Figure 8.3 Louis le Brocquy, *A Family*, 1951, oil on canvas, 147 x 185 cm. Courtesy of National Gallery of Ireland. ©Estate of Louis le Brocquy.

nostalgic nature of the subject matter of his painting and the fact that it was lauded by all factions of the establishment have resulted in his reputation as a conciliatory artist, very much in the Irish modernist mode.[11]

In 2001, the National Gallery accepted *A Family* (1951), a major painting by le Brocquy. In 1952, the painting had been notoriously refused by the Dublin Municipal Gallery of Modern Art (the Hugh Lane Gallery) before going on to win a prestigious award at the 1956 Venice Biennale (Figure 8.3). The ambitious and atypical work, painted in London, depicts a dysfunctional family dominated by a matriarchal figure in a claustrophobic interior. It pays homage to the work of Pablo Picasso, Henry Moore and Edouard Manet. Its eventual acceptance by the National Gallery of Ireland, where it became the only work by a living artist to be displayed as part of the permanent collection, was one of a number of events that seemed to mark a revolution in official attitudes toward Irish modernist art.[12] Earlier decades of neglect were finally being recompensed by a more enlightened, sophisticated and affluent establishment. The controversial past of *A Family* was referred to at the ceremony welcoming it into the National Gallery when the chairman of the board asserted that its acceptance into the state's collection marked the close 'of an unfortunate episode in our cultural history'.[13] Now, unlike 1952, the Irish were comfortable with the idea that, through art, a complicated representation of the nation's inner life might emerge. According to the chairman, le Brocquy's 'is an utterly compelling and authentic voice that traces a direct line from our Celtic past to our present in modern Europe'.[14]

The Hugh Lane Gallery's acquisition of Francis Bacon's studio in 1998 and its staging of a major exhibition of his work, *Francis Bacon in Dublin*, curated by David Sylvester in 2000, were part of a related impetus to reclaim major international artists as Irish and thereby to reinforce a more substantial association between Irish visual art and mainstream modernism.[15] It has been argued that the installation of the Bacon studio, in particular, represented the closure on the city of Dublin's rejection of Hugh Lane's plans for a gallery of modern art a hundred years previously.[16] Having been unable to secure a permanent home for the collection of European and Irish art from Dublin Corporation, Lane left, upon his premature death in 1915, 39 of the most significant of his French paintings to the National Gallery, London. This controversy continues to provide another modernist afterlife within the Irish art world. The installation of Bacon's studio in perpetuity in Ireland certainly demonstrated a more amenable attitude on the part of Dublin Corporation toward modernist art. However, it raised as many questions as it answered. First, the dedication of a permanent space to an artist flies in the face of postmodernist museum practice. As well, Bacon's 'Irishness' is dubious. Although born in Dublin of English parents and spending part of his childhood in Ireland, the artist returned only once to the country after leaving at the age of 16 in 1925. He had no inclination to be considered Irish at any point in his subsequent career, although he did acknowledge the potential impact that various traumatic childhood experiences in Ireland might have had on his later work.[17]

The studio at the Hugh Lane Gallery has fortified Bacon's reputation, in Ireland at least, as an Irish modernist. His reclamation has also provided a much needed foil to the compliant and distinctly passive image of Irish modernist art. His work injects critical weight, corporeality and an open acknowledgement of violence and sexuality into the existing canon of Irish modernist art. The studio was archaeologically reconstructed with artefacts transferred directly from 7 Reece Mews, London, to the specially made site in Parnell Square, Dublin. While its new presentation in the gallery fetishizes the world of the modernist artist as disorganized genius, it also provides the potential for a more critical understanding of Bacon's practice. The studio contains a vast archive of material that defies any simplistic evaluation of the artist in terms of national identity. It has already revealed that, contrary to received opinion, the artist made detailed and copious studies for his paintings, and that he researched a wide range of sources.[18]

The intricate nature of the Bacon studio and its archive contrasts with the more conventional installation in the same museum of a permanent display of paintings by Sean Scully, another recruit to Irish modernism (Figure 8.4). Born in Dublin in 1945, brought up and educated in England, Scully became a citizen of the United States in 1983. His abstract grid paintings, made on constructions of wood and other material make reference to a range of

Figure 8.4 Sean Scully, *Figure in Grey*, 2004, oil on linen, 299.7x 256.5 cm. Courtesy of Sean Scully Studio and Dublin City Gallery The Hugh Lane.

modernist artists, including Henri Matisse, Mark Rothko and Frank Stella. The specially designed room that holds his collection, the centrepiece of the newly extended Hugh Lane Gallery, opened in 2006 and proclaimed the conversion of Dublin into a major repository of modernist art. Scully's gift of his paintings followed on the heels of the installation of the Bacon studio. It has also been interpreted as a closing of the circle begun by the Lane controversy. The installation of the Scully room coincided with a major relaunch of the gallery leading up to its centenary in 2008. It inevitably revived the ghost of its original founder. The current curator of the permanent collection linked Lane's 'deeply held beliefs that Irish and international art deserved to be seen, celebrated and appreciated in a gallery of modern art in Dublin', with the opening of the Scully room and the 'presence of a significant body of work by such an internationally renowned painter'.[19] The director of the Hugh Lane Gallery, Barbara Dawson, assured Scully that through this installation, his 'identity with the city of his birth is truly cemented'.[20]

Scully, an international artist working within the era of postmodernism, poses a challenge for those seeking to connect his work to that of Irish modernism. His status as a modernist artist is open to debate. The fact that he consciously disrupts the surface of his paintings and evokes sources from the contemporary world has led to Scully being described as producing a 'revisionist, almost late-modernist style' and of his practice taking an 'essentially non-modernist position but nonetheless antipathetic to aspects of postmodernity'.[21] His reliance on the grid to produce large-scale atmospheric abstract paintings and their display within the conventional modernist white-cube space, as presented in the Hugh Lane Gallery, arguably places his work within the boundaries of modernism. Incorporating Scully into the world of Irish art is equally problematic. His 'embrace of contingency and operational change, and his positive acceptance of imperfection' has been described as quintessentially 'American'.[22] However, the Irish critic Dorothy Walker counteracted such a view when she asserted that, 'In all that has been written about his work throughout the world, it is curious that the visible Celtic element has not been recognized. [Scully's ...] early 'grid' paintings of the 1970s seem to me to be direct descendants of Celtic interlacing, layered linearity in a dynamic large-scale version of Early Christian graphic art. The artist himself agrees with this interpretation; quite easily demonstrated with reference to Celtic manuscripts like the Book of Kells'.[23]

This Celtic model is based on a highly selective formalist construction that ties twentieth-century Irish art to stylistic precedents in Celtic art. 'Celtic' rather than 'Irish' allows for a more metaphysical sense of what might constitute Irish modernism. Celtic art refers to not only Iron Age La Tene artefacts but also to early Christian and medieval material produced in Ireland up to the seventeenth century and even as far back as the megalithic art of the Neolithic. It can be summarized as an applied form of ornamentation consisting of 'intricate swirls and spirals', in which the human figure plays a secondary role and as 'full of elliptical and opposing curves, combined in dynamic yet symmetrical patterns in relief [...]'.[24] In addition to the stylistic attributes of Celtic art, other features include a focus on mythical rather than historical time, as well as an ambiguous sense of space and a nebulous quality that verges on the abstract.

It was Hugh Lane who initiated 'Celtic branding' in an attempt to construct a separate identity for Irish art. He was only able to do this theoretically as, in practice, Irish artists at the beginning of the twentieth century were a disparate group more influenced by contemporary British and French art than Celtic interlacing, despite being nurtured within the bosom of the Celtic revival. In the catalogue of the *Exhibition of Works by Irish Painters*, the major show of Irish art held in 1904 at the Guildhall, London, Lane stated that prior to the twelfth century Irish visual art was more advanced than that of any country in Western Europe.[25] But, he argued, the disruptive nature of Irish history, beginning with the Anglo-Norman invasion, had prevented the development of this great and ancient tradition. Arguably, in the decades following Lane's commentary, the major preoccupation of Irish artists has been the retracing of this lost tradition, either consciously or unconsciously. Decades later, Walker summarized the notion of a Celtic origin for Irish modernist art: 'There is an underlying structural basis in Irish art which is more interesting in that it has persisted since prehistoric times, a paradoxically informal formalism which can be seen as far back as the great carvings of Newgrange'.[26]

The notion of vibrant 'afterlives' in art is an inherent part, not just of contemporary art by Cross and Lahart in their re-use of modernism, but seems to be built into Irish modernist art itself as seen in the reincorporation of Celtic art in the decades after independence. Irish artists interested in participating in international modernism, such as Mainie Jellett and Evie Hone, devoted much of their energies to producing an Irish or Celtic version of modernist art. Jellett's prolific radio broadcasts and lectures from the mid-1920s to early 1940s sought to convince a conservative public of the merits of modernism through its fundamental alignment to Celtic art. At a local level, cubism and abstraction offered an alternative to the academic art that dominated art practice and public expectations of art in early twentieth-century Ireland and which, for some, was tainted by its connection to colonialism. By contrast, cubism could be directly related to the Celtic tradition of art-making in Ireland. According to Jellett, both were concerned with 'the sense of filling and decorating a given space rhythmically and harmoniously'.[27]

The model of Celtic art provides a coherent and strategic way of bringing together a range of work produced by Irish artists during the era of modernism and up to the present day. Celtic art is the pre-eminent Irish visual art. Uncovered and brought to wide public notice by antiquarians in the nineteenth century, it was further validated by the Celtic revival which contended that Celtic art was central to the formation of a distinctive Irish identity.[28] This artistic style, celebrated as both pre-colonial and indigenous, was widely deployed in the ornamentation of ephemera and material culture associated with Ireland and Irish nationalism. As a primitive and a proto-abstract art,

Celtic art was easily assimilated into later, more elite, discourses surrounding modernism.

The exalted position of Celtic art within Irish cultural nationalism, and the general public's familiarity with it, made it invaluable as an example of the kind of abstract art that Jellett was trying to explain. Like much of her work, it had representational elements, but its primary emphasis was on its formal arrangement. It embodied the use of colour and a meandering and rhythmic line that approximated closely the dynamic that Jellett was attempting to produce in her own work. She declared that the

> Cubist artist is nearer the Early Irish Christian artist in ideals of artistic expression than the academic artist of his own time[. …] It is quite natural for the artist who follows non-materialist truths to be closer to the Celtic and Early Irish Christian artist who has done the same thing[. …][29]

Jellett's invocation of Celticism is echoed in later interpretations of Irish modernist art. Brian O'Doherty has linked post-war Irish painting to an 'Irish Imagination', a phrase that comes from an exhibition of Irish art of the years 1959 to 1971, held at the Hugh Lane Gallery as part of the 1971 *Rosc*.[30] *Rosc* was a series of major exhibitions of international modernist and later postmodernist art held in Dublin between 1967 and 1988. Sponsored by Bórd Fáilte the exhibitions showcased the best fifty artists working internationally in the previous four years and were selected by a jury of leading curators. The *Irish Imagination* satellite exhibition was dominated by proto-abstract painting by artists such as Patrick Collins, Patrick Scott and Louis le Brocquy. The ambiguous treatment of form found in their work came, O'Doherty suggested, out of a postcolonial suspicion of direct statement. He used the idea of an Irish or Celtic imagination to argue that modernist Irish art was quite distinct from modernist art being produced elsewhere, and that its development sprang from not only an unconscious Celticism but also from the peculiarly isolated circumstances surrounding the patronage of modernist art in Ireland. He described the art produced within this closed community of dealers, audience and artists as 'a last examination and confrontation of a certain minority or subject mentality that never responds to anything directly[, …] not consciously but as a natural outgrowth of an isolation that encouraged introspection'.[31] This community established the Irish Exhibition of Living Art in 1943, an open exhibition forum for modernist art and was crucial to the development of an art market in Dublin during World War II that permitted the nurturing of Irish modernist art.[32] This expansion occurred at a period in which post-independence cultural introspection had reached its zenith. The restricted but intense focus on Irish art by this sub-group was part of a wider reframing of Irish identity and its relationship to international modernism.

Unfortunately, visual art has remained isolated from wider debates on Irish modernism. This is partly due to the contexts in which art was exhibited and discussed in Ireland, contexts that are absolutely crucial to the meanings this art imparts. Displayed within small exhibition forums or private galleries, and largely excluded from public museums, modernist art in post-independence Ireland was demarcated and even more marginalized than modernist literature. Compounding this material separation, the development of international modernism in the post-war period encouraged the separation of disciplines as well as promoting the autonomy of art practice. This was especially virulent in Anglo-American art criticism, which impacted directly on the Irish art field through its close economic, social and cultural ties to London and the United States. The Celtic model flourished in this context as it provided a link between Irish modernist art and the transcendental notion of visual art promoted within the wider international discourse of high modernism.

A second legacy of Irish modernist art that made it problematic for a postmodern generation was its apparent conciliatory relationship to the state and the public. The model of Celtic art itself was partly selected by pioneering Irish modernist painters and critics because it was a widely known and admired style of visual art. This concern with the wider public appreciation of modernism seemed to fly in the face of the movement's supposed rejection of bourgeois values. In the 1940s and 1950s the cubist-inspired work of Hone and Jellett was lauded by the new Catholic elite, who dominated the patronage and the discourse on art in Ireland. In Irish modernist art, anarchism was completely overshadowed by this reconciliation of tradition with modernity. Rather than making an overt critique of the state and its dominant ideology of right-wing Catholicism, Irish modernist art made little if any reference to issues of sexuality or control. In fact, it embraced religion, or at least spirituality. This passivity was compounded by the 'indirect statement' found in the paintings of le Brocquy and Scott.[33] These politely avoided confrontation although, ironically, the fact that artists like Scott, in particular, chose to ignore nationalist rhetoric in favour of abstraction could and was interpreted as a courageous stance.[34]

The continual refusal of Irish modernist art to engage openly with contemporary culture contributed to its fragmentation in the 1960s and 1970s. Michael Farrell attempted to reinvigorate Celtic sources by using spiral and interlacing motifs to create hard-edged paintings and sculptures that defied any poetic reading. Farrell was one of a number of artists who argued that Celtic art was fundamentally a conceptual or problem-solving practice.[35]

According to Farrell, the Book of Kells dated to a period in which Irish artists had last concerned themselves with the problem of picture-making.[36] But, as already noted, Farrell was forced to reject Celticism and abstract art in favour of representational images in order to make political statements that reflected contemporary events. The immediate catalyst for Farrell's rejection of Irish modernism was the outbreak of violence in Northern Ireland, but it coincided with a wider crisis in modernism internationally.

A further reason for Farrell's change in practice was his growing disillusionment with the Irish art world. A precocious young artist, he had trained in London and spent a year studying in New York on an Arts Council fellowship. He, along with every other Irish artist, was excluded from the first two *Rosc* exhibitions in 1967 and 1971. He emigrated to France in 1971, partly in response to this.[37] While the early *Roscs* were massively influential in bringing the highlights of modernist art to an Irish public, the exclusion of Irish artists highlighted the provincial status of contemporary Irish art. Paradoxically, a major section of ancient Celtic art was included in *Rosc 67*.[38] (Irish artists were selected for later *Rosc* exhibitions from 1977 to 1988, by which time their practice and the exhibitions had moved firmly from modernism into postmodernism). The Irish government's close involvement in the early *Roscs*, and the fact that crucial motives behind their staging were educational and touristic, reinforced an existing idea that modernist art in an Irish context was a celebratory, uncritical activity, albeit a challenging and unconventional one.

While Farrell was fundamentally a modernist disillusioned by the failure of abstraction to communicate in any meaningful way, later Irish artists, equipped with a more critical understanding of their art practice, have rejected the premises of Irish modernist art with relative ease. The work of Lahart and Cross, for example, takes a sceptical stance on the ability of modernism to transcend lived experience while at the same time acknowledging its ongoing function as a reserve of strategies and conceits that can be revisited and redeployed. In contrast to this complex engagement with modernist art, the art establishment – in the form of collectors, board members and museum directors – has continued to promote a romantic or Celtic view of modernism that is tied both to the art market and to a rudimentary idea of Irish nationalism. The Celtic metaphysical mode, for example, has persisted in the incorporation of Bacon and Scully into the canon of Irish modernism over and above the material conditions that surrounded the production and reception of their work. The afterlives of modernism found in the work of contemporary Irish artists can offer an antidote to Celticism and a way of reclaiming a more balanced understanding of the potential of modernist art to critique, rather than to bolster contemporary experience.

Notes

1. Enrique Juncosa, 'A Theory of Seeing', in *Dorothy Cross* (Dublin: IMMA, 2005), 28–30.
2. Alyce Mahon, *Eroticism and Art* (Oxford University Press, 2007), 137–38.
3. www.nevanlahart.com
4. *Trove. Dorothy Cross selects from the National Collections*, IMMA, 3 December 2014–8 March 2015.
5. Michael Farrell, *Madonna Irlanda or The Very First Real Irish Political Painting* (1977, acrylic on canvas, Dublin City Gallery, the Hugh Lane).
6. Hilary Pyle, 'To be loved as a Cupboard: The Yeats Museum in the National Gallery of Ireland', *Eire-Ireland* 36, (2001): 212–25.
7. Hilary Pyle, *Jack B. Yeats. A Biography* (London: Routledge, 1970); Bruce Arnold, *Jack Yeats* (Yale University Press, 1998).
8. David Lloyd, 'Republics of Difference: Yeats, MacGreevy, Beckett', in *Samuel Beckett. A Passion for Paintings* (Dublin: National Gallery of Ireland, 2006), 52–59; Nicholas Allen, *Modernism, Ireland and the Civil War* (Cambridge: Cambridge University Press, 2009), 136–66.
9. Thomas MacGreevy, *Jack B. Yeats – An Appreciation and an Interpretation* (Dublin: Victor Waddington, 1945), 23; Ernie O'Malley, 'Introduction', in *Jack B. Yeats National Loan Exhibition Catalogue* (Dublin, 1945), reprinted in *Broken Landscapes: Selected Letters of Ernie O'Malley 1924–1957*, eds. Cormac O'Malley and Nicholas Allen (Dublin: Lilliput Press, 2011), 391–97. See Róisín Kennedy, 'Divorcing Jack [...] From Irish Politics', in *Jack B. Yeats: Old and New Departures*, ed. Y. Scott (Dublin: Four Courts Press, 2008), 33–46.
10. Samuel Beckett, 'MacGreevy on Yeats', *Irish Times*, 4 August 1945, 2; Lloyd, 'Republics of Difference: Yeats, MacGreevy, Beckett'.
11. Tricia Cusack, 'Neither Visionary nor Porpoise', *Circa* 79 (Spring 1997): 43–45.
12. Louis le Brocquy quoted in S. Bhreathnach Lynch, 'Louis le Brocquy's A Family: An Unwholesome and Satanic Distortion of Natural Beauty', *Recirca.com* (September 2002); Róisín Kennedy, *Made in England. Louis le Brocquy's A Family*, in *Third Text (Ireland Special Issue)* no. 76, 19, Issue 5 (September 2005): 475–87.
13. Michael O'Reilly, 'Tribute to Louis le Brocquy', Speech, 27 May 2002, National Gallery of Ireland dossier file.
14. Ibid.
15. Hugh Lane Municipal Gallery of Modern Art, *Francis Bacon in Dublin* (Dublin: HLMGMA, 2000).
16. Luke Gibbons, 'Visual Modernisms', in *Cambridge Companion to Irish Modernism*, ed. Joe Cleary (Cambridge University Press, 2014), 141.
17. Anthony Cronin, 'An Irish Fear of Death?', in *Francis Bacon in Dublin*, 24–26; Bruce Arnold, 'Francis Bacon in Dublin', *Irish Independent*, 3 June 2000. See also Frances Barber, 'Diffused Ground: Francis Bacon, Traumatic Memory and the Gothic', *Irish Review* 39, (Winter 2008): 125–38, 157; Lucy Cotter, 'Ambivalent Homecomings: Louis le Brocquy, Francis Bacon and Mechanisms of Canonization', *Field Day Review* 7 (2011): 170–201.
18. Margarita Cappock, 'Works on paper by Francis Bacon in the Hugh Lane Gallery, Dublin', *Burlington Magazine* 145, no. 1199 (February 2003): 73–81.
19. Jessica O'Donnell, 'Sean Scully: A Major Presence in Dublin', *Museum Ireland* 17 (2007): 135.
20. Barbara Dawson quoted in O'Donnell, 'Sean Scully: A Major Presence in Dublin', 136.

21 Aidan Dunne, 'Painting in Ireland Now', *Circa* 109 (Autumn 2004): 30.
22 David Carrier, 'Sean Scully. Washington', *Burlington Magazine* 137, no. 1110 (September 1995): 642–43.
23 Dorothy Walker, *Modern Art in Ireland*, 102.
24 Carl Waldman and Catherine Mason, *Encyclopedia of European People* (New York: Info Base Publishing, 2006), 157–58.
25 H. Lane, 'Preparatory Notice', in *Catalogue of the Exhibition of Works by Irish Painters* (London: Guildhall, 1904), ix–x. See F. Cullen, *Ireland on Show. Art, Union and Nationhood* (Farnham: Ashgate, 2012), 153–72.
26 D. Walker, 'Traditional Structures in recent Irish Art', *Crane Bag* 6 (1982): 41–44.
27 Mainie Jellett, 'A Word on Irish Art', 1942, in MacCarvill, *Mainie Jellett*, 103.
28 Jeanne Sheehy, *The Rediscovery of Ireland's Past: The Celtic Revival, 1830–1920* (London: Thames and Hudson, 1980).
29 Jellett, 'Modern Art and Its Relation to the Past', in MacCarvill, *Mainie Jellett*, 90.
30 Brian O'Doherty, *The Irish Imagination 1959–71* (Dublin: Hugh Lane Municipal Gallery of Modern Art, 1971). *Rosc* was an international exhibition of modernist art held in Dublin every four years from 1967 to 1988. See Róisín Kennedy, 'The Irish Imagination 1971 – Romanticism or Pragmatism', *Journal of Art Historiography* 9 (December 2013), http://arthistoriography.wordpress.com.
31 O'Doherty, *Irish Imagination*, 11.
32 S. B. Kennedy, *Irish Art and Modernism* (Belfast: Institute of Irish Studies, 1991).
33 Frances Ruane, *The Delighted Eye: Irish Painting and Sculpture of the Seventies* (Dublin: Arts Council of Ireland, 1980): unpaginated.
34 Róisín Kennedy, 'The White Stag Group: Experimentalism or Mere Chaos', in *Irish Modernism. Origins, Contexts, Publics*, eds. C. Taafe and E. Keown, Reimagining Ireland 14 (Bern: Peter Lang, 2009), 179–94.
35 Brian O'Doherty/Patrick Ireland has used Ogham lettering in his practice as a conceptual artist. See Brenda Moore-McCann, *Brian O'Doherty/Patrick Ireland. Between Categories* (London: Lund Humphries, 2009).
36 Michael Farrell, 'Artist's Statement' (1965), published in Cyril Barrett, *Michael Farrell* (Dublin: Douglas Hyde Gallery, 1979), 21.
37 Gerry Walker, 'Michael Farrell – Changing Perspectives', Dublin: National College of Art and Design, MA thesis, 1998.
38 See Kennedy, 'The Irish Imagination 1971 – Romanticism or Pragmatism'.

Chapter 9

'PARTICLES OF MEANING': THE MODERNIST AFTERLIFE IN IRISH DESIGN

Linda King

> Far from being a neutral, inoffensive artistic activity, design, by its very nature, has much more enduring effects [...] because it can cast ideas about who we are and how we should behave in permanent, tangible forms[; ...] the history of design is also the history of societies.[1]

The record of history is inherently problematic: it is subjective and fractured, making our understanding of any civilization inherently incomplete. Irish literature is one measure of Irish cultural history, but this chapter considers a parallel history of creative expression, Irish design, to explore how the modernist afterlife became manifest through architecture, graphic design and other popular forms. Design history is the study of ideas in material and visual form; it is not merely concerned with aesthetics and the skill of making, but with what objects and images reveal about the cultural, political and economic factors from which they emerge. In design terms, as in other realms, modernism as a historical and conceptual category is a term in flux. Despite modernism's stated intention to comprise a universal ideology, historians – including Martin Daunton and Bernhard Rieger – argue that modernity embodies both 'continuity and rupture', which necessitates the investigation of 'modernities' as opposed to understanding modernism as an all-encompassing and monolithic concept.[2] Design historian David Crowley expands this thesis by arguing that modernism is localized within specific cultural and national contexts. He regards the emergence of regional inflections and interpretations as 'national' or 'regional' modernisms,[3] an approach that speaks to the recent acknowledgement of a distinct Irish or vernacular modernism, a negotiated form of expression closely aligned with nation-building and state sponsored projects.[4]

If the afterlife of Irish literary modernism arises after the publication of Joyce's *Finnegans Wake* (1939), this marks the period when modernism in design came into its fullest expression. Modernism is somewhat easier to define in material and visual terms than in the context of literature or other fields where definitions can be contested. Design historian Peter Greenhalgh offers that there were three phases to historical modernism in relation to design: *Proto-Modernism*, which signalled the break with historicism that emerged in the materiality of the late nineteenth and early twentieth centuries; *Pioneering Modernism* (also known as *High Modernism*), which refers to the period from 1914 up to the closure of the Bauhaus by the Nazis in 1933, when a Eurocentric ideology arising from the experiences of World War I placed design at the forefront of societal improvements; and *International Modernism*, which comprises the early 1930s up to the 1970s and is defined by an aesthetic firmly aligned to mass manufacturing and the post–World War II ideology of nation rebuilding and regeneration. Both Greenhalgh and Christopher Wilk re-emphasize the established canon of design modernism as it is typically configured (around movements and individuals), wherein the centres of design activity comprise Britain, Continental Europe and the United States and are aligned to mass industrialization. Yet, as Crowley has noted, 'Modernism had a profound appeal to those states that wished to demonstrate their place in the modern world and shake off associations of a colonial or foreign-dominated past',[5] which reflects the Irish experience.

In recent years, an interest in Irish design as a discourse of modernism has been slowly growing. This is in part influenced by a maturing of the Irish design professions and their curiosity about the history of their own disciplines, as well as by the more general awareness of how design objects render cultural and political intent in a material form. This evolution allows for a rich exploration of Proto- and Pioneering Modernism in Irish design and how they relate to localized expressions of International Modernism. It also encourages exchange amongst academic fields once understood as discrete in order to identify similarities and differences between them. For instance, if literary modernism is preoccupied with the motif of self as an expression of universal concepts, design modernism was, and is, about the mass, democratic experience. If literary modernism was largely directed at select or specific audiences, modernism in design was always about the quotidian and mass experience. By positioning emblematic objects within an expanded definition of Irish culture, the analysis of design – as a discourse of modernity – and how it interacts with different manifestations of modernism, including literature, can be explored.

In addition, how designed objects exist as particles of related or alternative cultural meaning can also be revealed.

The Conditions of Irish Modernity: Pioneering Modernism and the Nation-Building Project, 1914–39

Wilk has offered that modernism is a loose collection of ideas, and that the term 'is widely used but rarely defined'.[6] Typically, it is easier to define what modernism is not – that its form and ideology are not 'traditional', 'conventional' and rooted in the past – than to arrive at an accepted definition of what it is or was. Contested definitions are due, in part, to the fact that modernism defines a mode of cultural expression that simultaneously exists in historical terms – as defined by the cultural movement of modernism as it emerged in the early twentieth century – and in contemporary terms, where to be 'modern' is a description that means to be 'present' and of the moment. Modernism is also a process of negotiation: Jürgen Habermas argues that all definitions of modernism are fluid, but all are arrived at by comparative analysis to the past. In terms of the 'modern movement', which he defines through architecture, but which can be extended to consider all design practices, he states that it 'was sustained through its engagement with the past, that Frank Lloyd Wright would be inconceivable without Japan, le Corbusier without classical antiquity and Mediterranean architecture, and Mies van der Rohe without Schinkel and Behrens'.[7] Wilk, in defining Modernism in art and design, states that its shared characteristics across disciplines include self-conscious attempts at innovation united in

> the vociferous rejection of history and tradition; a utopian desire to create a better world, to reinvent the world from scratch; an almost messianic belief in the power and potential of the machine and industrial technology; a rejection of applied ornament and decoration; an embrace of abstraction; and a belief in the unity of all the arts – that is, an acceptance that traditional hierarchies that separated the practices of art and design, as well as those that detached the arts from life, were unsuitable for a new era.[8]

It is easy to see how such definitions can be easily detected in the experiences of Continental Europe and the United States, where mass industrialization led to the rise of design practices – including urban planning and the creation, packaging and promotion of goods and services – as a discourse of modernity. Without strong industrial bases and the desire to harness new technologies to artistic creativity there would have been no Bauhaus in Germany (1919–33), De Stijl in Holland (1917–31) or Futurism in Italy (1909–44). Less-radical schools of thought emerged in Britain and the United States, although the United States greatly benefitted from the emigration of key modernists from Europe in the 1930s, particularly in architecture and graphic design. These included Ludwig Mies van der Rohe and Walter Gropius, who abandoned the socialist agenda that defined European modernism to produce architectural monuments to American capitalism. The trajectory of modernism is harder to locate and understand in Ireland. Without much by way of indigenous industry or radical artistic intent, combined with the country's unusual position within Europe – that of a colonized country surrounded by colonizing forces – a political and economic climate of flux and instability restricted the growth of the visual arts and the industrial base necessary for fostering innovation and developing design activity. Until well into the second half of the twentieth century, farming drove Irish economic activity. Consequently, industrial production was a relative anomaly within an economy based on agriculture, and examples of large-scale manufacturing were confined to the urban centres, specifically Dublin.[9] Thus, within both colonial and postcolonial contexts Irish modernization was slow to evolve and design practices, where they did exist, were often more concerned with adopting and adapting visual languages developed in other countries than on the creation of innovative forms.

By the early twentieth century Ireland was certainly far from the cutting edge of the modernist avant-garde. Much of what could be considered design production was dominated by the Irish Arts and Crafts movement, a Proto-Modernist movement in which local craft traditions and indigenous visual forms became conduits of cultural distinction. The movement peaked in Britain in the late nineteenth century, but in Ireland and Finland it had greater longevity and was used as a means to materialize cultural difference in the pursuit of independence. Dublin stained-glass artist and illustrator Harry Clarke was a central figure in the Irish Arts and Crafts movement and also exceled in book design. His illustrated volumes included Edgar Allen Poe's *Tales of Mystery and Imagination* (1919, 1923) and Goethe's *Faust* (1925), which through their macabre and psychosexual content reveal an innate, idiosyncratic cosmopolitanism within an inwardly focused artistic movement. This tendency is also demonstrated in his Geneva Window (1929), a commission from the Irish government as a gift to the League of Nations. Its vignettes represent writings by Joyce, Pearse, Shaw, Synge, O'Casey, O'Flaherty and Yeats, among others, and it was rejected by the government as an inappropriate expression of Irish identity due to its depictions of nakedness and inference of sexual and drunken behaviour. Nonetheless decorative stained glass and the gift book were very much a continuation of nineteenth-century Victorian artistic expression and demonstrate how out of step Ireland was with the evolution of the European avant-garde. By 1908, for example, Viennese architect Adolf

Loos had published his influential polemic 'Ornament and Crime' suggesting that 'the evolution of culture is synonymous with the removal of ornament from utilitarian objects. [...] We have outgrown ornament',[10] reflecting a zeitgeist from which the expression 'form follows function' became the mantra of design modernists.[11]

The Irish Free State (*Saorstát Éireann*) was established in 1922, the year Joyce published *Ulysses*. Little indigenous industry emerged during this period, and the focus on growing the Irish language through the school system to the exclusion of art education proved detrimental to the growth of professionalized design activity. Such decisions ensured that Ireland was hopelessly ill-equipped to embrace the 'art for industry' pedagogies that swept across Europe and the United States in the early decades of the twentieth century. Yet, against a backdrop of political and economic challenges, the first government, led by *Cumann na nGaedheal*, embarked on an ambitious project of nation building that demonstrated how design practices could be harnessed to the expression of political autonomy and infrastructural modernization. Key among these projects were the introduction of Free State coinage (1928) designed by British sculptor Albert Power under the direction of W. B. Yeats, and the building of Ardnacrusha, the monumental hydroelectric station on the Shannon (1925–29). These projects reveal how modernist design was found in everyday, common experiences and demonstrated the influence of Continental European design practices. Ardnacrusha was built by Siemens workers from Germany and reflects the influences of German architect and designer Peter Behrens and his work for Allgemeine Elektrizitäts-Gesellschaft Aktiengesellschaft (AEG, 1909–), the German electricity provider and manufacturer that at the time was at the forefront of European infrastructural architecture, product and graphic design. Ardnacrusha was a hugely ambitious project for the nascent state, so much so that it was marketed as the 'eighth wonder of the world' and drew huge crowds and international media exposure. In this project, we see the merger of a romanticized Irish ideal with pragmatic Europeanism to produce a distinctive example of Irish design that architectural historian Hugh Campbell notes reflected the rhetoric of Patrick Pearse in its literal and symbolic harnessing of the rivers of Ireland.[12]

Ardnacrusha exposes the relative lack of consideration awarded Irish design as an expression of modernity when compared to its literary counterparts. In his history of twentieth-century Irish culture, Terence Brown states that: 'the conservatism of Irish society in the 1920s [...] lacked any great positive passion. No architectural splendours can be pointed to as expressions of a confident, assertive self-regard in a society persuaded of its own newly independent traditional strengths'.[13] Brown mentions Ardnacrusha and other milestones of architectural modernism, including Desmond Fitzgerald's Dublin Airport (1940) and Michael Scott's Dublin bus depot, Busáras (1953), as curious emblems of modernity within an environment that was intensely insular and conservative. Brown further comments on the limited exposure of the Irish population to modernism, stating that from the 1930s through to the 1950s the public 'was made aware of these inroads of artistic modernism by the occasional building commissioned by official bodies that displayed knowledge of developments in European architecture'.[14]

However, as other authors have demonstrated, including Seán Rothery, Campbell and most recently Rolf Loeber and others, modernist architecture in Ireland was far from 'occasional'.[15] The first two Free State governments initiated many major urban and rural infrastructural projects during the 1930s, including hospitals, schools, housing and factories. These were typically modernist in both intent and aesthetics and were influenced by Irish architects who had travelled to Continental Europe and returned to Ireland, where they tempered existing design paradigms for local conditions. Indeed, Campbell notes that the placement of many of these structures within the rural landscape was the opposite of practice in other countries, where architectural modernism was largely an urban experience. Architectural historian Ellen Rowley suggests that this 'enormous achievement' of infrastructural development was highly 'innovative'[16] and, indeed, Irish modernist architecture was also not always derivative. Rothery suggests, for example, that Fitzgerald's airport terminal is of international importance, stating that it is an 'original exercise' and 'not derivative of any other single modern building in Europe or America'. This same commitment to modernist innovation was evident when, in 1936, the Architectural Association of Ireland invited Bauhaus founder Gropius to Dublin, where he delivered an address on 'The International Trend of Modern Architecture'. This invitation suggests that Ireland was, at least in architectural terms, more engaged with modernism than might be assumed.[17]

The patronage of a notoriously conservative government, under Taoiseach Éamon de Valera, supported these and other groundbreaking projects, as well as promoting Irish architectural modernism both nationally and internationally. Scott's iconic 'Shamrock Pavilion' for the New York World's Fair (1939), for example, is an effective example of modernism having been modified for national circumstances and projected onto an international stage (Figure 9.1). The pavilion was a showcase of contemporary Irish industrial output and quite conservative artistic achievement as represented by artists including Evie Hone and Mainie Jellett. When viewed from above, the pavilion's shamrock shape provided observers with one of the most recognizable and conventional motifs of Irish identity, although at ground-floor level it expressed the radical visual

Figure 9.1 Michael Scott, Irish Pavilion at the 1939 New York World's Fair. Image courtesy of Irish Architectural Archive.

language of International Modernism through the expansive use of glass and concrete. During the 1930s cities and towns throughout Ireland experienced the widespread development of privately funded buildings, including cinemas, factories, offices and retail outlets that used the modernist vocabulary of Art Deco. This hybrid style found popularity during the interwar years in Britain, France and the United States and tempered the hard edges of International Modernism with decorative details that referenced contemporary preoccupations with the abstractions of technology and speed. Art Deco provided a material register of international cultural events, including the interest in Egyptology that emerged after the discovery of Tutankhamun's tomb (1922), Aztec and Mayan art after the Mexican Revolution (1910–20), and the rising popularity of jazz music. Thus, far from being culturally peripheral, architecture as a practice of design was a significant conduit for the discourses of modernism and modernity in Free State Ireland.

If design is the subaltern within Irish creativity, and women are the subaltern within the history of design, it is somewhat surprising that Ireland's most significant design achievements happened outside of the island and were led by a woman, Eileen Gray. Moving to London and then to Paris before settling in the South of France, Gray absorbed influences from the avant-garde practices of de Stijl and the Bauhaus. Her radically modernist home at Roquebrune-Cap-Martin, E.1027 (1929) was celebrated internationally as a ground-breaking example of *Gestamkunstwerk* (or 'the total artwork'), which synthesized architecture, furniture, textile and graphic design in a pioneering expression of modernist intent, although her work was frequently attributed to the male architects within her social and professional circles, including her lover Jean Badovici and le Corbusier. Through her work, Gray explored radical ideas of space, materials and form, producing prototypes derived from personal necessity that embodied the modernist dictum of form following function. Gray's focus on the self as a conduit for the universal, her personalization of European modernism, her absorption of the zeitgeist to produce work that is entirely innovative and her self-imposed exile from Ireland, prompt certain parallels with the life and work of James Joyce. Certainly, like Joyce, she could not have produced such radical work if she had stayed in Ireland, and her independent wealth gave her the freedom to pursue her own idiosyncratic path.

Dublin-born artist Stella Styne also sought design innovation outside of Ireland and lived in Paris on and off for five years (1926–31), where she met Joyce, Beckett and Sylvia Beach. In 1929, Joyce commissioned her to illustrate *Finnegans Wake* (serialized as 'Continuation of Work in Progress') for the literary publication *transition*. Like Gray, Styne's financial freedom provided the pragmatic means to connect directly with the European avant-garde and subsequently she enrolled at the Bauhaus in Dessau (1931–32), the most radical art school of the twentieth century. There, Styne studied graphic design during the tenure of Mies van der Rohe as director and had Kandinsky, Klee, Bayer, Albers and Moholy-Nagy among her teachers. She produced magazine covers and typographic studies, however, she later described this engagement with high modernism as a 'false move' that had the effect of turning her attentions back to more 'traditional' forms of painting, specifically impressionism and post-impressionism (Figure 9.2). Like Gray, once she emigrated Styne never returned to live in Ireland.[18]

The Modernist Afterlife in Irish Design: International and Vernacular Modernism 1933–79

Literary modernism may have reached its apogee by the beginning of World War II, but design – as a discourse of utopianism and cultural improvement – evolved and expanded after the war. Up to the 1930s, Pioneering Modernism offered design prototypes that suggested how a new world could be materialized but, after World War II, International Modernism put these experiments

Figure 9.2 Stella Steyn, *Rn nnn* 1931–32. Image courtesy of The Molesworth Gallery, Dublin.

into practice, particularly in the areas of architecture, urban planning and graphic design, and aligned these to socialist agendas. Ireland did not have to rebuild post-war, and state infrastructure continued to develop. Political thinking gradually shifted from economic and cultural protectionism to opening up to external connections and, as a result, the modernization of the tourism industry became a central concern of economic development and new relationships between artistic creativity and industry slowly emerged. The 1940s began with ambitious attempts to physically link Ireland with wider spheres of influence. The completion of Dublin Airport was followed by the first commercial transatlantic flights into Ireland by TWA and Pan Am (1945) and by the opening of Shannon Airport (1947), where employee Brendan O'Regan, conscious of exploiting an American gaze for the purchase of Irish commodities, revolutionized touristic consumerism by inventing the duty-free concept. Internally focused infrastructural projects were also ambitious and included the start of the Rural Electrification Scheme (1946) and the consolidation of public transport in the form of Córas Iompair Éireann (CIÉ, 1946).

The 1950s in Ireland witnessed unsurpassed levels of unemployment and emigration, but the period was also characterized by a notable growth in design activity, much of which arose through immigration or was allied to tourism development. The dormant company, Waterford Glass, for example, was re-established by Czech manufacturer Charles Bacik and glass designer Miroslav Havel; renamed Waterford Crystal (1950–2009), it became an important driver of tourism spending. Welsh-born designer Sybil Connolly and Danish-born designer Ib Jorgenson opened haute couture fashion businesses in Dublin in 1953 and 1958, benefitting from the support of Córas Tráchtála Teo (CTT), the Irish export authority, which successfully championed the promotion of Irish fashion in North America. Connolly excelled in marrying international fashion trends with Irish textiles, and Jacqueline Kennedy chose one of her dresses for her official White House portrait (1970). However, the most significant design developments as a consequence of immigration occurred in the field of graphic design. Beginning in 1950, graphic designers from Dutch airline KLM were enticed to Ireland to work on advertising campaigns for the Irish national airline, Aer Lingus (Figure 9.3). This decision to reach beyond Ireland's borders for more experienced designers had a profound effect on the nascent profession as a whole. The Dutch brought with them a graphic modernism that was highly influenced by Bauhaus teaching and combined the visual language of European and American design with local references.[19] As the decade progressed these designers were much sought after and worked for many indigenous companies of which Guinness and RTÉ are two further examples. In the post–World War II climate of aviation expansion, Aer Lingus began to enlarge its network of European routes and in 1958 also established a transatlantic route. In its combined roles of de facto tourism authority, flag carrier and transportation agent, the airline was a principal agent of modernization and crucial to how Ireland was viewed internationally and nationally. A parallel history of emigration had an important influence on the spread of Irish design worldwide, particularly in the areas of architecture and engineering, as many Irish designers sought opportunities abroad. These included structural engineer Peter Rice, who worked on the Sydney Opera House (1973) and the Pompidou Centre (1977), and architect Kevin Roche, who with partner John Dinkeloo designed headquarters for numerous institutions and corporations in the United States, including the U.S. Post Office (1969) and John Deere (1978), and additions to the Metropolitan Museum of Art (1967–) and the United Nations Plaza (1969).

It was also in the United States, specifically New York, that the most radical and sympathetic repackaging of Irish literary modernism occurred. In the 1930s, the city became the hub of European modernism as many fled the hostilities in Europe. Influenced by these events, a distinctly American

Figure 9.3 Jan de Fouw, *Britain*, 1959, screenprinted poster. Image courtesy of Aer Lingus, Dublin.

interpretation of modernism emerged in the 1940s and 1950s that combined European rationalism and order with informality. This visual language was expressed through strong blocks of colour, photomontage, collage and illustration and typically sans serif typography. Graphic designers working in this idiom evolved a visually precise but metaphorically rich aesthetic that became particularly adept at capturing the narrative of modernist discourse in fiction. These designers included Paul Rand for Alfred A. Knopf, who designed covers for books by Camus, Mann and Mencken, and Alvin Lustig for New Directions, who designed for Arthur Miller, Nabokov, Tennessee Williams, Kafka and Lorca. Lustig designed one cover for a work by Joyce, *Exiles* (1947), in which he captured the drama's tense relationship between the three protagonists by visualizing them as stick figures trapped in a web of frenetic scribbles (Figure 9.4). Grove Press became a champion of Beckett, and its designer, Roy Kuhlman, gave visual form to the anarchic and oblique language of Beckett's writing through expressionist typography and crude mark making. In covers for *Malone Dies* (1956), *Murphy* (1957), *The Unnamable* (1958), *Krapp's Last Tape* (1960) and *How Is It* (1964), Beckett's linguistic exploration of self and the fragmentation of the inner psyche are exteriorized through the cover designs and conveyed to a mass audience. Similar conceptual approaches to book cover design became popular in Ireland in the 1960s and 1970s, and Dutch immigrant Kor Klassen was among those leading the vanguard.

Design advocacy slowly emerged in Ireland, even though the infrastructure to support design activity was limited. The Arts Council was established in 1951, and it employed Britain's Design Research Unit to produce small touring exhibitions based on the principal of 'art applied to industry', showcasing the best of indigenous and international design, replicating patterns of design advocacy that had emerged in Britain, Europe and the United States. By the late 1950s the gradual shift of focus from political and economic insularity to greater international engagement accelerated with the publication of TK Whitaker's Programme for Economic Expansion (1958). This was supported by one of Ireland's great modernizing influences, Taoiseach Seán Lemass (1959–67) and paved the way for economic development through greater engagement and trade relations with Europe, culminating in Ireland's application (1961) for, and acceptance to, EEC membership (1973). In the coming decades design activity became a central concern in the packaging of goods and services aimed at international markets, and design practices became the material expression of an Ireland that was modernizing and becoming more international in outlook.

The visual evidence of such modernization was particularly apparent in Dublin, which experienced an architectural boom expressed through a modernist idiom. In the later years of the mid-century, Ireland was comfortably

Figure 9.4 Alvin Lustig, book jacket for *Exiles* by James Joyce (New Directions Books, 1947). Image courtesy of Elaine Lustig Cohen.

integrating modernist paradigms developed earlier in the century into its contemporary design practices. As Rowley has noted, extensive urban planning expanded the city's borders, while office developments and new corporate headquarters redefined its fabric.[20] The United States Embassy by American architect John Johansen (1964), who trained under Gropius, is a potent example of localized modernism with its references to indigenous forms and use of Irish materials, including Connemara marble and granite. The Bord Fáilte headquarters by Robin Walker (1961), the RTÉ headquarters (1960–ca. 1975) and the Bank of Ireland headquarters by Ronald Tallon (1978) are also emblematic in their adaptations of International Modernism to local circumstances. Designed by architects who trained for periods in the United States, they modified archetypes by such pioneers as Mies van der Rohe and Gropius for the more modest scale of Dublin city and its suburbs. Catholic church building also experienced a boom because of the reforms of Vatican II (1962–65); this initiated a vigorous programme of which Liam McCormick's Burt Chapel in Donegal (1967) is an idiosyncratic example that exemplifies a vernacular modernism that materializes the localization of Catholic religiosity the reforms encouraged.

While architectural practices were intent on adopting international ideas, other areas of design practice also moved with this tide of change. Following criticisms of standards in design education in Ireland, a group of Northern European designers (including Kaj Franck and Åke Huldt) were invited by CTT to survey contemporary provisions in manufacturing and design education. After World War II the Nordic region had successfully reconfigured much craft and small-scale manufacturing to suit a more industrialized climate, and it was hoped that Ireland could learn from these experiences. The resultant observations, published as *Design in Ireland* (more commonly known as the *Scandinavian Report*, 1962), were highly critical of Irish design standards and called for widespread reform and the establishment of more industry-aligned design courses. In part a response to the report, the Kilkenny Design Workshops (KDW, 1963–88), the first government-sponsored design agency in the world, was established as a subsidiary of CTT. KDW focused on the training, modernization and promotion of industrial, graphic and craft design and made sustainable links with extant Irish manufacturers and small-craft initiatives. In other words, it reflected the forms and ideology of International Modernism in improving everyday life through synthesizing modernist aesthetics with functionality. In summary, KDW was a conscious attempt to stimulate design development in a country where such activities had not organically occurred. Corporate identity systems for semi-state companies were a particular strength, and the abstractions of infrastructural modernization were expressed through either the language of International Modernism – for example the Department of Posts and Telegraphs (1968) logo – or through a vernacular, adapted modernism – for example the Office of Public Works (1973) logo – both by Damien Harrington. Other projects in the areas of food packaging and street furniture ensured that KDW's designs mainstreamed modernist design within the everyday experiences of the Irish public. KDW's model of design advocacy and stimulation was exported to developing nations, including the Philippines and Africa, and its legacy with respect to the development of Irish design education and professionalization was substantial.

Conclusion

The conditions of Irish modernity are unusual when compared to other European countries and North America. What was understood to be revolutionary in Ireland was likely to be considered as 'safe' in other jurisdictions. In the main, modernist expression was not as expansive in Ireland as elsewhere, but the 'particles' of modernist design activity that did exist were more expansive than has been previously acknowledged. Irish modernist designers routinely adapted international paradigms in the creation of a vernacular modernism, and this is particularly evident when the patrons for their designs were either political or religious organizations. This is principally manifest in architecture, where the experiments of the early twentieth century ushered in a realized utopian expression from the mid-twentieth century onwards, demonstrating that the design afterlife was far from a 'ghostly' presence but comprised the apex of modernism in Ireland and was a vibrant material manifestation of earlier ideals and aspirations. Irish design modernism was imitative in the main, although there are notable exceptions to this tendency, for example, Gray. However, when the material expression of design did pull against the conservative national tendencies, it produced exciting new forms that spoke to indigenous and foreign audiences. By closely examining these forms and the designers who imagined and produced them, extant historical narratives can be challenged – such as the parochialism of mid-century Ireland or the marginal place and limited influence of women in design history. To visualize and materialize modernity is not merely thinking about modernism, it is to be modern. What that means in the context of Irish cultural history has yet to be sufficiently explored and understood.[21]

Notes

1. Adrian Forty, *Objects of Desire: Design and Society since 1750* (London: Thames and Hudson, 1995 reprint), 6–8.
2. Martin Daunton and Bernard Rieger, *Meanings of Modernity: Britain from the Late-Victorian Era to World War II* (London: Bloomsbury, 2001), 4–5.
3. David Crowley, 'National Modernisms' in *Modernism: Designing a New World, 1914–1939*, ed. Christopher Wilk (London: V&A, 2006), 340–61.
4. See for example Linda King and Elaine Sisson, *Ireland, Design and Visual Culture: Negotiating Modernity, 1922–92* (Cork: Cork University Press, 2011).
5. Crowley, 'National Modernisms', 347.

6 Wilk, 'Introduction: What Was Modernism', 12.
7 Jürgen Habermas, 'Modernity: An Unfinished Project', in *Habermas and the Unfinished Project of Modernity: Critical Essays on the Philosophical Discourse of Modernity*, eds. Maurizio Passerin d'Entreves and Seyla Benhabib (Cambridge, MA: MIT, 1997), 38–39.
8 Wilks 'Introduction: What Was Modernism', 14, 12.
9 This largely comprised brewing, distilling, biscuit-making and paper production.
10 Adolf Loos, 'Ornament and Crime', in *The Design History Reader*, eds. Grace Lees-Maffei and Rebecca Houze (Oxford and New York: Berg, 2010), 98.
11 This phrase is attributed to the Chicago-based architect Louis Sullivan.
12 Hugh Campbell, 'Irish Identity and the Architecture of the New State', in *Ireland – Twentieth Century Architecture*, A. Annette Becker et al. (Munich and New York: Prestel Verlag, 1997) 82–88.
13 Terence Brown, *Ireland – a Social and Cultural History, 1922–1985* (London: Fontana Press, 1985), 136.
14 Brown, *Ireland – a Social and Cultural History*, 1985, 234. The comments remain in the revised edition, 2004.
15 Seán Rothery, *Ireland and the New Architecture: 1900–1940* (Dublin: Lilliput, 1991); Rolf Loeber et al., *Architecture: 1600–2000: vol. IV of Art and Architecture of Ireland* (Yale University Press: New Haven, 2014).
16 Ellen Rowley 'The Conditions of Architectural Modernism in Ireland, 1900–1970: Between Aspiration and Production', in *The Moderns: The Arts in Ireland from the 1900s to the 1970s*, eds. Enrique Juncosa and Christina Kennedy (Dublin: The Irish Museum of Modern Art), 422.
17 Rothery, *Ireland and the New Architecture: 1900–1940*, 215, 127–29.
18 S. B., Kennedy, *Stella Styne* (Dublin: Gorry Gallery, 1995) 10, 16.
19 For further discussion, see: King: '(De)Constructing the Tourist's Gaze: Dutch Influences on Aer Lingus Tourism Posters, 1951–61', in King and Sisson, 165–87.
20 See also Rowley 'From Dublin to Chicago and Back Again: An Exploration of the Influence of Americanised Modernism on the Culture of Dublin's Architecture, 1945–1975', in King and Sisson, 210–31.
21 Thanks to Elaine Sisson and Paige Reynolds for their generous insights into this chapter. Alternative overviews of Irish design can be found in: Linda King and Lisa Godson 'Design in Ireland: 1900–2000', in *Twentieth Century: vol. V of Art and Architecture of Ireland*, ed. Catherine Marshall and Peter Murray (New Haven: Yale University Press, 2014) 120–34; and Linda King 'Irish Design: History, Context and Possibilities, 1900–2011' and 'Irish Design Timeline', in *Pivot: Dublin's Bid for World Design Capital 2014* (Dublin: Dublin City Council, 2011), 396–414.

Chapter 10

ANIMAL AFTERLIVES: EQUINE LEGACIES IN IRISH VISUAL CULTURE

Maria Pramaggiore

> The sound of hooves in Irish art [...] seems highly unlikely to die out; it is part of the national psyche, admit it or not.
>
> Brian Fallon, *Irish Arts Review*

For centuries, the horse has functioned as a compelling symbol within Irish mythology, literature and visual culture, often serving as an emblem of national identity. From the imposing steed that conveys Oisín to Tír na nÓg, the land of eternal youth, and the horses that appear alongside humans in the 'Book of Kells', to Art O'Leary's white-nosed mare, the Pegasus-like phantom in W. B. Yeats's 'Easter, 1916', and the grey charger of *Into the West* (1992), the horse stands with humans as a partner in work and war, a near-equal who transports objects and conveys humans, often to supernatural worlds. This notion of transportation, not only physically moving people and objects between locations but also moving human beings spiritually, emerges as a central trope of the horse in ancient and modern Irish culture.

In formal terms, the horse figure's animal afterlife emanates from its persistence across the centuries and from its privileged relationship to temporal and spatial liminality. Linked to movement and mediation, the horse simultaneously invokes the romantic and the modern, the rural and the urban, the earth-bound past and a heavenly future. The horse functions as the quintessential anachronism: an antiquated throwback and a figure of timeless endurance that is almost always pictured as out of sync with whatever present moment it is used to signify. Enlightenment modernity gave birth to notions of historical progress and temporal homogeneity, and literary and cultural modernisms called into question that Enlightenment project through the representation, in language and images, of the radical break, crisis and fragmentation. The horse engages both regimes, its physicality expressing both the measured sequential rhythm of the military march and the sublime transcendence of the leap. The horse is able to call up a backward-looking nostalgia and a forward-looking aspiration. In its double signification – and without even beginning to address the role and plight of actual, embodied horses within Irish economic and cultural history – the horse can be recruited to explore modernity's fundamental contradictions.[1]

The fictional Irish horses that most prominently speak to these contradictions appear in Jonathan Swift's fictitious Enlightenment travelogue, *Gulliver's Travels* (1724), a tale that culminates in Lemuel Gulliver's encounter with the hyper-rational horse society of the Houyhnhnms. Swift's work presciently comments on the temporal reversals inherent within the Enlightenment project: its aspirations toward a rational, scientifically regulated order and its designation of the non-European periphery as primitive in order to establish the superiority of European civilization and progress. Philip Armstrong argues that *Gulliver's Travels* employs two notions of inhumanity: one is associated with non-European populations and the other is linked to the 'moral degradation' arising from the greed and instrumentalism that animates British imperialism.[2] At the conclusion of his travels, after his expulsion from Houyhnhnm Land because of his likeness to the enslaved humanoid Yahoos, Gulliver eschews human contact and sleeps with his horses in 'a droll reversal of the historical progress of separation between farmers and animals that marked the rise of the modern agricultural system'.[3] Gulliver's horses not only suggest temporal disjunction and reversal – challenging the meanings of civilization and backwardness, for example – but also project the notion of the end of time itself, as they toy with the possibility of human eradication, presaging twentieth-century practices of eugenics and genocide. The Houyhnhnms propose to castrate Yahoos as a way of putting an end to the species without 'destroying life', a plot twist which makes reference to a proposed 1719 statute in Britain that would have permitted the castration of Irish men.[4] Swift's gimlet-eyed critique of Enlightenment modernity thus embeds within its equine ecology a tension between concepts of movement and generativity on the one hand and intransigent temporalities on the other.

Fredric Jameson argues, 'the moderns were obsessed with the secrets of time'[5] and offers a materialist approach to modernism's 'sensitivity to deep time'[6] through a generational model that speculates about the lived experience of the first modernists.

> I want to conjecture that the protagonists of those aesthetic and philosophical revolutions were people who still lived in two distinct worlds simultaneously;

born in those agricultural villages we still sometimes characterize as medieval or premodern, they developed their vocations in the new urban agglomerations with their radically distinct and 'modern' spaces and temporalities.[7]

Gulliver's Travels foreshadows the movement between 'backwardness' and 'forwardness' that Jameson writes about in broad terms here, yet these disruptive rhythms and momentums also evoke Irish culture in very particular ways. A number of Irish studies scholars characterize Irish political and literary temporalities as disruptive of chronology[8] and as heterogeneous.[9] These contradictory alternatives to Enlightenment linearity are often embodied in the figure of the horse. The horse's status as victim of, and organic counterpoint to, the industrialized war machines of World War I has emerged in narratives such as Nick Stafford's 2007 play, *War Horse*, in which the contrasting temporalities of field and trench are dramatized through puppetry that visually articulates the ways that horses, like soldiers, served as machines for the transport of weapons and as cannon fodder.

The Irish horse in the twentieth century accords with Jameson's two 'socio-economic temporalities', resonating with the diurnal rhythm of the farm across a still heavily agricultural island, while also conforming to the clockwork timetable of the city streets. In Dublin, horses were used for postal transportation from 1789 onward. They towed boats along the canals and carried passengers in coaches. Trams replaced double-decker carriages in 1872. Although the trams were fully electrified by 1904, the horse maintained a key presence in the city as a working and leisure animal, even making a dramatic appearance at the Easter Rising. Alfred West's eyewitness account begins with the observation that the corpses of two dead horses (the mounts of British cavalry) lying in Sackville Street served as 'testament to a skirmish'.[10]

The horse appears as a frequent subject in early twentieth-century visual art in Ireland and Europe as a traditional, or even classical, subject reconfigured by modernist abstraction. Horses join the placid human figures in Georges Seurat's pointillist *Horses in the Water* (1883), they grace the landscape of Natalia Goncharova's *Bathing Horses* (1911) and they transport the gods in Odilon Redon's symbolist paintings of Apollo's chariot (ca. 1910). Franz Marc, a founder of *Der Blaue Reiter* and later condemned by the Nazis as a degenerate artist, produced numerous horse paintings, including *Landscape with Horses*, which was rediscovered in Munich in 2012 with other works confiscated by the Nazi regime. The work possesses a cubist abstraction, attention to colour, and expressionist style that prefigures the paintings Irish artist Mainie Jellett (1897–1944) produced in the 1940s.

The tendency to conflate old and new can be identified in the work of Jellett, who was a member of the somewhat staid Society of Dublin Painters and yet also worked with the avant-garde White Stag group after their relocation from London. Her *Achill Horses* (ca. 1941) are modern, sculptural, graphically abstract and lyrical; their lack of connection to literal environments contrasts with the colourful impasto horses that her contemporary, Jack B. Yeats (1871–1957) situates within very traditional Irish settings. Yeats's horses acquire a modernist patina when given an expressionist treatment in paintings such as *A Horseman Enters a Town at Night* (1948). In both Jellett's and Yeats's work, horses are traditional subjects transported far beyond the well-established traditions of equestrian portraiture from the eighteenth and nineteenth centuries.

Jack B. Yeats, whom Brian Fallon describes as 'scarcely conceivable without the horse' depicted horses in oils and watercolours throughout his career.[11] He is in many ways a model for Jameson's modern, with his experience of both the country (Sligo) and the city (London and Dublin). His work was heralded by his friend, poet Thomas MacGreevy, as the 'consummate expression of the spirit of his own nation at one of the supreme points in its evolution'.[12] Yeats's work is typically associated with romanticism and the west of Ireland because it often depicts the Sligo of his youth. Like his brother's poetry, however, Yeats's visual art formally and in its subject matter captures tense, transitional, uncomfortable moments between life and death, day and night and traditional and modern Ireland. An early work, *The Swinford Funeral* (1918) is a sombre study of a working horse in motion, lifting one hoof as it pulls the cart that carries away the deceased. The horse's arrested movement embodies a moment of temporal indeterminacy when a human life recedes before an uncertain future. Yeats's horses mediate nineteenth-century realism and modernist abstraction, especially in terms of style: his early work is dominated by illustration and linearity, whereas his work after 1920 in oils is characterized by an expressionist emphasis on colour and texture. 'Jack Yeats was less interested in the anatomy of horses', argues Brian Fallon, 'than he was in them as expressions of a kind of "spirit energy"'.[13] Lines disappear, as evidenced in *The Cavalier's Farewell to his Steed* (1949). Yeats applied the paint directly to the canvas, without linseed oil and turpentine, using a palette knife and building up the surface, joining painting and sculpture.

Gordon Armstrong notes the importance of the equine in communicating emotional experience in Yeats's writing as well.[14] A passage from the novel *Sligo* (1930) reinforces the horse's characteristic motion and its occupation of the liminal zone between heaven and earth:

> To get the full feeling of a horse race, one should lie on the grass, to get a low horizon and let the horse go thudding by you with their bodies between you and the sky.[15]

Both of the Yeats brothers return again and again to images of horses that exemplify tensions between rural and urban, past and future that Jameson describes as the spatiotemporal legacy of this generation of modernists. W. B. Yeats's early and late poetry is laced with equine imagery, from the supernaturalism of 'Dhoya' (1891) to the shadowy horses of disaster in 'Michael Robartes bids his Beloved be at Peace' (1899), to *Two Plays for Dancers* (1919), 'Nineteen Hundred and Nineteen' (1921), and 'Easter, 1916' (1920).

Anthony Cuda describes W. B. Yeats's repeated engagement with horses by foregrounding the poet's fascination with the ninth-century Japanese painter Kose Kanaoka, whose horses were purported to be so lifelike that they seemed to free themselves from the confines of his canvases. For Cuda, this tale represents a 'passion scene' that demonstrates the emotional engagement of modern artists like Yeats with the act of creation. Despite the fact that he never visited Japan, Yeats 'pursue[d] the imaginary painted horses in both his life and his art with an impressive persistence'.[16] They 'always retain the emotional connotations of turbulence, fear and anxiety'.[17] Using terminology that accords with my reading of the ways in which horses signify diverse temporalities through rhythm, movement and transportation, Cuda defines Yeats's passion as being moved, an experience marked by the often involuntary nature of the creative process.

Beyond poetry and painting, the horse enjoys a unique relationship to the most modern of art forms, the cinema, a medium that transports spectators visually and imaginatively, if not physically. It was the horse that Eadweard Muybridge subjected to serial photography in 1878 to satisfy the curiosity of horse breeder and railroad magnate Leland Stanford. This choice was no accident, I would suggest, but instead reflects the way the horse, as experienced by humans, captures the rhythms and also the disjunctions of modern life. Lynne Kirbly links the train to the silent cinema as industrial technologies that 'annihilate time and space'.[18] Yet the horse is the organic prototype for the train (once also known as the 'Iron Horse') and thus should be understood as a technology of temporality as well: one whose influence persists from the cinema of the twentieth century into the digital images of the twenty-first.

Eisenstein's *October* (1928), a re-enactment of the 'July Days' of the Russian Revolution of 1917, crystallizes the way the cinematic horse disrupts the neat progression of past, present and future. The film depicts a white horse that falls victim to a skirmish between revolutionary workers and counter-revolutionaries. The horse remains yoked to an empty carriage, lying across a drawbridge that links the city to the workers' quarter. According Robert Rosenstone, Eisenstein focused on the raising of the bridge because the act produced a potent visual metaphor for the widening gap between the Provisional Government and the revolutionaries.[19] As the bridge is raised, the dead horse dangles precariously from its carriage. Eventually, the animal's carcass breaks free and descends to the river below, a moment that is shot from two perspectives. The plummeting animal's horrific downward flight is the uncanny obverse of the motion of a winged Pegasus. Rapid cuts to images of dead revolutionaries and to the tattered revolutionary flag link the horse to the plight of the still-oppressed workers. Murray Sperber writes '[the horse's] plunge into the Neva implies the abuse of nature and the end of a decadent era. [...] The Provisional Government does not care about the loss of human and animal life'.[20] This aestheticized death, endowed with what Vivian Sobchack has described as 'the charge of the real', acts as a metaphor for the loss of connection between the people and the Provisional Government, yet it also functions as a sacrifice that paves the way for the eventual October Revolution.[21] Here, the horse, engaged in movement even after its death, occupies the space and time of both the past and the future, its involuntary movement becoming a metaphor for history itself.

A living Irish horse serves a similar historicizing function in John Ford's *The Quiet Man* (1952), a film in which Irish-born American Sean Thornton, who has immigrated to Ireland to escape his past, experiences a flashback to the mortal blow he dealt his opponent in the boxing ring in Pittsburgh. For Luke Gibbons, at this pivotal moment film editing signifies the transportation of trauma across space and time. Gibbons argues that the editing proposes equivalence between violence in the United States and in Ireland. Editing brings the past into the present with an immediacy that, for Gibbons, discourages romantic nostalgia: 'the cinematic device of flashback, at its most intense, works decidedly against romantic nostalgia in that it prevents any detachment from the past'.[22]

The Irish draft horse, Napoleon, is an equally important element that connects the past, present and future, however. Michaleen's horse represents a form of transportation that, like film editing, mediates spatial and temporal relationships. Prior to Sean's flashback, the horse sutures past and present by physically returning Sean to his family's ancestral cottage, White O'Morn. Sean arrives in Castletown by train; significantly, the train and the horse cross paths as he leaves the station in the cart, suggesting divergent trajectories of the modern and the archaic. Peter Stowell argues that this moment marks the passage from cinematic realism to Sean's 'dream of returning to Ireland'.[23] The temporal compression and psychological complexity of the encounter between present and past is suggested when Sean first gazes at his birthplace, a gesture accompanied by the voice of his deceased mother.

Scholars rightly emphasize the significance of the bridge where Sean pauses as he contemplates the cottage: it serves as a spatial metaphor for the conjunction of past and future.[24] Yet the horse, the living beast of burden that has conveyed Sean to this point, is what first enables the man's sentimental gaze upon the Irish homestead. Later, Napoleon prepares the way for the future by participating in the courtship ritual between Sean and Mary Kate Danaher, only to be supplanted by the tandem bicycle. Unlike the flashback, a cinematic technology that effaces its own work, the horse represents an embodied intrusion of the persistent past into the affairs of the present day. Napoleon intrudes into the filmic space, functioning as an element of cinematography, *mise en scène*, and narrative as an organic machine of transport that carries human bodies through heterogeneous temporalities to real and imaginary locations.

In the second half of the twentieth century and moving into the twenty-first, horses appear frequently in Irish and Irish-themed films. Elsewhere, I have explored the way horses in Celtic Tiger era films function as a proxy for a masculinity perceived as being endangered, arguing that the depiction of the horse in the city demonstrates the continuing negotiation of modernity and masculinity through the axis of rural and urban experiences.[25] This synecdoche turns on the fact that the modernization of Dublin city centre in that period required that horses, animals that had long resided within the city, be deemed inappropriate interlopers within urban environments.

Equine examples drawn from contemporary art projects and videos further demonstrate the way the horse experienced an animal afterlife during the Celtic Tiger era and continued to negotiate modernist anxieties. The Celtic Tiger boom and bust economy brought about significant changes in Ireland, disruptions with a significant temporal orientation. Gerry Smyth observes that 'there was much talk in all walks of Irish life about "new times", about the necessity of orienting the nation towards the future rather than towards the past'.[26]

Like their predecessors, contemporary horse representations do not merely serve as placeholders for nostalgia. Instead, they generate political and economic critiques of Celtic Tiger culture and resist the notion that the march of chronological time can always be equated with progress.

The equestrian statue *Misneach*, commissioned as part of the Ballymun Regeneration project in 2006, memorializes the tradition of horse ownership by the local youth in this blighted urban housing estate. John Byrne's monumental bronze statue challenges the tradition that honours victors and colonizers on horseback by instead depicting a teenaged girl sitting bareback on a stallion.

The decision to honour a marginalized population at the peak of the economic boom – its dramatic crash had occurred by the time the statue was unveiled in 2010 – was not a coincidence. The temporal contestation around the statue became apparent during a debate regarding whether the statue belonged to the past or the present, whether it reinscribed 'old' (pre-Celtic Tiger, impoverished, criminal) Ballymun or, instead, validated the strength of a typical working class girl, echoed in the use of the Irish *misneach* (courage) and in the selection of a 16-year-old local girl as the model.

Furthermore, two popular music videos from the 1990s and 2000s use comedy to explore anxieties surrounding Irish Europeanization, and indeed globalization, while also forwarding the trope of the horse as a nexus of temporal indeterminacy. 'My Lovely Horse' (1996) from the television programme *Father Ted*, and 'Horse Outside' by the Rubberbandits (2010) mark, respectively, the moment of Ireland's Eurozone membership (confirmed in December 1995, although not implemented until 1999) and the disastrous austerity after the financial crisis of 2008.

Father Ted's 'My Lovely Horse' aired in 1996 on an episode entitled 'A Song for Europe'. The narrative involves a musical farce that speaks to Ireland's new position in Europe, not only as a prospective Eurozone member, but also as a cultural equal in the Eurovision contest. The episode refers to the fact that in 1994, Ireland had won the Eurovision contest two years running: something that national broadcaster RTÉ publicly lamented because of the high cost of hosting the next year's event, which the winning nation is obliged to do. Some speculate that the choice of the Irish act in 1994 – 'The Rock 'n' Roll Kids' (Paul Harrington and Charlie McGettigan) – was intended to be a losing entry. As it happened, the intermission performance of *Riverdance*, which was not in competition, stunned the appreciative audience and ultimately garnered global success. Against all odds, the uninspiring Irish entry won, possibly because of the popularity of *Riverdance*.

On *Father Ted*, two priests consigned to Boggy Island for misdeeds and incompetence, enter the 'Eurosong' contest to thwart the ambitions of their rival, Father Dick Byrne. Ted and Dougal compose a song extolling the virtues of their lovely white horse, but it lacks a suitable melody. After complications force them to abandon their original tune, Ted revives the bid by plagiarizing music from an obscure Norwegian winner from the 1970s.

The episode's narrative aligns with the overall approach adopted by the programme because it suggests the ability of the past to colonize the present. Although produced in the 1990s, *Father Ted* intentionally courts a 1970s visual aesthetic in sets and costuming, suspending its characters out of time. Ted borrows a 20-year-old tune for his masterpiece, only to learn subsequently that the song has had its own afterlife when he hears the plagiarized tune whistled by a stagehand and also piped into an elevator: the return of the not-so-repressed as *muzak*. Fearing they might be exposed as frauds, Ted and Dougal perform their original number instead and, miraculously, they win. They lose at the European competition, however: the anticipated costs of hosting the contest proved too great for the small Irish economy to bear and thus the competition is rigged (by the Irish) to prevent the Irish entry from winning. Here, European politics and the questionable implication of the Irish in their own undoing emerge in an eerie foreshadowing of the 2008 banking crisis.

At the centre of the episode, afterlives of the modern and the postmodern collide: the campy traditionalism of rural Irish horse culture (depicted in the video by the priests wearing classic jumpers in lurid green pastures), intersects with the tinsel and glitter of the Eurovision competition, a Europe-wide if not global media event. Furthermore, the popularity of the episode endures, suggesting its continuing salience. In May 2014, a petition was submitted to the Irish parliament to submit 'My Lovely Horse' as the Eurovision song contest entry for that year.[27]

A second video that speaks to contemporary Irish identities through the device of the horse is 'Horse Outside' the phenomenal hit by the Rubberbandits, a Limerick comedy and hip-hop team pairing, Dave Chambers (Blindboy Boatclub) and Bob McGlynn (Mr. Chrome). The two rappers typically conceal their identities by wearing plastic shopping bags over their faces, which, in addition to presenting an uncanny visual element, suggests a vaguely sinister connection to terrorism.[28] In 2010, the pair rose to international prominence as a result of 'Horse Outside'. The video debuted on the Republic of Telly and went viral on YouTube. By early 2011, it had reached the top of Irish Billboard Charts.[29]

The video makes a mockery of an extremely traditional event: an Irish wedding. The two trash-bag-faced bandits crash a church where the nuptials are taking place; one is intent upon seducing the bridesmaid, played by model Madeline Mulqueen. The currency that mediates McGlynn's challenge to his rivals for Mulqueen's attention is the hipness of their modes of conveyance: 'Fuck your Mitsubishi, I've a horse outside' sing the Rubberbandits, satirizing the cultural over-investment in branded automobiles and the class hierarchy that places nearly every locale in Ireland at a disadvantage in relation to the wealthy urbanism of Celtic Tiger Dublin. The fact that the video is set in Limerick offers a clue as to the layered irony at work: the 'posh' people that the singers are challenging are clearly scrambling toward upward mobility themselves. It is no accident that the brand-name commodities mentioned are Mitsubishi, Subaru and Honda. As economy cars rather than luxury vehicles, they are mocked on two fronts because they function as signifiers of masculinity – the three rival suitors appearing self-satisfied when they are identified with their cars – and yet these particular brands occupy a somewhat humble status in the world of automobile fetishism.

As the song attacks the pride and piety of those assembled, the singers praise the advantages of owning a horse: the owner pays no taxes and has no need for a parking space. The song pays respects to horses of the Irish past, including the real racehorse, Shergar, and the mythical Tír na nÓg, while also mocking contemporary popular culture by comparing the horse's face to that of English actress Billie Piper of *Dr. Who* fame.

The song resolves in a pun on the colloquial use of the verb 'to ride' as a euphemism for sex, as the bridesmaid agrees to leave with the bag-faced singer. The video's troubling gender politics are worthy of mention: the song depicts competition for the attention of a woman based on the ownership of and identification with machines of transport. The bridesmaid asserts her agency at the song's conclusion by asking her would-be-lover to 'take me by the pony tail and ride me like a horse'. She and two women are then shown dancing with horse heads obscuring their faces, a highly problematic image. Although we may be reminded that the Rubberbandits themselves are wearing plastic garbage-bag face masks, the easy slide from human to animal, in the context of becoming a ride rather than having a ride, is a disturbing moment in which the woman is shown to voluntarily cross the human–animal divide.

In an interview, McGlynn comments on the way the video was interpreted against the backdrop of the post–Celtic Tiger bust and downplays the song's critique: 'Ireland was signing an austerity treaty with Germany at the time and everyone called us "the voice of the poor". The amount of stuff people thought that song was about! It was a song about a horse'.[30] And yet, as journalist Brian Logan points out, the song addresses conflicts within Irish culture related to regional and economic realities and fantasies. 'Their act came about partly in response to Limerick's reputation as a poverty-stricken place', he writes, acknowledging the international dimensions of Limerick's reputation: '(it's where Frank McCourt's misery memoir, *Angela's Ashes*, is set), riven with gangs, drugs and crime (it's also Ireland's murder capital)'.[31]

'Horse Outside' not only scrambles time in giving precedence to the horse over high horse-powered cars; it also identifies Ireland's rural and urban divide as a continuing source of conflict, despite urbanization and Europeanization. In the closing line, the singer tells the bridesmaid he will take her to Mullingar, a bucolic town in the rural midlands. When the bridesmaid accepts the ride, the horse conveys the two lovers, serving as a viable contemporary challenger to the automobile: not a ghost of the past but a living creature still engaged in negotiating Irish identities.

In conclusion, the figure of the Irish horse not only symbolizes a pastoral and an urban heritage and the possibilities of spatial and temporal transcendence, the creature experiences modernist afterlives in twentieth- and twenty-first-century Irish visual culture as it continues to confound claims of progress and obsolescence, and to animate modernism's jagged rhythms and reveal the irregularities within the Enlightenment's project of linear temporality.

Notes

1 In this chapter, I focus on the figural horse. As Jonathan Burt reminds us in *Animals in Film* (Reaktion Books, 2004), this is never the whole story. This is especially true for horses, which literally appear 'in' film in the form of gelatin. For an account of the Irish horse that more fully addresses the relationship between screen image and animal life, see my essay 'The Celtic Tiger's Equine Imaginary', in *Representing Animals in Irish Literature and Culture*, eds. Kathryn Kirkpatrick and Borbala Farago (London: Palgrave Macmillan, 2015), 270–91.
2 Philip Armstrong, *What Animals Mean in the Fiction of Modernity* (Abingdon and New York: Routledge, 2008), 25.
3 Philip Armstrong, 28.
4 Philip Armstrong, 25; C. Rawson, *God, Gulliver, and Genocide: Barbarism and the European Imagination, 1492–1945* (Oxford: Oxford University Press, 2001), 230.
5 Fredric Jameson, 'The End of Temporality', *Critical Inquiry* 29, 4 (2003): 697.
6 Jameson, 699.
7 Jameson, 699.
8 Declan Kiberd, *Inventing Ireland: The Literature of a Modern Nation* (New York: Vintage, 2009), 294.
9 Gregory Dobbins, 'Constitutional Laziness and the Novel: Idleness, Irish Modernism and Flann O'Brien's *At Swim-Two-Birds*', *Novel: A Forum on Fiction* 42, 1 (2009): 87.
10 Thomas M. Coffey, *Agony at Easter: The 1916 Irish Uprising* (New York: Pelican/Penguin, 1971), 38.
11 Brian Fallon, 'Horse Power', *Irish Arts Review* 25, 2 (2008): 96.
12 Quoted in Karen Brown, 'Thomas MacGreevey and Irish Modernism: Between Word and Image', *Irish Modernism: Origins, Contexts, Publics (Reimagining Ireland, vol. 14)*, eds. Edwina Keown and Carol Taafee (Brussels: Peter Lang, 2009), 99–100.
13 Fallon, 96.
14 Gordon Armstrong, *Samuel Beckett, W.B. Yeats, and Jack Yeats: Images and Words* (Selinsgrove, PA: Bucknell University Press, 1990), 182.
15 Quoted in Gordon Armstrong, 67.
16 Anthony Cuda, 'The Turbulent Lives of Yeats's Painted Horses', in *Yeats Annual 17: Influence and Confluence* (Basingstoke, London and New York: Palgrave Macmillan, 2007), 14.
17 Cuda, 9.
18 Lynne Kirby, *Parallel Tracks: The Railroad and Silent Cinema* (Durham, NC: Duke University Press, 1997), 9–10.
19 Robert Rosenstone, 'October as History', *Rethinking History: The Journal of Theory and Practice* 5 (2001): 270.
20 Murray Sperber, 'Eisenstein's *October*', *Jump Cut: A Review of Contemporary Media* 14 (1977): 15–22.
21 Vivian Sobchak, *Carnal Thoughts: Embodiment and Moving Image Culture* (Berkeley: University of California Press, 2004), 278.
22 Luke Gibbons, *The Quiet Man* (Cork: Cork University Press, 2002), 50.
23 Quoted in Gibbons, 77.
24 Natalie Harrower, 'Cityscapes of Fluid Desire', in *Genre and Cinema: Ireland and Transnationalism*, ed. Brian McIlroy (New York: Routledge, 2012), 219.
25 Pramaggiore, 270–91.

26 Gerry Smyth, 'Irish National Identity after the Celtic Tiger', *Estudios Irlandeses* 7 (2012): 134–35.
27 Lizzie Dearden, 'Petition to make Father Ted's "My Lovely Horse" Ireland's Eurovision song turned down', *The Independent*, 26 June 2014.
28 Logan, Brian, 'The Rubberbandits: comedy, prank CDs [...] and the IRA'. *The Guardian*, 16 January 2013.
29 'Hits of the World', 2011. *Billboard*, vol. 123, Issues 1, 2, 3, & 4. January and February: 51, 55, and 67.
30 See Logan.
31 See Logan.

Chapter 11

CHOREOGRAPHIES OF IRISH MODERNITY: ALTERNATIVE 'IDEAS OF A NATION' IN YEATS'S *AT THE HAWK'S WELL* AND Ó CONCHÚIR'S *CURE*

Aoife McGrath

Although movement is often viewed as forming the 'kinetic basis' of the modern age, the analysis of movement practices such as dance is often neglected in theories of modernity.[1] Dance theorists such as André Lepecki (2006) and Randy Martin (1998) have argued for an awareness of how the kinaesthetic politics of modernity perform a colonization of space and bodies in their constant drive toward movement and mobility. This chapter examines how an analysis of two dance works by Irish artists, one from the early twentieth century and one from the early twenty-first century, can contribute to these discussions of modernity and dance, and how the works might illuminate connections between dance and politics in Ireland in their alternative approaches to these modernist kinaesthetic politics. Taking a brief, contextualizing look at an early dance play by William Butler Yeats, the chapter then focuses on what echoes, or afterlives, can be found from this early modernist work in a piece by contemporary dance theatre choreographer Fearghus Ó Conchúir. In both works we see the ability of dance to create an alternative space within the pervading discourses (or movements) of a sociopolitical and cultural landscape that allows the spectator – through a visceral connection with a dancer – to experience a different perspective on the 'idea of a nation'.[2]

In his revisionary study of modern dance, Mark Franko argues that modernist accounts of modern dance history, 'perform the telos of aesthetic modernism itself: a continuous reduction to essentials culminating in irreducible "qualities"'.[3] In this chapter's discussion of what 'afterlives' a modernist dance piece in Ireland might have in the work of a contemporary Irish choreography, there can be no danger of such reductions being performed, as the (very) few examples of historical modern dance to be found are so thoroughly different from each other from a formalist perspective.[4] However, this discussion does attempt to find echoes from a modernist work from the early twentieth century in a contemporary dance theatre piece – not from a formalist perspective, but through an examination of how these works engage in a 'modernist cultural politics'.[5] In his questioning of the familiar modernist narrative of aesthetic modernism's 'absolute' – 'the reduction of art to the essence of its own formal means' – Franko proposes, instead, a modernist cultural politics that calls into question the notion that modern dance operates on some aesthetic plane divorced from sociopolitical and cultural realities.[6] This approach challenges the idea of modern dance as being 'ahistorical, abstract and autonomous' and encourages the links between modernist choreographies and the societies they emerged from (and are commenting on) to be considered.[7]

Both Yeats's and Ó Conchúir's works can be viewed as political responses to changes, and wished-for changes, in Irish society. Yeats (1865–1939), a resistive poet and dramatist, was committed throughout his life to decolonization.[8] In his work he looked to ancient Irish myths for inspiration in his imagining of a de-Anglicized Irish culture, and he constantly searched for new forms of artistic expression to communicate 'the idea of a nation'. Dancer and choreographer Ó Conchúir's work also grapples with issues of Irish identity and the moulding of corporealities. Much of Ó Conchúir's work explores the relationship between individuals and determining sociopolitical and cultural structures. His most recent works have focussed on an exploration of the influence of religion, specifically the Catholic Church, on the formation of corporeality in an Irish context, and the work discussed in this chapter deals with the recent collapse of sociopolitical and cultural structures in contemporary, recessionary Ireland. In both of the works discussed here, although they were created almost a century apart, we can see dance functioning as a 'privileged site for defining the lived experiences of modernity';[9] in the case of Yeats's work, the struggle to imagine and embody a de-colonized Irish corporeality, and in the case of Ó Conchúir's, the re-imagining and rehabilitation of a sick and damaged corporeality in the current climate of recessionary collapse.

At the Hawk's Well

As Ramsay Burt proposes, modernist dance has a 'visceral quality and powerfully moves the spectator in ways she or he doesn't always understand, but nevertheless responds to'.[10] This 'visceral quality' of the dancing body is an 'aspect of the affective power of the body and poses a problem for ways of thinking that are conditioned by the Judaeo-Christian value system [and its] dualistic ways of thinking, [in which] the body is generally marginalized and ignored although it may occasionally be wildly overdetermined'.[11] This dualistic approach to the corporeal is clearly evident in Ireland when dance is considered. During the Gaelic Revival movement at the end of the nineteenth century, the necessity to construct an 'Irish' corporeality that was distinct from that of its colonizer created a need to strictly control danced expressions of nationality.[12] Step dancing, renamed 'Irish' dancing by the Gaelic League in 1893, became the only morally acceptable dance form, and its tight regulation by the *Comisúin le Rincí Gaelacha* (Commission for Irish Dance) could certainly be seen as an instance of 'overdetermination' of the body.[13] Regulations in the competitive step dance form stress the importance of a continual feeling of 'upness' in Irish dancers' movements, and a connection can perhaps be made to a striving toward moral rectitude and upward social mobility.[14] Other forms of social and theatrical dance were considered morally dubious,[15] and so, in this ideologically frosty environment, it is perhaps not so surprising that modern dance – as practiced, for example, by U.S. and German choreographers and dancers such as Isadora Duncan (1877–1927), Mary Wigman (1886–1973) and Martha Graham (1894–1991) – did not thrive in Ireland. However, there are nevertheless important, if isolated, examples of modern dance to be found. One example is the dance plays of Yeats. These works harnessed the dancing body's 'affective power' to bring to the fore bodily realities – corporealities – in a deeply conservative Irish society in which bodies were limited in their capacity as creative agents because of acceptable forms of corporeal expression being restricted to articulations that supported state and church views.

After being introduced by Ezra Pound to a collection of Japanese Noh play texts in 1913, Yeats collaborated with modern dancer and choreographer Michio Ito for the first staging of one of his four dance plays, *At the Hawk's Well*, in Lady Emerald Cunard's drawing room in London in 1916. The dance play would later have its Irish premiere at the Peacock Theatre in Dublin in 1933, with Ninette de Valois adapting and performing Ito's role. Ito, a Japanese dancer who had not had any substantial Noh training, but whose interest in modern dance had led him to study at the Dalcroze Institute in Hellerau, was helping Pound with the translation of Noh texts.[16] After seeing Ito perform one of his 'dance-poems', Yeats recognized a possibility to synthesize poetry, music and dance into a new mode of expression that could communicate beyond the 'limits' of language. Yeats reimagined the Zeami Noh play, *Yoro*, to tell a tale of mythological Irish warrior Cúchulainn, and his adventure at a magical ancient well, the waters of which lend immortality to those who drink from it when it appears, a well that is guarded by the mysterious Hawk woman (danced by Ito). Inspired by the writings of Stéphane Mallarmé on the image of the dancer as the embodiment of the convergence of form and meaning, the *'incorporation visuelle de l'idee'*,[17] Yeats's collaboration with Ito created an early dance theatre work that re-envisioned how Irish myths, and Irish identity, could be embodied outside the confines of a (in Yeats's opinion) stifling conservative realism that was prevalent on the Irish stage at the time.[18]

This was largely achieved through Ito's choreography and performance. Yeats writes of his reaction to seeing Ito perform: 'he was able, as he rose from the floor, where he had been sitting cross-legged or as he threw out an arm, to recede from us into some more powerful life. Because that separation was achieved by human means alone, he receded, but to inhabit as it were the deeps of the mind'.[19] This perceived ability of Ito's to bring the spectator to a different, 'more powerful', reality through movement, allowed for an unfamiliar experience of Irish mythology to be created. It produced an alternative affective experience of a performance of nationalist narratives that allowed a glimpse of a different 'idea of a nation'; one that embraced an articulate, creative dancing body. Ito's Hawk woman dance, which consisted of 'tense, continuous movement with subtle variations on its monotony, inducting a trancelike state in both personages and audience',[20] was certainly a challenge to the modernist colonization of the Irish dancing body with its ever upward and forward striving movements in its performance of mobility and nationalism.[21] Considering this work of Yeats and Ito as an early example of dance theatre in Ireland, a thread, or 'afterlife', can indeed be traced from this pioneering piece to the choreographies of contemporary dance theatre artists working in Ireland today. The rest of this chapter will examine one such example.

Cure

The solo performance, *Cure*, danced by Fearghus Ó Conchúir, premiered in Dublin at the Project Arts Centre's Space Upstairs in 2013. As explained earlier, Ó Conchúir's work often explores the relationship between individuals and determining sociopolitical and cultural structures. Following a series of works exploring the interface between bodies and buildings/architecture, which took place in various locations in the United States, China and Europe, his more recent works have focussed on an exploration of the influence of religion, specifically the Catholic Church, on the formation of corporeality in an Irish context. These works include the dance film *Mo Mhórchoir Féin* (2010) and *Tabernacle*, a piece for five dancers that premiered at the Dublin Dance Festival in 2011.[22] *Mo Mhórchoir Féin* was created by Ó Conchúir in collaboration with film director Dearbhla Walsh for RTÉ's (Ireland's national television and radio broadcaster) *Dance on the Box* series. As Ó Conchúir explains about the work:

> [T]he title is from the Confiteor, the part of the Catholic mass where the congregation confesses "to Almighty God and to you my brothers and sisters, that I have sinned through my own fault, in my thoughts and in my words, in what I've done and what I've failed to do". In Irish we say not only 'through my own fault' but 'through my grievous fault'. I proposed to make a film about the role of religion in the creation of the Irish body and I guess, in particular, in my body. There have been many words written about the bodies of young children traumatised and abused by the Catholic Church. I wanted to understand the wider impact of the Church but not through words. Dance seems a more appropriate language for that physical investigation.[23]

Tabernacle continued this exploration of the role that religion plays in the moulding of Irish corporealities. This work, in Ó Conchúir's own words, was 'about the Catholic Church and the making of the Irish body, [...] investigat[ing] authority, control and the individual search for purposeful living'.[24] The piece that will be focused on here, *Cure*, can be seen to have developed out of these two previous works, with the focus shifted from exposing the traumas inflicted on Irish bodies by the Church, to the rehabilitation and healing of injuries in a time of recovery. *Cure*, is, as Ó Conchúir explains, 'about the process of getting over challenges, about what's needed to survive and about the journey in hope as much as the arrival. It's a work that emerges from the experience of collapse – personal, political, moral, economic – and, wondering what next, invites many different perspectives to look for the way ahead'.[25] Within the context of contemporary, recessionary Ireland, in which economic, social and political structures have suffered seismic change and disintegration, Ó Conchúir wanted the work to make a connection between both a personal and a societal experience of collapse and the efforts made to recover, and how each of these levels of experience might inform each other. Some of the seismic changes in Irish society that have occurred during the past decade include: the collapse of the moral authority of the Catholic Church following the publication of a number of government-commissioned investigations into child abuse in Church-run institutions (e.g., the *Ryan Report* and the *Murphy Report*, both 2009); the collapse of the economy when Ireland entered severe economic recession in 2008; and the collapse of the leading political party, Fianna Fáil, in 2010. As Ó Conchúir explains, in *Cure* he wanted to investigate 'how the macro context is experienced personally as well as how the individual experiences (psychological, physical and emotional) of weakness, loss, survival and recovery might teach us about what's going on at a political and social level'.²⁶

As one way to access and embed different perspectives on 'cure' in the piece, Ó Conchúir asked the five dancers and the visual artist that he worked with on *Tabernacle* to each create a ten-minute solo for him over a two-week period on the theme of 'recovery'. He had been thinking about this subject while working on and touring *Tabernacle*, but felt that he 'couldn't ask the dancers to carry questions about sickness and cure in their bodies [...] while they were carrying *Tabernacle*', and that 'maybe [he] was able to carry those questions in [his] own body'.²⁷ The six solos were then assembled by Ó Conchúir during a final two-week period to create the finished work, which he presented as an hour-long solo performance. In *Cure* the stage is bare, but lighting and sound design create an ever-shifting series of locations and moods. Each solo requires a distinct movement vocabulary that generates a very different atmosphere although, as the solos are all interpreted by the same dancer, there is a coherence of movement quality throughout. Some solos are lighter in mood, with Ó Conchúir playing with hospital-type woollen blankets to transform himself into a delicately gesturing geisha, or into a caped crusader who dashes gleefully with fast, shuffling feet and comical, small leaps across the space. Another depicts a group-therapy session with an angry, flailing body restricted and contained by a circle of chairs. Another shows a broken figure, quivering with effort and engulfed by muscle spasms as it tries to pick itself up from the ground, failing and falling, yet trying again and again.

It is a moment from the penultimate solo that the rest of the chapter will focus on. This section begins with Ó Conchúir creating the outline of a large circle with sand in the centre of the space. In the following dance within the circle he draws attention to the fragility and impermanence of the circle's outline through movement phrases that carefully skirt the perimeter, taking care not to disturb the sand, while echoing its shape within his body. At the end of this sequence he collects a rough lump of concrete from the upstage area and, carrying it downstage, kneels on the edge of the circle facing the audience. Then placing the concrete on the ground just outside the circle's perimeter, he starts to force his body to retch. Crouched over the piece of concrete, his body heaves audibly and repeatedly until he succeeds in vomiting onto the concrete. Watching this sequence was a discomforting experience. A strong moment of kinaesthetic empathy caused my own stomach to feel queasy and I felt concern for the performer's wellbeing, even though I knew that he was ultimately in control of what he was doing and could make it stop whenever he wanted to. But, simultaneously, I also felt myself withdrawing from my, until that moment, untroubled immersion in the performance. Although there was nothing gratuitous about how Ó Conchúir performed this action, it was as if this instance of jarring physical reality, this literal sickness, burst some bubble of trust that had been created between the spectator and the performer, altering the affective environment.

The expulsion of bodily fluids (urination, defecation, vomiting) is of course nothing particularly innovative in contemporary performance.[28] So why was it so disturbing in this setting? Perhaps it was the connection that was established very early on in the performance between the performer and the spectator that created a context in which this moment became so troubling. At the beginning of the piece, after an opening dance section, Ó Conchúir seats himself on the floor in front of the audience and, addressing us directly, explains that a cure is not something that can be easily shown, but that he thinks it is something that 'you need to experience for yourself'.[29] He tells us that during their research for the piece, both he and the choreographers spent a lot of time thinking about body practices that are used to help people recover from various traumatic experiences such as Tai Chi and Qigong, Yoga, Feldenkrais, Alexander Technique and transformational breathing. Explaining that they found a focus on breath to be a connecting element important to all of these practices, he then led us, the audience, in a group breathing exercise, which he prefaced by stating that 'focussing on breath isn't only about connecting to ourselves, there is an in-breath and an out-breath, so the breath connects to you, but it also connects beyond you, to the world outside you, to other people, and to what's going on'.[30] This simple breathing exercise at the beginning of the piece brought attention to how the shared air of the performance space, something not normally at the forefront of awareness, connected the performer and the spectator in a comforting and encompassing structure of recovery. Similar to Ito's trance-inducing dance in *At the Hawk's Well*, this breathing exercise transported us, with the dancer, to another state of awareness.

On some level I continued to breathe with Ó Conchúir throughout the piece, and so the scene of retching and vomiting ruptured my comforting narrative of recovery, allowing a glimpse of a harsher reality in which these protective structures (perhaps represented here by the sand circle) momentarily lost their immunizing power against the harsh realities of everyday life, in which recovery is not always possible, or comes too late for some. This moment brought awareness to the dance's creation of an alternative affective environment, as in Ito's performance in *At the Hawk's Well*. A space had been forged in which a structure of recovery was built and felt, based on an awareness of shared space and shared experience. *Cure*, like Yeats's dance play, does not engage in an explicit sociopolitical critique. However, just as the project of decolonization provides the backdrop to Yeats's experiments so, too, do the precarity and instability caused by the collapse of economic and social structures in Ireland create the backdrop to Ó Conchúir's work. Yet, both pieces nevertheless create a site in which hopeful movements toward freedom (Yeats) and recovery (Ó Conchúir) could be rehearsed outside of the usual circulations of affect; in the case of *At the Hawk's Well*, the surrounding discourse of colonial oppression, and in the case of *Cure*, the surrounding discourse of burst economic bubbles, bailouts and loss of sovereignty.[31] However, the moment of 'real', if choreographed, illness in *Cure*, functioned to highlight and underline the importance, and simultaneous fragility, of dreamed-for realities and the ability of dance to embody them. Through dance, both Yeats and Ó Conchúir bring their audiences to an alternative space. Yeats's dance plays, as Christopher Murray reminds us, are dream plays, which places their action 'at one remove from the audience […] in some space beyond the real'.[32] Ó Conchúir also creates an alternative space, but he punctures any dreamlike quality with an intrusion of bodily realities.

Concluding Thought

In the first of his *Spheres* trilogy, *Bubbles*, philosopher Peter Sloterdijk argues for a spatial understanding of our being in the world. He proposes that, in the development of modernity, the 'increasing removal of safety structures from the traditional theological and cosmological narratives' of Western society that gave people a sense of their place in the world, has 'brought the people of the First World the loss of the cosmological centre, and subsequently set off an age of progressive decentralizations'.[33] Modernity, then, is 'characterized by the technical production of its immunities' that were once provided by the belief in traditional structuring systems such as religion.[34] This progression has great resonance with recent developments in Ireland, where belief in the traditional 'safety structures', to use Sloterdijk's term, such as the Church and the government, has largely collapsed, leaving people searching for other ways to centre themselves in the world. Sloterdijk acknowledges that it is now 'too late to dream ourselves back to a place under celestial domes whose interiors would permit domestic feelings of order'.[35] Indeed, in the context of Ireland, decades of societal blindness to the deep veins of corruption in the Church and state structures that created societal order has led to such grief that there can never be a desire to go back, and Yeats's mythological imaginings from the early twentieth century seem very far away. The body practices researched and performed by Ó Conchúir and the choreographers of *Cure*, can then perhaps be seen as the 'technical production of immunities' that, in times of collapse, are turned to in order to build a structure for recovery. However, the moment of real sickness in the piece highlights the performance's creation of a space for an alternative affective experience. It punctures any easy consumption of an ever forward-progressing modernist narrative of recovery and reminds us of the harsh realities experienced by many in everyday life. It also functions as a kind of inoculation against a forgetting of our fragility, and how the forging of a new and better world must be a shared, inclusive experience. The alternative affective experience created in *Cure* simultaneously shows both our continuing need for belief in protective, comforting rituals and for something to replace 'the old homely, immunizing cosmos', and for the cold 'realities' of our enlightened understanding of a diseased and corrupted, but hopefully not incurable, Irish society.[36]

Notes

1 See Gabriele Klein and Sandra Noeth, *Emerging Bodies: The Performance of Worldmaking in Dance and Choreography* (Bielefeld: Transcript Verlag, 2011).
2 W. B. Yeats, *Autobiographies* (London: Macmillan, 1956), 493.
3 Mark Franko, *Dancing Modernism/Performing Politics* (Bloomington: Indiana University Press, 1995), ix.
4 The two most obvious examples being Yeats's collaborations with choreographers Michio Ito and Ninette de Valois, and the works of Erina Brady. Brady, whose father was Irish, was a modern dancer and choreographer. She is believed to have trained with some of the most important European modern dance innovators – Rudolf von Laban, Mary Wigman and Émile Jaques-Dalcroze – before arriving in Dublin in the late 1930s and founding the Irish School of Dance Art at Harcourt Street in Dublin in 1939. See Aoife McGrath, *Dance Theatre in Ireland: Revolutionary Moves* (Houndmills: Palgrave Macmillan, 2013).
5 Franko, ix.
6 Franko, x.
7 Ramsay Burt, *Alien Bodies: Representations of Modernity, 'Race' and Nation in Early Modern Dance* (London: Routledge, 1998), 128.
8 His commitment often took the form of institution building, as evident in his co-founding of the Irish Literary Society and Abbey Theatre.
9 Burt, front matter, unpaginated.
10 Burt, 6.
11 Ibid.
12 See McGrath and Barbara O'Connor, *The Irish Dancing: Cultural Politics and Identities, 1900–2000* (Cork: Cork University Press, 2013).
13 In 1927 the Gaelic League set up *An Comisiúin le Rincí Gaelacha* (The Commission for Irish Dance), which in 1930 became a centralized organization with regulatory authority that continues today in its role of creating and enforcing rules of competition and examination, both in Ireland and internationally. See Helen Brennan, *The Story of Irish Dance* (Dingle: Brandon Press, 1999).
14 See Frank Hall, *Competitive Irish Dancing: Art, Sport, Duty* (Madison, WI: Macater Press, 2008).
15 See Brennan.
16 Émile Jaques-Dalcroze was a professor of music who developed a system for teaching music that explored the relationship between musical and bodily rhythms. He developed a series of physical exercises, known as *Rhythmischen Gymnastik* (rhythmic gymnastics) that translated musical scores into physical movements.

17 Stéphane Mallarmé, *Oeuvres Complétes*, 306, cited in A. J. Bate, 'Yeats and the Symbolist Aesthetic', *MLN*, 98, no. 5 (December 1983): 1218.
18 For a discussion of theatre from this period, see Christopher Murray, *Twentieth Century Irish Drama: Mirror up to Nation* (Manchester: Manchester University Press, 1997).
19 W. B. Yeats, cited in Sylvia C. Ellis, *The Plays of W. B. Yeats: Yeats and the Dancer* (London: Macmillan, 1995), 130.
20 Helen Caldwell, *Michio Ito: The Dancer and his Dances* (Berkeley: University of California Press, 1977), 45.
21 See McGrath for a more detailed discussion of *At the Hawk's Well*.
22 Fearghus Ó Conchúir, 'Tabernacle', *Fearghus*, 4 April 2014, http://www.fearghus.net/projects/tabernacle/.
23 Fearghus Ó Conchúir, 'Mo mhórchoir féin: London Buddhist Arts Centre', *Fearghus*, 23 February 2010 (accessed 7 April 2014), http://www.fearghus.net/mo-mhorchoir-fein-london-buddhist-arts-centre/.
24 Ibid.
25 Fearghus Ó Conchúir, cited from the promotional video for *Cure* (accessed 10 April 2014), http://vimeo.com/67955475.
26 Fearghus Ó Conchúir, 'Yearly Archives 2012', *Fearghus*, 9 December 2012 (accessed 4 April 2014), http://www.fearghus.net/2012/.
27 Fearghus Ó Conchúir, 'Yearly Archives 2012', *Fearghus*, 23 September 2012 (accessed 20 May 2014), http://www.fearghus.net/2012/.
28 For example, urination in Jerome Bel's *Jerome Bel* (1995), or urination and defecation in Matthew Barney's *Guardian of the Veil* (2007).
29 *Cure*, Project Arts Centre, Dublin, 2013.
30 Ibid.
31 After the collapse of the Irish economy following the onset of global recession in 2008, the EU and the International Monetary Fund (IMF) agreed to lend the Irish state €85 billion in 2010. This bailout loan was seen by many Irish people as having resulted in the loss of Irish financial sovereignty.
32 Murray, 26.
33 Peter Sloterdijk, *Bubbles: Spheres 1*, trans. Wieland Hoban (Los Angeles: Semiotext(e), 2011), 20.
34 Sloterdijk, 25.
35 Sloterdijk, 28.
36 Sloterdijk, 29.

Chapter 12

THE MODERNIST IMPULSE IN IRISH THEATRE: ANU PRODUCTIONS AND THE MONTO

Emilie Pine

Anu Productions is a site-specific Dublin theatre company run by director Louise Lowe and visual artist Owen Boss. Founded in 2009, Anu explores the history of particular sites in economically deprived inner-city locations, with an inside-out approach, prioritizing local memory and experience over grand historical, or literary, narratives. The work the company is best known for is its Monto tetralogy of plays set in north inner-city Dublin and named for the area around the former Montgomery Street (now called Foley Street). The Monto tetralogy includes: *World's End Lane* (2010), *Laundry* (2011), *The Boys of Foley Street* (2012) and *Vardo Corner* (2014). As a company, Anu is dedicated to developing work that is highly collaborative, interdisciplinary and provocative, both theatrically and politically. Although predominantly identified with inner-city Dublin, Anu has also made work in the city of Limerick and in the United Kingdom. By using formal strategies and emphasizing the power of affect, both aimed at increasing audience participation and questioning agency, Anu forces an interrogation of positions of 'self' and 'other' and, the company hopes, makes visible people who otherwise are 'invisible to the world [they] live in'.[1] An encounter with Anu's work does not immediately suggest modernism as an interpretive framework, particularly given the ways in which the company's work consistently violates the critical distance, or detachment, often associated with modernist work. Yet, equally, this juxtaposition newly demonstrates the strong resonances of contemporary avant-garde drama with the modernist engagement with form as meaning, as a mode of expressing and understanding trauma.

Anu's tetralogy is set in the 'Monto', an area of Dublin that Joyceans are familiar with from the 'Circe' episode of *Ulysses*. One way of approaching the

Monto trilogy is thus as a theatrical reimagining of 'Circe' for a twenty-first-century audience. Certainly Anu is very aware of Joyce, viewing its work as building on, as well as rebutting, a literary and social tradition, reflected in his novel, of viewing the Monto area as a chaotic and 'other' space of sexual and moral deviance.[2] The formal difficulty of the 'Circe' episode is mirrored in Anu's approach, while the company's combination of affecting and disorienting spectators mirrors and extends Bloom's encounter with the Monto. In this sense, then, the afterlife for modernism within contemporary and avant-garde Irish theatre is as a still-persistent, ghostly presence.

Rather than merely cataloguing echoes between Joyce and Anu, I focus in this essay on how the tetralogy is staged, exploring the idea that form is meaning. Anu's performance style is aggressively experimental and very obviously avant-garde, particularly in an Irish theatrical tradition still largely dominated by the text and the writer. Anu's avant-gardism represents a political challenge to the idea of the spectator as a passive viewer of an active performance: a transformation effected through affect and formal experimentation, decentred and multiple perspectives, fragmentation, subjective voice and sensory experience.[3] So far, so modernist. However, Anu's performers also directly address and implicate the audience, often using violence as both a thematic and formal practice, emulating the chaos they seek to represent, and reversing (indeed, rejecting) the aesthetic distance that is most usually ascribed to modernism. Anu's practices as a company may thus seem diametrically opposed to the ideals of modernist impersonality, yet in the creation of an 'intimate violence' in their work – as I show in my reading of *The Boys of Foley Street* – they mirror modernist preoccupations with representational strategies for traumatic experience and the affective implications of violence.[4]

The Active Spectator

Anu's emphasis on the role of the spectator emerges from a sense of the audience member as interpreter and explorer. In the Monto trilogy, the line between reality and artifice is constantly blurred, and often it is only the audience's presence that can be said to constitute these performances as art. The audience member has to continually decode and react to the scene before her: for example, in *The Boys of Foley Street* the spectator stands on the street, waiting for the performance to commence, when she is propositioned by an actor, who is playing a homeless man. The street location, the lack of any formal 'lights-up' device to signal the beginning of the performance, and the actor's direct address all suggest, however, that the spectator is being approached by a real homeless person and not an actor. This fine distinction between reality and artifice makes the spectator and critic far more alert to techniques and modes of illusion, with the effect of changing the relationship between the 'stage' and the 'audience'. In many ways, Anu thus mimics the aims of avant-garde dramatists before them, from Jarry to Brecht, whose manifestos so strongly challenged the convention of the 'fourth wall'. Anu lays down this challenge with a particular ethical focus, generating, through this process, an active and critical 'seeing'. The Monto area, its streets and buildings, are places where many spectators, both local and nonlocal, would not be accustomed to pausing and looking around. Instead, the Monto is an area that suffers from being unseen, both literally as the passer-by moves swiftly through the streets, and also figuratively, as this area of north inner-city Dublin is desperately politically disenfranchised and economically marginalized. And so Anu's emphasis on active seeing and interpreting represents an ethical and political intervention into a culture of not-seeing.

Throughout Anu's work, the spectator is engaged as an active witness, highlighting the generative relationship between spectacle, spectator and 'art'. Anu's work goes beyond the Artaudian idea of 'theatre that wakes us up' to theatre that implicates the spectator in the theatrical scene. As Susan Bennett argues, writing in relation to Brechtian *Verfremdungseffekt*, 'Performance, hitherto almost hermetically sealed, demanding of the audience only the role of receiver, became essentially a co-operative venture. Thus a role of activity was established for audiences, and their centrality to the dramatic process acknowledged'.[5] How a spectator reacts to this will be enormously varied, from feelings of discomfort to enjoyment, from alienation to inclusion, from disempowerment to agency. Spectating in these productions necessitates involvement in the co-production of meaning. Tim Etchells argues that 'witnesses are produced especially when performed events are not only presented in a challenging, open-ended way but also when they have a connection to the real'.[6] In Anu's work the 'real' is abundantly provided through the combination of *mise-en-scène* (from streets to cars to council flats) and the involvement of the spectator as a component of the scene. Audience members thus become, in Karine Schaefer's term 'spectatorial witnesses'.[7] This reality value adds a further layer of complicity and provocation; what is being performed is often unethical (in *Boys of Foley Street* this can be generally categorized as 'drug-related violence', from assault to rape), so the spectator's involvement in the scene troubles the ethical boundary between spectacle and spectator, highlighting the (moral) inertia of being a bystander rather than an active witness.

The Boys of Foley Street

In *The Boys of Foley Street* the audience members congregate in a small group of four people, before being divided into pairs and then, after a few minutes, being led off singly. The show is dominated by male actors, with an emphasis on violence. It is performed in a range of spaces, from Foley Street itself and its surrounding alleyways, to a derelict car, to an almost derelict flat in a council block. These are spaces of fear, and acting as a witness thus takes on frightening, as well as ethical, dimensions. The performance spaces are also linked to different time periods – the derelict car is resonant of the bombing of nearby Talbot Street by Loyalist terrorists in 1974; the alleyways are the site of a drug-related fight in the present day; the squalid council flat is the stage for the 1975 heroin epidemic and its attendant casualties. There is an incredible layering of urban experience, history and memory, and a real sense of the simultaneity of these layers and spaces within a singular place – the Monto. The structure of the show mirrors in some ways the structure of memory, interconnecting narrative fragments in an associative and imagistic methodology. In not re-enacting the past as a nostalgic journey, Anu instead explores the far-reaching impact of traumatic events on memory, both individual and collective. Indeed, in using a site-specific approach, Anu inscribes these memories in the architecture of the area, so that the streetscape the spectator is guided through is also a 'memoryscape'. This mélange of memory is not, however, a postmodern flattening of time and space, as there is a strong sense of causal progression within *The Boys of Foley Street*, creating a co-present past and present in a multiply voiced and periodized narrative.

To talk about *The Boys of Foley Street* is to talk about personal experience. When I attended a production in October 2012, I found the theatrical cliché that a show is different for every audience thrillingly and challengingly true. At the beginning of the show, I was led away from my fellow spectator by two men I hoped were actors, and I was incredibly nervous. We walked down a blind alleyway, which seemed so unwise that I kept stopping, until they shouted at me to continue walking. A large part of me wondered why I would pay to endure this, as well as noted how automatically – out of my comfort zone but still operating as a theatre spectator – I followed their directions. Those thoughts did not go away for the entirety of the experience. At the end of the alleyway was a young man who seemed even more nervous than I, and my two male companions, to my initial relief, turned their attention to him. Then they started to beat him and to harass him about drugs and money. They took his mobile phone from him. They gave it to me. They told me to film them as they beat him up.

In this scene there is a clear ethical choice for the spectator as to whether you comply and collude with the aggressors. This collusion is a free choice, yet it is not without a sense of coercion. And in the use of a mobile phone, rather than a camera, the spectator also understands that the film she is making is not restricted to this moment, but will likely be replayed via online media.

This intersection of violence with personal action and public consumption, as mediated through technology, resonates with modernism's concern with the ways that technology corrupts our construction of selfhood and our relationship to the world. It also underlines what Carl Lavery has described as avant-garde theatre's tendency toward a 'dramaturgy of trauma'.[8]

The most disturbing element of this scene is, obviously, the violence: the way this young man is victimized seemed all too real, yet not only did I not intervene (though occasionally spectators *do* intervene) but I accepted the mobile phone and the injunction to film it, and this seems even worse (although I pointed the camera away from the violence, this was hardly a moment of resistance). In a discussion with Anu,[9] some of the actors expressed surprise at the regularity with which audience members accepted their roles as recorders in this scene, yet, as theatre critic Lyn Gardner argues in relation to immersive theatre, 'our fear of doing the wrong thing – of behaving in a way that potentially destroys the intended performance – remains very strong. We worry that we will make a performance out of ourselves. It renders us impotent'.[10] Instead of creating agency, scenes such as the alleyway encounter underscore how even active audiences can be passive, how witnessing can be itself an unethical subject position, and how difficult it is (in the theatre, in real life) to transform witnessing into ethical action.

The Active Witness

In every show, Anu creates junctures at which the audience is required to make ethical choices. Not doing anything, being passive and allowing yourself to be taken to the next scene, is revealed as also being a choice. There is an enormous pressure put upon the audience at these moments, particularly given each audience member's isolation from the group. The issue here is not restricted to what you should do as an individual, or indeed how individuals react in stressful situations. One of the primary goals of *The Boys of Foley Street* is to open up a closed world and simultaneously put the present moment into dialogue with the past. But why is the presence of a witness so vital?

The emphasis on witnessing suggests the ghostly presence of Bishop Berkeley's famous maxim: to be is to be perceived. I want to extend the concept that perception and identity are linked by inserting memory into the matrix. The anxiety that one is not being perceived and thus does not exist underlines much modernist culture, iconically summed up in the uncertainty of Beckett's Vladimir in *Waiting for Godot* (1953): '[T]ell him you saw me'.[11] Forty years later, avant-garde British playwright Sarah Kane ventriloquized this line in her 1995 play, *Blasted*, when the Soldier says to journalist Ian, moments before his suicide, 'Tell them you saw me / Tell them [...] you saw me'.[12] Vladimir's existence is verified by having been seen. However, his insistence on having been seen is not just about the present, but is angled at tomorrow: 'You're sure you saw me, you won't come and tell me tomorrow that you never saw me!' (86). Vladimir's persistent anxiety reveals that existence is verified through a combination of perception *and* remembrance, with the understanding that the act of perception is enacted in the present, while remembrance – far from being oriented to the past – is future-oriented, as the re-enactment of perception. To be is to be perceived now and tomorrow. Vladimir, and the Soldier, realize that to be forgotten is to be rendered retrospectively unseen.

Of course this dictum takes on particular significance in a play that is based on the twin premises of audience and future repetition. As an audience, there is a certain knowing pleasure in the joke that we know the same boy *will* come again tomorrow and tell Vladimir that he *did not* see him. For Berkeley, there is always God, the ultimate presence and perceiver. For Beckett and Kane that role is played by the audience members who, through their presence, verify the existence of the onstage world. In an Anu production, the relationship between the spectacle and the spectator seems even more vital (and precarious) when the spectator is regularly outnumbered by the actors. Furthermore, the subject and the sites Anu chooses suggest, like Beckett's tramps, that perception cannot be assumed by those marginalized or disenfranchised by modern – and in Anu's case, urban – society. Although not explicitly articulated in the same way that Kane embeds Beckett's modern anxiety into her script, Anu implicitly builds the same questions into the structuring of its work, with the purpose of forcing the audience to answer the question: Did you, or did you not, see? Anu, however, is aware that to ask for validation in this way is not a guarantee of anything. The recognition of this insecurity of identity is a further dimension of Anu's stylistic practice of using formally challenging and open-ended theatre as a mode of engaging and troubling the spectator so that, although the audience members may leave Foley Street once the performance is over, the show remains imprinted on their memories.

Form and Meaning

The Boys of Foley Street's challenging aesthetic is created through a fusion of immersive theatre style and the subjects being dramatized, from drug crime to terrorist bombing to sex work. The three main scenes the audience witness are the alleyway fight, the aftermath of the 1974 Talbot Street bombing and a brothel. Spectators are brought one by one from scene to scene: in order to maximize the size of the show's audience, and to create a non-linear theatrical world, spectators encounter scenes in seemingly random order.[13] This means that there are up to four spectators 'in' the show at any one time, with the actors following a complex and tightly timed 65-minute cycle to make sure that each spectator experiences a scene before being moved onto the next scene, with no overlap between spectators (except at the beginning and the end). This cycling is aesthetically essential to the show's sense of simultaneity – the idea that the city is a space of multiplicity that, as a layering of palimpsests, contains and reveals collective histories and individual stories. Moreover, the order in which the spectator encounters scenes will affect how she perceives each segment and, of course, her building impression of the overall show.

The 1974 Talbot Street bombing was the second scene I saw. After the alleyway encounter I was taken to a broken-down shed and told to sit in a derelict car. A soundtrack of the bombing played as a silent and staring woman slid over the bonnet and front and back windows of the car. Although this is a gentler evocation of the past than the other scenes and represented a welcome respite from the violence of the alley, the car scene nevertheless evokes a feeling of traumatic memory and requires an equal level of witnessing. The absence of explanation provokes the spectator to question the space, the action and the meaning, so that the spectatorial experience chimes with the disorientation caused by the bomb's explosion.

From the relative security of the derelict car I was brought to a 1970s-style council flat that acted as both a family home (a mother, father and daughter live there) and a brothel. This shift is the most unsettling of the entire show and depicts the play's worst violence, including beatings, rape, and entrapment. At moments in the flat I was asked for help and at other times ordered around. I was even offered tea, but this seemed an expression of hostility rather than hospitality. Indeed, my reaction to the tea – refusing it – suggests the extent to which the production was successful in making spectators question otherwise 'normal' social situations. After watching the brothel scene unfold for some minutes, I was brought into the front hall of the flat and pushed into the tiny bathroom, where a young woman asked me to help pin her ripped dress together. She appeared to have been beaten and was shaking – she asked me to help her leave the flat and escape her forced position as a sex worker. Immediately, the door opened. I was ushered out of the room into the hall and out the front door, while the young woman was pushed back into the main room. I did not protest and, again, I had failed the challenge to understand that ethical spectatorship requires intervention rather than passive viewing. I had interacted with the show but not intervened, out of fear, out of a sense of propriety as a witness not an actor, and out of a feeling of disempowerment generated by not knowing the boundaries of my situation. Instead, I allowed myself to be 'rescued' by anti-drugs vigilantes, and brought back to my original audience group and the start of the journey on Foley Street.

In an empty room, at the close of the production, we were left to look at photographs taped up on the walls taken of us and other audience members during the show without our awareness. In this instance, the spectator became the spectacle and again technology and surveillance operate in tandem to affect our sense of personal agency. Being an audience member at *The Boys of Foley Street* was an emotionally challenging experience; it was the most difficult piece of theatre I have ever been part of as a spectator, including the other shows in the Monto tetralogy. *The Boys of Foley Street*, intended by Anu to be the most confrontational of the four works, successfully creates a viscerally challenging form that opens up a history of abuse, from physical and drug abuse, to the political abuse of neglect and disenfranchisement.

A Dramaturgy of Trauma

This show is a piece of immersive theatre designed to test spectator reactions to challenging events. But we might also read its traumatic content and ramifications as mirroring the psychoanalytic process in which a confrontation between the self and the traumatic past is a required, if gruelling, necessity. Anu's work mirrors the underlying paradox of psychoanalysis: that past traumas are the source and cause of present pathological neuroses, and only through remembering the trauma can those neuroses be cured. For Anu the neuroses are less individual and more social; the desired move from melancholia and haunting to mourning and resolution centres on social change rather than personal catharsis in a quest to provoke civic responsibility. *The Boys of Foley Street* shows the process of theatre-going as a double journey, into both the collective past and the social psyche.

Anu's work then ultimately enacts another paradox – that trauma represents not only rupture but also connection, both destruction and creation. Because trauma is not often discussed as a creative force, I want to stress this point: at the same time as something is being destroyed through trauma, something else is always being made. *The Boys of Foley Street* expresses this point doubly; first, the form creatively embodies the trauma that it represents and, second, the mode of performance directly affects the audience, bringing trauma into the experience of the spectator so that she is transformed from Bloomian voyeur to active witness. This transformation is made possible, even unavoidable, by flattening the distance between spectator and spectacle and creating affect through this sense of contact. However, even though this is extremely powerful, both emotionally and intellectually, this dramaturgy raises a question: How effective is this for audiences? Jill Dolan argues that utopian performances 'inspire moments in which audiences feel allied with each other, and with a broader, more capacious sense of a public, in which social discourse articulates the possible, rather than the insurmountable obstacles to human potential'.[14] The grinding poverty and extreme violence that pervades *The Boys of Foley Street*, and the dividing up of the audience into solo spectators, may in fact create a theatre of cruelty rather than of utopian possibility, a theatre where the audience is only capable of perceiving the 'obstacles to human potential'. Moreover, the show provokes a profound disorientation, partly as a result of the constant violation of social and spectating norms, and partly by being brought round the backstreets of Dublin at high speed. The spectator's inner compass – both moral and literal – is sent into a tailspin, resulting in what Laura Doyle has called a 'horizon reversal' typical of postcolonial modernism.[15]

This reversal not only involves the citizen's relationship to the physical and social geography of Dublin's inner city, but also the spectator's expectation of theatre and performance. Using techniques that are at the heart of modernism – decentred narratives, fragmented form, an exploration of the relationship between interior subjectivity and the urban environment (of the spectator, rather than the character) – Anu aims to radicalize the theatre audience to arrive at a Brechtian *Gestus* in which social relationships are crystallized. Yet Anu does this not by *reflecting* the chaos of a broken society, but by *enacting* it, and even participating in it. This is a major difference between the 'classic' modernist texts of fiction, poetry and the visual arts, which create a calculated instability that produces both reflection and alienation. In contrast, Anu collapses the critical distance necessary to contemplation and embraces alienation. In other productions of the tetralogy, such as *Laundry* and *Vardo*, and some of the *Thirteen* mini-productions, the company created silent spaces for spectators to process and react thoughtfully. However, in *The Boys of Foley Street*, immediacy and viscerality are the dominant dramaturgical and aesthetic strategies, emulating the 'savage' confrontation of Jarry rather than the controlled angst of Beckett.

Modernist Spectacle?

To identify modernist traces in avant-garde theatre (a genre that is often conspicuously absent from discussions of modernism) helps us, as theatre critics, to see how the form and the production of meaning are interrelated. Yet, as is clear from my discussion above, Anu's work also contains many elements not aligned with modernism, particularly in their preference for direct confrontation over distanced reflection. So what does this mean for thinking about both Anu's theatrical identity and the category of modernism itself – especially given the fact that the company acknowledges its debt to many theatrical and literary traditions, including Joyce, but would never identify itself as modernist? Indeed, in a review of the first part of the tetralogy, Helen Meany set Anu in contrast to modernism, stating, 'There's no danger of nostalgia here, or some Joycean pageant'.[16]

It is at this point, I think, that the term modernism breaks open in two distinct ways. First of all, the association of modernism with a distanced and reflective aesthetic is not always the case, which is evident in the links between *The Boys of Foley Street* and 'Circe'. Indeed, as Sarah Cole argues, 'works of the modernist period were profoundly shaped by the call of violence: to answer its challenges, to seek out new representational strategies, to find a conceptual register cued to its brutalities'.[17] This description would be equally fitting for Anu's approach to staging contemporary and historical Dublin; indeed, what links all the scenes in *The Boys of Foley Street* is the common experience of violence. If we accept Cole's point, which she expands to argue that modernism portrayed violence through intimacy as well as shock, then framing Anu's work within a modernist aesthetic reveals much about modernism. For, although it is commonplace to read modernism as a reaction to the hyperviolence of two world wars, that reading tends to position modernism as a turn against, or retreat from, violence rather than reading high-modernist form as an embodiment of a crisis of representation in the wake of violent trauma. By stressing form as meaning, we can see how modernist work attests to the creative power of violence while simultaneously being horrified by its effects.

And, second of all, by classifying Anu as a post hoc form of modernism, the modernist aesthetic is redefined as a practice rather than a historically limited canon, a process rather than a set of rules, a verb not a noun. The afterlife of modernism is not ghostlike, as I initially suggested, but resurgent through a reconceptualization of modernism as multiple rather than singular.

In its attempt to stage trauma, Anu perhaps inevitably calls on a technique of representational practices associated with modernists working in post-war contexts wherein the artist became the witness and the artwork became the fulcrum of witnessing. This technique signifies a lineage of representing violence as more than a literary mono-cultural tradition, a lineage that is apparent in the echoed emphasis on witnessing between Beckett's high modernism, Sarah Kane's 'in-yer-face' theatre and Anu's site-specific shows. This lineage suggests an evolution of representing traumatic violence that is so increasingly experiential that the aesthetics of Anu and Beckett could not seem further from each other. Yet this grouping demonstrates the ways that theatre that aims to express trauma and to redefine the heroic as a continuation of performance in the wake of trauma, shares certain representational aims and practices, even if diverging in other respects. One of the central practices in enacting trauma continues to be via a modernist aesthetic that strives to represent the unrepresentable and to acknowledge the challenges within that project. Modernism thus continues to live within ostensibly nonmodernist works because of the continued need to shape art in relation to the social – often violent – contexts it is made out of. Anu takes this to one extreme, refusing the shelter of the traditional theatre and bringing art to the streets. But perhaps in fact, it is the other way round and, like modernists before them, Anu works by bringing the streets to the art. Anu's approach can, finally, be read as palimpsestic, both historically and stylistically and, through this reading, the Monto tetralogy becomes the most recent modernist inscription upon both the Dublin landscape and its literary and theatrical traditions.

Notes

1 See http://anuproductions.ie/index.php?/productions/down-the-valley/
2 In discussion with cast and director during the Now-Then-Now Symposium on the work of the tetralogy, 7 October (part of the 2014 Dublin Theatre Festival programme), actor and artist Una Kavanagh included *Ulysses* as a key text in her formation of the characters she played in all four parts.
3 In their use of affect, Anu mirrors Jill Dolan's conception of affect as a socially, as well as theatrically, transformative possibility. See Jill Dolan, *Utopia in Performance* (Ann Arbor, MI: University of Michigan Press, 2005). However, as discussed below, Anu's work does not mirror the utopian performatives as set out by Dolan.
4 See Sarah Cole, *At the Violet Hour: Modernism and Violence in Ireland and England* (Oxford: Oxford University Press, 2012), 5.
5 Susan Bennett, *Theatre Audiences: A Theory of Production and Reception* (London: Routledge, 1997/2005), 30.
6 Etchells, paraphrased by Karine Schaefer, 'The spectator as witness? *Binlids* as case study', *Studies in Theatre and Performance*, 23, 1 (2003): 5–20 (6).
7 Schaefer, 7.
8 Carl Lavery, 'The Dramaturgy of Trauma', keynote lecture, Spaces of Memory and Performance, 21 June 2014, University of East London. Lavery discussed avant-garde dramatic representations of trauma – in this case, the 'Disappeared' of Argentina – which mirror the originary trauma and (advertently or inadvertently) expose its audience to traumatic experience.
9 Discussion with cast and director during the Now-Then-Now Symposium.
10 Lyn Gardner, 'Should immersive theatre audiences accept greater responsibility?', *Guardian Theatre Blog with Lyn Gardner*, 12 November, 2014, accessed 6 December 2014, http://www.theguardian.com/stage/theatreblog/2014/nov/12/immersive-theatre-audiences-take-responsibility-bordergame-the-privileged.
11 Samuel Beckett, *Waiting for Godot*, in *The Complete Dramatic Works* (London: Faber and Faber, 1990), 86.
12 Sarah Kane, *Blasted*, in *Sarah Kane: Complete Plays* (London: Methuen, 2001), 48.
13 While confusing to the spectator, this is highly controlled, with a 'master clock' that controls which scenes are happening in which locations at what time.
14 Dolan, *Utopia*, 2.

15 Laura Doyle, 'Geomodernism, Postcoloniality, and Women's Writing', in *The Cambridge Companion to Modernist Women Writers*, ed. Maren Tova Linett (Cambridge: Cambridge University Press, 2010), 140.
16 Helen Meany, review of *Worlds End Lane* (Dublin Fringe Festival, 2010), *Irish Theatre Magazine*, accessed 9 December, 2014, http://www.irishtheatremagazine.ie/Reviews/Dublin-Fringe.aspx?review=26.
17 Cole, 5.

AFTERWORD: THE POETICS OF PERPETUATION

David James

The 'artist's job', claimed John Banville, 'is not to say the thing itself, but to speak about it. Narrative is all'. He adds that '[g]reatness in this conception of art is achieved not through form, but content'.[1] Two rather different things are being proposed here. Initially, Banville appears to back obliquity: be circuitous, he advises, speak 'about' something, rather than give too much away by addressing head on 'the thing itself'. However, he then prioritizes substance over style in ways that, on the surface, steer him away from modernism, or at least from that particular conception of modernist writing that assumes form and content are indissolubly linked. And the plot thickens. More recently, Banville has been very much *for* the idea of excavating experience 'through form', claiming that while '[l]iterary art cannot hope to express' the complex 'congeries of selves' that make up one's personhood, 'it can, by the power of style, which is the imagination in action, set up a parallel complexity which, as by magic, gives a sufficiently convincing illusion of lifelikeness'.[2] It is a quintessentially Banvillian sentence, becoming at once accretive and sinuous without marring its own euphony. But it also reveals something fruitfully discrepant about Banville's own position on modernist aesthetics. Writers change their minds, of course, as Zadie Smith's career makes clear.[3] In Banville's case, though, shifting standpoints matter because his work is a key port of call for discussions about modernism's presence in contemporary Irish fiction. For him to admit that 'I don't know if there's much to do after Nabokov and Proust, but one does one's little bit', sounds deceptively modest,[4] especially in light of how he has enabled us – rather like J. M. Coetzee has done for scholars of postcolonial and world Anglophone fiction – to rethink the formidable yet still-generative influence of the likes of Beckett, James and Kafka. Banville thereby speaks, contradictions and all, to that broader sense in contemporary Irish culture, as Paige Reynolds describes it, of 'the enduring potentiality of modernist forms, themes and practices'.

Proof of this potentiality can be found in Banville's *The Sea*, winner of the 2005 Man Booker Prize. At first glance, formal audacity does indeed seem to take second place to the novel's intrigues of retrospection. *The Sea* braids lyrical reminiscence with destabilizing flashbacks as our narrator, Max, recalls his distress in caring for his terminally ill wife, Anna. Integral to this anguish is his acknowledgment that Anna was not only someone consumed helplessly and beyond comfort by disease, but also irreducibly someone *else* altogether. What Phibsborough-born Iris Murdoch once called the 'opacity of persons' materializes in *The Sea*'s striking episodes of reflexive self-assessment,[5] prompting Max to admit that he's 'beginning to forget' Anna despite his efforts to 'think of her' as 'lodged in' him much 'like a knife':

> I have come to realise how little I knew her, I mean how shallowly I knew her, how ineptly. I do not blame myself for this. Perhaps I should. Was I too lazy, too inattentive, too self-absorbed? Yes, all of those things, and yet I cannot think it is a matter of blame, this forgetting, this not-having-known. I fancy, rather, that I expected too much, in the way of knowing. I know so little of myself, how should I think to know another?[6]

In accent and diction alike, Banville captures here the traits of epistemological self-doubt that would be familiar to any reader of Conrad's Marlow, Ford's John Dowell, or Jean Rhys's Sasha Jensen. Tracking valences of unknowing, *The Sea* exemplifies what Alex Davis defines as 'ideational modernism' in his discussion of Padraic Fallon, which involves the 'appropriation of modernist topoi rather than the adoption and development of avant-garde devices'. For the later Banville is certainly no avant-gardist, however baroque and mellifluous his syntax can be. In the passage above, Max's blend of repeated queries in looking back – along with those hesitant, elaborative, qualifying clauses – epitomize *The Sea*'s concern with the modernist topos of bewilderment. Inattention, uncertainty, and their dissection via recollection become the source of dramatic action rather than the signatures of formal innovation. Through its rhetoric of 'not-having-known', then, the novel dexterously dramatizes 'the subject', as Max himself describes it, 'of observing and being observed', unpacking as he does his own lack of self-knowledge despite his knack for tenacious and frank observation.[7] Still, Banville's exquisite technique is never far from the spotlight. Paradoxically eloquent on the subject of his own incomprehension, Max in fact provides an occasion for showcasing what Banville himself is formally capable of – regardless of Banville's earlier assertions about the priority of 'content' over 'form'. A protagonist's cognitive and affective incapacities catalyse and confirm his creator's linguistic virtuosities.

The Sea offers a titular echo of Iris Murdoch's own Booker winner from 1978, *The Sea, the Sea*. Yet Banville's understated salute reaches more substantially beyond setting alone. Through his self-scrutinizing narrator, he extends Murdoch's insistence, in her essay 'Against Dryness' (1961), that post-war writers should strive for what she called 'a new vocabulary of attention' in order to convey a 'renewed sense of the difficulty and complexity' of being ethically attentive to others with whom we interact.[8] Now, Murdoch was often hostile toward modernism, because of the sorry state in which it had left the twentieth-century novel – in her view, luring post-war writers to perpetuate a 'crystalline' aesthetic that consoled readers with its compositional self-perfections. Banville, however, reveals another side to her claims about the fate of modern fiction. While zeroing in on what Murdoch termed the 'unutterable particularity' of another person's moral being, *The Sea* also takes aesthetic aim at what she called 'the apprehension of something else, something particular, as existing outside us' – surely a distinctly modernist target.[9]

That this process of apprehension – of taking on the challenge of evoking the psychological 'opacity of persons' – had long been modernist fiction's standard fare shows how Banville's *The Sea* is doubly significant for revealing affinities between Murdoch and modernism that she herself would refute. And what this brief case study hopefully implies is that our reconstruction of modernism's afterlives is often compelled to navigate such complex crosscurrents of affiliation and dissent. Dialogues with modernism's legacies depart from as often as they reinforce our portraits of modernism's ruptural modes and moments. Sheer variety introduces further interpretive considerations. For how do we coordinate the alignment of critically prominent figures with other emerging, though potentially key, players in the story of modernism's legacy in Irish fiction? What would be the stakes in adopting modernism as a rubric for grouping very different innovators from successive generations, anywhere from Frank O'Connor to Anne Enright? Moreover, there is the intervening matter of form to ponder. For what sort of comparative framework could tackle the urban textures, multi-character focalizations, panoramic agility and episodic commotion of Colum McCann's *Let the Great World Spin* (2009), for example, alongside the poised tribute to Jamesian perspectivism in Colm Tóibín's *The Master* (2004)? Is McCann more of a modernist for writing without any obvious precursors, in comparison to Tóibín's explicit homage, one that Jesse Matz has characterized quite pointedly as an example of 'pseudo-Impressionism' – a mode that sails dangerously close to pastiche?[10] In any case, what challenges do we face in engaging both diegetic and formal elements of such idiosyncratic novels while sustaining the critical scope that comparison provides? In what terms can such distinct novelists be brought together so that their incongruities are as edifying as their complementarity? And how might they then help us to recognize that the modernist 'inheritance a writer receives', in Sarah McKibben's phrase, is 'not fixed but subject to challenge' because 'the possibilities to be extracted are not finite but unbound'?

Modernist Afterlives in Irish Literature and Culture offers incisive and energetic answers to such methodological questions. While contributors show that affinities between formal procedures separated in time do not automatically equal congruence between their generative aesthetic aims, they nonetheless find ways of demonstrating how modernist 'knowledge', as Laura Marcus puts it, 'is transmitted from one text to another and across the decades', acknowledging the degrees of ideological, intellectual and artistic distance that separates divergent modernisms from their equally diverging legatees.[11] Retaining the epithet *modernist* as a modal (and mobile) category throughout time can have the consequence – limiting for some, liberating for others – of leaving modern*ism* unanchored to any periodizable movement. Yet, the payoffs of relaxing modernism's temporal coordinates have generally outweighed the risks of diluting its historical purchase. Neil Lazarus, for one, discovers modernist commitments in late twentieth-century postcolonial writers who provocatively reveal that 'some of the most adamantine and far-reaching resistance to the violence and repressiveness of the postcolonial state has been undertaken precisely in the name of alternative nationalisms'. These 'different national imaginings' mobilize 'the *ongoing* critical dimension of modernist literary practice' in texts that 'situate themselves very explicitly and self-consciously in terms of the nation's experience'.[12]

This experience remains central to any account of modernism's continuities in Irish literature: an emphasis that might at first seem unfashionable, but which turns out to be pertinent as modernist scholarship today posits transnationalism at the leading edge of the field's own advancement. Recent work in Irish studies has shown how modernist dynamics gain political traction and aesthetic precision in the context of decolonization, and such arguments have reinvigorated rather than displaced a focus on national culture at mid-century. In his 2013 *Empire's Wake: Postcolonial Irish Writing and the Politics of Modern Literary Form*, Mark Quigley argues that '[f]undamental to Irish late modernism are the ways it extends an earlier modernist critique of the colonial state to the postcolonial state so as to address the newly invigorated discourses of "tradition" and modern subjectivity'. Moreover, he points out that 'the extent to which the essentialism and primitivism of revivalist modernism has increasingly been overtaken by the rank commodification of "tradition" in the postcolonial era serves as an important impetus for late modernism's critique'.[13] To notice modernism's regional potency in this fashion at specific cultural–historical junctures helpfully moves the discussion of modernism's persistence (as the preceding chapters do here) beyond questions of aesthetic influence alone. Quigley joins scholars of world literature – in addition to Lazarus, I'm thinking especially here of acute interventions from Derek Attridge, Rita Barnard and Rebecca L. Walkowitz – who have purposively defended the political efficacy of modernist strategies for later writers concerned with the aftermaths of decolonization, resurgent nationalisms and diverse expressions of cosmopolitanism.[14]

Where Quigley's argument resounds in an even more timely fashion, however, is on the issue of scale. 'Attending to the details of more "localized" modernisms', he suggests, 'does not mean simplifying analyses of modernist form or producing accounts of modernist aesthetics that have only narrow critical relevance'. On the contrary, regional optics can enable us 'to consider what we might see as the negative dialectics of modernism', capitalizing on 'the insights of postcolonial studies so as to re-evaluate the fixity of "local" categories such as "the nation" and "tradition" while at the same time challenging the inevitability and desirability of a refurbished "global" orientation'.[15] Politically and methodologically speaking, there's nothing *inherently* progressive about expanding modernism (whether spatially or temporally), just as there's nothing axiomatically reactionary about teaching or writing on the comparatively localized or 'nationalist' concerns of some rural and provincial writers.[16] Clearly, if one *is* going to call 'modernist' the technical achievements in rhythm, lyricism and scenic luminosity in John McGahern's *That They May Face the Rising Sun* (2002) or in Tóibín's spare, domestically focused *Nora Webster* (2014) – to choose two of the more seductively indefinable examples of postmillennial Irish fiction – we may find ourselves working against the grain of the field's 'refurbished global orientation'. This need not be a sign of tacit retrogression; rather, it's simply an attempt to do some justice to these texts – stylistically and politically – on their own terms, irrespective of injunctions about modernist studies' need for spatiotemporal enlargement. Arguments for repudiating Eurocentric models of modernism's historical provenance and evolution are indubitable; but the internationalization of modernism as a manifold, illimitable concept does not necessarily make it more intrinsically useful as a paradigm for particularizing inventive contemporary writing at a global scale.

Idea or movement; mode or moment; irrepressible ethos or receding flashpoint; period-breaching impulse or historically discrete revolution – modernism's competing definitions will always play at least some role in fresh stories of its persistence. Although we cannot simply dispense with these definitional conflicts, the present collection shows that we need not feel theoretically constrained by them, either. In so doing, it affords a critically compelling set of reasons why we should continue to articulate modernism's perpetuation, without conceptually overhauling modernism itself to an extent that it becomes historically vacuous or artistically all-embracing. To borrow Lucy Collins's phrase, this book offers perspectives that don't just prove the 'existence of an afterlife' for modernism, but that also enact 'a subtle refutation of such fixed ideas of progression and chronology' with respect to modernism's development, before and beyond mid-century. That this volume operates within a national context of cultural production furthers rather than discounts modernist studies' recent efforts to embrace the transnational genesis and translational reception of multiple modernisms across time. For, together, the authors here demonstrate that combination of cultural particularism and multidisciplinary flexibility required to make sense of modernism's continuities, all the while being mindful of the geohistorical unwieldiness to which the notion of any movement's 'afterlife' is prone.

Indeed, now is a time when the field of modernist studies might find it all the more desirable to reconcile its particularist and expansionist inclinations, in order to renew the vital work of recuperating hitherto marginalized writing and reassess the neglected sites, means and social implications of aesthetic experimentalism as modernism's temporal borders become porous. As Anne Fogarty incisively observes, 'microhistories of the modern are necessary in order to achieve a more nuanced account of the ways in which women writers engaged with the structures of modernism and selectively and purposefully made their own of them'. Microhistorical analyses of this kind also remind us of course that we cannot simply abandon periodization, or assume that it is somehow politically advantageous to do so – for quite the opposite may be true. This volume is too shrewd to indulge that critically self-consoling tactic of pluralizing modernism as a convenient means of reiterating the fact that modernity is not a Western invention; and it's too thickly historicized and attentive to medium-specific permutations to assume that diffusing modernism's periodicity has an immediately democratizing effect on the selections and scope of our research. If anything, this book can be seen as 'complicating and enriching discourses about periodization', in Reynolds's phrase; and it does so without lampooning periodization's legitimacy or consigning its endurance to the supposedly retrogressive corners of the field's current conversations about its own future. As they embark on polytemporal quests for modernism's transcultural whereabouts, the most expansive accounts of what modernist art, literature and performance do in the *longue durée* will thus profit from the subtlety of this book's ambitions.

Notes

1 John Banville, 'A Talk', *Irish University Review* 11, 1, Special Issue: John Banville (Spring 1981): 16.

2 John Banville, 'Grave Thoughts from a Master', review of *Everyman*, by Phillip Roth, *The Guardian, Review*, 29 April 2006, 7.
3 Not only am I hinting here, of course, at Smith's essay collection, *Changing My Mind: Occasional Essays* (London: Hamish Hamilton, 2009), but also at the way each successive novel since *White Teeth* (2000) radically departs from its predecessor. Such a creative trajectory is a testament to Smith's experimental verve, something I discuss in 'Worlded Localisms: Cosmopolitics Writ Small', in *Postmodern Literature and Race*, ed. Len Platt and Sara Upstone (Cambridge: Cambridge University Press, 2015), 47–63.
4 John Banville, Interview by Ben Ehrenreich, in *The Believer Book of Writers Talking to Writers*, ed. Wendela Vida (San Francisco: Believer Books, 2005), 54.
5 Iris Murdoch, 'Against Dryness' (1961), in *The Novel Today: Contemporary Writers on Modern Fiction*, ed. Malcolm Bradbury (London: Fontana, 1977), 30.
6 John Banville, *The Sea* (London: Picador, 2005), 215.
7 Ibid., 127.
8 Murdoch, 'Against Dryness', 30.
9 Iris Murdoch, 'The Sublime and the Good', *Chicago Review* 13, 3 (Autumn 1959): 51–52.
10 Jesse Matz, 'Pseudo-Impressionism?', in *The Legacies of Modernism: Historicising Postwar and Contemporary Fiction*, ed. David James (Cambridge: Cambridge University Press, 2012), 114–32.
11 Laura Marcus, 'The Legacies of Modernism', in *The Cambridge Companion to the Modernist Novel*, ed. Morag Shiach (Cambridge: Cambridge University Press, 2007), 96.
12 Neil Lazarus, *The Postcolonial Unconscious* (Cambridge: Cambridge University Press, 2011), [70, 30, 71].
13 Mark Quigley, *Empire's Wake: Postcolonial Irish Writing and the Politics of Modern Literary Form* (New York: Fordham University Press, 2012), 7.
14 Derek Attridge, *J. M. Coetzee and the Ethics of Reading: Literature in the Event* (Chicago: University of Chicago Press, 2004), see esp. Chapter 1, 'Modernist Form and the Ethics of Otherness'; Rita Barnard's recent work toward her forthcoming book, *South African Modernisms*, including 'Post-Apartheid Modernism and Consumer Culture', *Modernist Cultures* 6, 2 (2011): 215–44; and Rebecca L. Walkowitz's account of modernist aesthetics as a vehicle for 'critical cosmopolitanism', in her Introduction to *Cosmopolitan Style: Modernism Beyond the Nation* (New York: Columbia University Press, 2006), esp. 14–23.
15 Quigley, *Empire's Wake*, 9.
16 I have reflected on the position of rural fiction in the new modernist studies elsewhere: see 'Capturing the Scale of Fiction at Mid-Century', in *Regional Modernisms*, eds. Neal Alexander and James Moran (Edinburgh: Edinburgh University Press, 2013), 104–23.

NOTES ON CONTRIBUTORS

Lucy Collins is lecturer in English literature at University College Dublin. Recent publications include *Contemporary Irish Women Poets: Memory and Estrangement* (2015) and the anthology *Poetry by Women in Ireland 1870–1970* (2012). She has published widely on individual poets from Ireland, Britain and the United States and has a particular interest in gender issues and in ecocriticism. She is also editor of *Poems: Sheila Wingfield* (2013) and (with Andrew Carpenter) *The Irish Poet and the Natural World: An Anthology of Verse in English from the Tudors to the Romantics* (2014).

Alex Davis is professor of English at University College Cork. He is the author of *A Broken Line: Denis Devlin and Irish Poetic Modernism* (2000) and of many essays in anglophone poetry from decadence to the present day. He is coeditor, with Lee M. Jenkins, of *Locations of Literary Modernism: Region and Nation in British and American Modernist Poetry* (2000), *The Cambridge Companion to Modernist Poetry* (2007) and *A History of Modernist Poetry* (2015); and, with Patricia Coughlan, of *Modernism and Ireland: The Poetry of the 1930s* (1995). He is currently writing a book on the Edwardian Yeats.

Leah Flack is an associate professor of English at Marquette University. She works on comparative modernism (Anglo-Irish, American, Russian), modern and contemporary Irish literature and classical receptions. She has published in *The James Joyce Quarterly* and *Modernism/Modernity*. Her first book, *Modernism and Homer: The Odysseys of H.D., James Joyce, Osip Mandelstam, and Ezra Pound*, was published in 2015.

Anne Fogarty is Professor of James Joyce Studies at University College Dublin and founder and coeditor with Luca Crispi of the *Dublin James Joyce Journal*. She has been director of the Dublin James Joyce Summer School since 1997. She is coeditor with Timothy Martin of *Joyce on the Threshold* (2005), with Morris Beja of *Bloomsday 100: Essays on 'Ulysses'* (2009), with Éilís Ní Dhuibhne and Eibhear Walshe of *Imagination in the Classroom: Teaching and Learning Creative Writing in Ireland* (2013) and with Fran O'Rourke of *Voices on Joyce* (2015). She is currently completing with Marisol Morales Ládron a coedited collection of essays on the Northern Irish novelist, Deirdre

Madden, and a monograph on the politics of cultural memory in James Joyce's *Ulysses*.

David James is reader in modern and contemporary literature at Queen Mary, University of London. Author, most recently, of *Modernist Futures* (2012), he has edited several books, including *The Legacies of Modernism* (2012), *The Cambridge Companion to British Fiction since 1945* (2015) and *Modernism and Close Reading* (2017). An associate editor of the journal *Contemporary Literature*, he also coedits the book series Literature Now. His new book, *Discrepant Solace: Contemporary Writing and the Work of Consolation*, is forthcoming.

Róisín Kennedy is lecturer in School of Art History and Cultural Policy at University College Dublin. She is former Yeats Curator at the National Gallery of Ireland 2006–8 and curator of the State Collection at Dublin Castle, 1998–99. Her research focuses on modern Irish art and its contexts. She has published widely on the subject in edited collections and in *Circa*, *Irish Arts Review*, *Third Text* and *Journal of Art Historiography*. She has recently completed a book on the reception of modernist art in Ireland, which is in preparation for publication, and is coediting a book on art censorship due to be published in 2018.

Linda King is design writer and researcher and co-programme chair of the BA (Hons) Visual Communication Design, at the Institute of Art and Design, Dublin. Her research interests focus on where design analysis informs cultural history, with specific reference to post-colonial politics, the visual culture of tourism (specifically the design strategies of the former national airline, Aer Lingus) and the development of design professionalization. She is coeditor (with Elaine Sisson) of *Ireland, Design and Visual Culture: Negotiating Modernity, 1922–92* (2011), the first in-depth analysis of design culture within Irish Studies.

Andrew A. Kuhn is a doctoral candidate in the English Department at Boston College. His research is in British and Irish modernism and print culture. His current project examines modernist literary institutions in the works of Yeats, Joyce, Gissing and Woolf. He is the editor of *Dubliners Bookshelf* and author of articles on literary representations of the British postal service in Ireland, the print culture of rural nineteenth-century Ireland and the poetry of Ciaran Carson.

Aoife McGrath is lecturer in the Drama Department, Queen's University Belfast. She has worked as a dancer and choreographer and as dance adviser for the Irish Arts Council. She is the coconvenor of the Choreography and Corporeality working group of the International Federation for Theatre Research. Recent publications include her monograph *Dance*

Theatre in Ireland: Revolutionary Moves (2013) and a forthcoming edited collection on contemporary dance in Ireland, *Dance Matters* (2017).

Sarah McKibben is associate professor of Irish language and literature at the University of Notre Dame. She is author of *Endangered Masculinities in Irish Poetry, 1540–1780* (2010) and has contributed to *Éire-Ireland*, *Irish University Review*, *Eolas: The Journal of the American Society of Irish Medieval Studies*, *The Irish Review*, *Proceedings of the Harvard Celtic Colloquium*, *Research in African Literatures* and various collections.

Ellen McWilliams is lecturer in English literature at the University of Exeter. She is the author of *Margaret Atwood and the Female Bildungsroman* (2009) and *Women and Exile in Contemporary Irish Fiction* (2013). She has received a number of awards for research, including an Arts and Humanities Research Council Fellowship and a Fulbright Scholar Award. Her third book, *Irishness in North American Women's Writing: Transatlantic Affinities*, is forthcoming.

Emilie Pine lectures in modern drama at University College Dublin. She is the author of *The Politics of Irish Memory: Performing Remembrance in Contemporary Irish Culture* (2011), editor of the *Irish University Review* journal, and director of the Irish Memory Studies Network. She was a judge for the 2014 Irish Theatre Awards. Her work explores the performative aspects of ethical memory and witnessing, and she currently leads the Industrial Memories project (2015–18) on historical child abuse in Ireland.

Maria Pramaggiore is professor and head of Media Studies at Maynooth University. Her most recent book – and the work that inspired her to take a closer look at Irish horses – is *Making Time in Stanley Kubrick's Barry Lyndon* (2014). She is at work on a book on horses in modern visual culture.

Paige Reynolds is professor in the Department of English at the College of the Holy Cross in Worcester, Massachusetts. The author of *Modernism, Drama, and the Audience for Irish Spectacle* (2007), and editor of "Irish Things," a 2011 special issue of *Éire-Ireland*, she has published on topics related to modernism, modern and contemporary Irish literature, drama, performance and periodical culture.

INDEX

Abbey Theatre 96
Achill Horses (Jellett) 144
advertising 134
AE (George William Russell) 96
Aer Lingus 134
African-American poetry 2
afterlives
   animal portrayals and 7, 141, 147, 149, 150
   art and 116, 119, 122
   dance and 153, 156
   Irish design and 125, 139
   Irish women poets and 24, 25
   Irish women writers and 6
   literary institutions and 93
   literary temporalities and 23
   literature and culture and 3, 7
   modernism and ix, 3, 4, 172, 177, 180
   poetry and 5, 24, 25, 65
   theatre and 164
'Against Dryness' (Murdoch) 177
airport terminals 130, 132
Albers, Josef 132
Alfred A Knopf (publisher) 136
Allgemeine Elektrizitäts-Gesellschaft Aktiengesellschaft (AEG) 129
alternative space, in dance 153, 160
Angela's Ashes (McCourt) 150
Anna Livia, in *Finnegans Wake* 57
Anu Productions 7, 163–73
'Antaeus' (Heaney) 38
Arc & Sill (Lloyd) 65
Architectural Association of Ireland 130
architecture 7
   examples of milestone of modernism in 129
   Free State infrastructural projects and 130
   German design influence on 129
   Gray's leadership in 131

   importance of emigration to development of 128
   International Modernism and 133
   modernist afterlife in 125
   modernist innovation in 130
   Shamrock Pavilion, New York World Fair, as example of 130
Ardnacrusha, hydro-electrical station, Shannon River, Ireland 129
Arendt, Hannah 6, 12–13
Armstrong, Gordon 144
Armstrong, Philip 142
Arnold, Bruce 113
art. *See* Irish art; *individual artists*
Art Deco 131
art education 129
Art Nouveau movement 107
Arts and Crafts movement
   English 95, 98
   Irish 128
Arts Council of Ireland 122, 136, 184
Astrophil and Stella (Sidney) 69
At the Hawk's Well (Yeats) 7, 105, 153, 154–56, 159, 160
'Athair' (Father) (Ó Conghaile) 75, 81–86
   coming out narrative in 6, 81–83
   Irish modernist heritage of 81
   modernist irony and ambiguity in 6
   queer modernism and 81
Attridge, Derek 179
Austen, Jane 53
avant-garde
   art and 76, 112, 113, 144
   Gray's architecture and 132
   Ireland out of step with 128
   poetry and 63, 64, 69
   Steyn's exposure to, in Europe 132
   theatre and 7, 61, 163, 164, 165, 167, 171

Bacik, Charles 134
Bacon, Francis 116, 122
Badovici, Jean 132
Ballymun Regeneration project, *Misneach* equestrian statue in 147–48
Bank of Ireland 138
Banville, John 175, 176
  The Sea 176–77
Barnacle, Nora 53, 55–57
Barnard, Rita 179
Baskin, Leonard 105
Bathing Horses (Goncharova) 143
Bath-sheba (Bible) 68
Bauhaus 126, 127, 130, 132, 134
Baume, Sara 4
Bayer, Herbert 132
Beach, Sylvia 132
Beal Bocht, An (O'Brien) 98
Beat Drum, Beat Heart (Wingfield) 30
Beckett, Samuel
  Dolmen Press and 96
  European exile of 3, 132
  Grove Press and 136
  high modernism of 172
  How Is It 136
  Irish modernism and 4, 76, 94
  Jack Yeats's achievements and 114
  Krapp's Last Tape 136
  legacies of 107
  Malone Dies 136
  Murphy 136
  poetry of 63
  rethinking influence of 175
  trauma enacted in 172
  typographical design in printing of 136
  Unnamable, The 67, 70, 136
  Waiting for Godot 167, 168
Behrens, Peter 127, 129
Beja, Morris 51
Bell, The (journal) 62, 96
Benhabib, Seyla 12, 13
Bennett, Susan 165
Berkeley, George, Bishop 167, 168
Biggs, Michael 98
Blasted (Kane) 167
Bluemel, Kristin 2
Bodley Head 95
Boey, Kim Cheng 41

'Bog Queen' (Heaney) 38
Boland, Eavan 65
Book as World, The (French) 58
book design. *See also* publishers and publishing
  aesthetic qualities versus commercial aspects of publishing and 98
  Clarke and 128
  collaborative approach to, at Dolmen Press 103
  contemporary Irish design and 7
  Dolmen Press approach of 98
  Dun Emer Press and 95
  Elizabeth Yeats and 95, 98
  experimentation in 103
  Morris and Arts and Crafts movement influence in 95, 98
  poetic experimentation and 103
  reinvention of tradition in, by Cuala Press 93
  typography in 95, 98, 103, 136
Book of Kells
  book design and 103
  Colum's poem on 97
  Farrell on picture-making in 122
  horse imagery in 141
  Irish modernists and 4
  Literary Revival and 98
  Scully's art and 118
'Book of Kells, The' (Colum) 97–98
book publishing. *See* Cuala Press; Dolmen Press; private presses; publishers and publishing; *specific publishers*
Bord Fáilte 120, 138
Borges, Jorge Louis 106
Boss, Owen 163
Bowen, Elizabeth 6, 15, 16–18, 95
  background of 16
  Irish feminist modernism and 4, 20
  Last September, The 16
  To the North 11, 16–18, 20
Boys of Foley Street, The (Anu Productions) 7, 163, 165–67, 170, 171, 172
Brady, Andrea 70
branding 7, 119
Brecht, Bertolt 7, 165
Broadsheet, A (Cuala Press) 97

INDEX

Brown, Terence 23, 129, 130
Browne and Nolan (publisher) 96
Bubbles (Sloterdijk) 160
Buch, Robert 26
Buile Suibhne 43
'Burren, Co. Clare' (Coghill) 28
Burt Chapel, Donegal, Ireland 138
Burt, Ramsay 154
Burton, Richard 58
Busáras bus depot, Dublin 130
Bush, Ron 51
Byrne, John 147–48
Byron in Love (O'Brien) 51
Byron, George Gordon, Baron 51

Campbell, Hugh 129, 130
Campbell, Joseph 63
Cantos, The (Pound) 61, 62
    Canto LXXIV 66
Casanova, Pascale 1
Cat and the Moon, The (Yeats) 68
Cathleen ni Houlihan (Gregory and Yeats) 3
Catholic Church
    child abuse and moral authority of 157
    Ó Conchúir's work exploring 154, 156, 157
    Vatican II and building boom in 138
Catholicism, Irish modernist art and 121
Catullus 41, 43
'Cavalier's Farewell to his Steed, The' (Yeats) 144
Cavanagh, Clare 37
Celtic Tiger 3, 108, 113, 147, 149
Centenary Papers, The (Miller) 103, 105, 106
Certain Noble Plays of Japan (Fenollosa) 105
Chambers, Dave 149
Change of State (Lloyd) 68–69
'Chekhov on Sakhalin' (Heaney) 38
choreography. *See At the Hawk's Well* (Yeats); *Cure* (Ó Conchúir); dance
Clarke, Austin 49, 61
Clarke, Harry 128
Clé (Irish Book Publishers' Association) 107
Cleary, Joe 3
'Coat, A' (Yeats) 62
Coetzee, J. M. 175
Coffey, Brian 63, 103

Coghill, Rhoda 6, 25, 28, 32
coinage design 129
Cole, Sarah 25, 172
Collins, Lucy 6, 7, 23–32, 180
Collins, Patrick 120
Colum, Padraic 96
    'Book of Kells, The' 97–98
    Ten Poems 96, 97, 98
Comisúin le Rincí Gaelacha 155
Commission for Irish Dance 155
Connolly, Sybil 134
Conrad, Joseph 176
'Conversation about Dante' (Mandelstam) 40–41, 44
Córas Iompair Éireann (CIÉ) 133
Córas Tráchtála Teo (CTT) 134, 138
Costello, Peter 51
Counter-Revivalism 80, 81
Country Girl (O'Brien) 49, 50, 52, 55, 57–58
Country Girls, The (O'Brien) 51, 52, 54, 55
Coupures (Lloyd) 67, 68, 69
Coyle, Kathleen 6, 18–2018
    Flock of Birds, A 11, 18–20
    Irish feminist modernism and 20
craft traditions
    Irish design and 128
    Irish manufacturers and modernisation of 138
'Crediting Poetry' (Heaney) 45
Cross, Dorothy 6, 112, 113, 119, 122
    Teacup 111, 113
Crowley, Aleister 68
Crowley, David 125, 126
CTT (Córas Tráchtála Teo) 134, 138
Cuala Industries 3
Cuala Press 6, 24, 94–95
    book design approach of 103
    Dolmen Press's resurrection of strategies of 98
    international audience and 105
    legacy of 95
    literary approach of 103
    modernism and 93, 94
    politics and ideologies of 95
    Yeats and 93, 95, 96, 98, 103, 105
Cúchulainn 155
Cuda, Anthony 37, 145

cultural nationalism 76, 95, 120
Cumann na nGaedheal 129
Cure (Ó Conchúir) 7, 156–60

Danae myth 68
dance, 153–61, *See also At the Hawk's Well*
    (Yeats); *Cure* (Ó Conchúir)
    afterlives in 153, 156
    idea of a nation communicated in 153,
        154, 156
    Irish dancing (step dancing) 155
    Ito's dance play 155
    Mallarmé's writings on 4, 155
    politics and 153
    theories of modernity and 153
dance plays of Yeats 155, *See also At the
    Hawk's Well* (Yeats)
dance-poems (Ito) 155
Dante
    Heaney on 37, 40
    Mandelstam on 40–41, 44, 45
'Darkness' (Wingfield) 31
Darwin, Charles 94
Daunton, Martin 125
David, King (Bible) 68
Davis, Alex 4, 5, 6, 61–70, 176
Dawson, Barbara 118
de Paor, Louis 77
De Stijl movement 127, 132
de Valera, Éamon 130
de Valois, Ninette 155
'Dead' (Coghill) 29
'Dead, The' (Wingfield) 30
Deane, Peter. *See* Hinkson, Pamela
decolonisation
    modernism in Irish literature and 178
    writers' concern with aftermatchs
        of 179
    Yeats and 154, 159
Deoraíocht (Exile) (Ó Conaire) 79
'Delusion and Dream in Jensen's *Gradiva*'
    (Freud) 70
Dépôts de savoir et de technique
    (Roche) 68
Derrida, Jacques 70
design. *See also* book design; graphic design;
    Irish design
    meaning of modernism in 125

design education 138, 139
*Design in Ireland (Scandinavian
    Report)* 138
Design Research Unit 136
Devenport O'Neill, Mary 6, 25, 27, 29,
    30, 32
Devlin, Denis 63
'Dhoya' (Yeats) 145
Dickson, E. Jane 57
Dinkeloo, John 134
'Divided Mind, The' (Kinsella) 63
Dolan, Jill 170
Dolmen Press 6, 93, 96–105
    book design approach of 98, 103
    Colum's work with 97, 98
    Cuala Press's strategies
        ressurected by 98
    international audience and 106, 107
    Joyce and 96, 103
    modernist revival of 98–105
    poetic experimentation and 103
    role in publishing Irish works in a global
        world 105, 106
    Yeats and 96, 98, 103, 106
Dolmen Press Yeats Centenary Papers, The
    (Miller) 103, 105, 106
Douglas, Lord Alfred 84
Doyle, Laura 171
Dreaming Dust, The (Johnston) 7
Dublin Airport terminal 130,
    133
Dublin Corporation 116
Dublin Magazine 25
Dublin Municipal Gallery of
    Modern Art. *See* Hugh Lane
    Gallery, Dublin
Dublin Yeats Society 105
Dubliners (Joyce) 52, 103
Dun Emer Industries 94
Dun Emer Press 94, 95
Duncan, Isadora 155
Dutch graphic designers 134
Duty Free concept 133

E.1027 villa, Roquebrune-Cap-Martin,
    France 13, 132
Ear of the Other, The (Derrida) 70
'Easter, 1916' (Yeats) 68, 141, 145

editors, book publishing
  Ellmann's duties as, for Stanislaus Joyce's book on James Joyce 50
  legacies of 93
  male level of control of 24
  Pound as, for Ezra Fenellosa 105
  Yeats as, at Cuala Press 103, 105
editors, film 146
editors, magazine, women as 24
EEC (European Economic Community) 136
Eisenstein, Sergei 145–46
Eliot, T. S. 4, 5, 64
  Dante and 37, 40
  Heaney and legacies of 35, 36, 37, 39, 40, 41, 65
  Introducing Joyce 52
  'Little Gidding' 37, 65
  Mandelstam compared with 41
  O'Brien's encounter with Joyce and 52
  relevance to contemporary Irish poets of 62, 63
  '*Ulysses*, Order, and Myth' 2
Ellmann, Richard 50, 54
'Émaux et Camées' (Gautier) 64
... engine is left running, the (Salkeld) 27
Enlightenment 141, 142, 143, 150
Enright, Anne 177
Envoy (journal) 96
Etchells, Tim 165
ethnography, and modernist literature 105
European Economic Community (EEC) 136
European Union 3
Eurovision Song Contest 148, 149
Eurydice myth 29, 70
Exhibition of Works by Irish Painters, Guildhall, London, catalogue 119
Exiles (Joyce) 136

'Fade' (Lloyd) 65–67
Fáilte Ireland 120, 138
Fallon, Brian 144
Fallon, Padraic
  'Journal' 62
  modernist poetic practice and 61, 62, 63, 176
  Pound and 63
Farrell, Michael 113, 121–22

Father Ted (television programme) 148–49
Faust (Goethe) 128
Feis Ceoil 94
Fenollosa, Ernest 105
Fianna Fáil 157
film. *See also* videos
  horses portrayed in 7, 145–47
film editing 146
Finland, Arts and Crafts movement in 128
Finnegans Wake (Joyce)
  Colum's involvement with printing 97
  Edna O'Brien on 57
  Flann O'Brien on 49
  literary modernism 1, 2, 126
  Steyn's illustration of 132
'First Gloss, The' (Heaney) 43
First World War 15, 19, 20, 26, 143
Fisherman's Wake (Lane) 26
Fitzgerald, Desmond 130
FitzGerald, T. D. 63
Flack, Leah 5, 35–45
Flaherty, Robert 111, 113
flashbacks, in film 146, 147
Flock of Birds, A (Coyle) 11, 18–20
Fogarty, Anne 5, 6, 11–14, 24, 55, 180
Ford, Ford Madox 64, 176
Ford, John 146–47
'form follows function' dictum 129, 132
Forster, E.M. 81
Franck, Kaj 138
Franko, Mark 153, 154
Free State
  design of coinage in 129
  Irish architects and modern infrastructure design in 130, 131
  isolationism during early years of 24
  lack of indigenous industry in 129
French, Marilyn 58
"Fresh Images Beget: Art Nouveau & Irish Books" (Miller) 107
Freud, Sigmund 70
Futurism 127

Gaelic Alphabet, A (Biggs) 98
Gaelic League 94, 155
Gaelic literature. *See* Irish-language literature
Gaelic Revival 75, 76, 77, 78

Gaeltacht
  marginalization of 80
  Ó Conaire's stories and 79
  Ó Conghaile's stories and 85
  Pearse's stories and 80, 85
  Revival and 78, 80
Gardner, Lyn 167
Gautier, Théophile 64
Gébler, Ernest 53
Gehenna Press 105
Geneva Window, League of Nations 128
German design, influence of 127, 129, 132
Gestamkunstwerk 132
Gibbons, Luke 146
Gill (publisher) 96
Gillespie, Michael 54
'Glanmore Sonnets' (Heaney) 69
global literary scene, Irish publishing and 105–106
Goethe, Johann Wolfgang von 128
Golden Bough, The (Frazer) 61
Goldsmith, Kenneth 69
Goncharova, Natalia 143
Gonne, Maud 3
Gore-Booth, Eva 25
Government of the Tongue (Heaney) 36
Gradiva (figure in Surrealist poetry) 70
Gradiva (Jensen) 70
Graham, Martha 155
Grania (Gregory) 2
Grania (Lawless) 2
graphic design. *See also* book design
  Aer Lingus advertising and 134
  German influence on 132, 134
  Gray's E.1027 villa and 132
  importance of emigration to development of 128
  International Modernism and 133
  modernist afterlife in 125
  Steyn's study of 132
  typography in 136
Gray, Eileen 131–32
  E.1027 villa of 13, 132
  European exile of 132
  Irish modernism and 13
  public and private sphere and 6, 12, 13
Gregory, Lady Augusta 2, 3, 118
Gropius, Walkter 128, 130, 137, 138

Grove Press 136
Guildhall, London 119
Gulliver's Travels (Swift) 142, 143

Habermas, Jürgen 127
Harmon, Maurice 96
Harper's Bazaar 56
Harrington, Damien 138
Harrington, Paul 148
Haughton, Hugh 64
Havel, Miroslav 134
Heaney, Seamus 5
  'Antaeus' 38
  'Bog Queen' 38
  'Chekhov on Sakhalin' 38
  'Crediting Poetry' 45
  Fallon and 63
  'First Gloss, The' 43
  'Glanmore Sonnets' 69
  Government of the Tongue 36
  'Hercules and Antaeus' 38
  'Impact of Translation, The' 35
  'M.' 45
  North 37–38, 43
  'On the Road' 44
  'Punishment' 38
  'Settle Bed, The' 37
  'Shelf Life' 38
  Spirit Level, The 45
  Station Island 36, 38–39, 44
  'Station Island' 38–39, 61, 64–65
  'Sweeney Redivivus' 38, 39, 43–44
  'Tollund Man, The' 38
'Hercules and Antaeus' (Heaney) 38
high modernism ix, 1, 2, 3, 5, 6, 7, 61, 94, 96, 121, 126, 132, 172
Hilliot, Dana 68
Hinkson, Pamela 6, 11, 12, 14–16
  Irish feminist modernism and 20
  Ladies' Road, The 11, 15–16, 20
Home Rule, campaigning for 76
Homer 4
  Mandelstam on 42, 43, 45
Hone, Evie 119, 121, 130
'Horse Outside' (Rubberbandits) 148, 149–50
'Horseman enters a town at night, A' (Yeats) 144

horses
  critiques of Celtic Tiger culture
    using 147–50
  film and 145–47
  Gulliver's Travels and meanings of 142
  Irish mythology and 141,
    150
  Jack B. Yeats's painting and 144, 145
  Misneach equestrian statue 147–48
  national identity and 141
  ninth-century Japanese painting
    and 145
  twentieth-century painting and 7,
    143–44, 145
  W. B. Yeats's writing and 144–45
Horses in the Water (Seurat) 143
How Is It (Beckett) 136
Hugh Lane Gallery, Dublin
  Bacon's studio installation at 116
  le Brocquy painting refused by 115
  Rosc exhibitions at 120
  Scully's paintings at 116–18
Hugh Selwyn Mauberley (Pound) 64, 65
Huldt, Åke 138
Hyde, Douglas 96

'I Gather the Limbs of Osiris'
  (Pound) 64
ideational modernism 63, 176
identity. *See* Irish identity
'Image from Beckett, An' (Mahon) 61
Imagism 63, 64
'Impact of International Modern Poetry
  on Irish Writing, The' (Montague) 63
'Impact of Translation, The' (Heaney) 35
impressionism, in painting 132
'In the Court of Queen Edna' (Dickson)
  57
industrialization 126, 127
'Insomnia. Homer. Taut sails'
  (Mandelstam) 42, 43
International Book Year 107
International Modernism 126, 131, 132,
  138
'International Trend of Modern
  Architecture, The' (Gropius) 130
Into the West (film) 141
Introducing Joyce (Eliot) 52

'Íosagán' (Pearse) 80, 86
Irish art 111–22, *See also specific artists*
  afterlives of 116, 119, 122
  Anglo-American art criticism and 121
  avant-garde in 76, 112, 113, 128, 144
  Celtic origins of 113, 118, 119, 120, 122
  international art scene and 107, 113
  Irish identity and 120, 128
  Jack Yeats's contribution to 113
  Lane on Celtic branding of 119
  modernism in 113
  new Catholic elite and 121
  Scully paintings permanent installation
    and 116–18
Irish Arts and Crafts Movement 128
Irish Big House novel 15
Irish dance. *See also* dance
Irish dancing (step dancing) 155
Irish design 125–39, *See also* architecture;
    book design; graphic design
  importance of emigration to 134
  industrial production and slow
    development of 128
  influence of Continental European
    design practices on 129
  international and vernacular modernism
    in 132–39
  Irish Arts and Crafts Movement and
    128
  lack of art education and 129
  modernist afterlife of 125
  nation building using 129
  phases of historical modernism in 126
  Shamrock Pavilion, New York World
    Fair, as example of 130
  Steyn's innovation in 132
Irish Exhibition of Living Art (1943),
    Dublin 120
Irish Free State. *See* Free State
Irish identity
  Bacon's paintings and 116
  Beckett and 114
  Celtic art as central to 119
  Counter-Revivalism and 80, 81
  Cross's *Teacup* video and 111
  Cuala Press and 106
  dance and 154, 156
  Dolmen Press and 106

Irish identity (*cont.*)
  horse as symbol of 141, 149, 150
  Irish government on art and 128
  Irish literature and 5
  Irish modernist art and 121, 128
  Lane on Celtic branding and 119
  male homosexuality and 85
  Scully's paintings and 118
  Shamrock Pavilion, New York World Fair, and 130
Irish language. *See also* Gaeltacht
  Gaelic Revival and 76
  loanwords in 85
  teaching of 129
  word 'gay' in 6, 82, 85
Irish-language literature
  audience for 77
  modernism and 6, 75
  Ó Conghaile's 'Athair' (Father) and 6, 75, 81–86
  Pearse and 80
  Revival and 76
  style and form of 78
  teaching of 80
Irish Literary Theatre 94
Irish literature. *See also specific writers*
  afterlives of 3, 7
  debates about future of 24
  Dolmen Press's support for 96, 98, 105
  Irish identity shaped by 5
  modernism and 93, 178
Irish Museum of Modern Art (IMMA) 112
Irish mythology. *See* myths and mythology
Irish Strategies (Borges) 106
Irish theatre. *See also Boys of Foley Street, The* (Anu Productions); *specific writers and plays*
  afterlives of 164
  avant-garde in 7, 61, 164, 165, 167, 171
  modernism in 163–73
Ishibashi, Hiro 106
Ito, Michio 155, 156, 159

James, David 2, 3, 7, 11, 36, 39, 175–80
James Joyce (Beja) 51
James Joyce (Ellmann) 50
James Joyce (O'Brien)
  early reviews of 54
  influence of Ellmann's biography of Joyce on 50
  O'Brien's arrangement of bibliography in 54
  O'Brien's Byron biography contrasted with 51
  Penguin Lives series publication of 53, 54
  strategies used in writing 50
  treatment of Joyce's mother in 55
  treatment of Nora Barnacle in 53, 55–57
James Joyce Quarterly 54
James Joyce: The Years of Growth (Costello) 51
Jameson, Fredric 142, 143, 144, 145
Jarry, Alfred 7, 165, 171
jazz music 131
Jellett, Mainie 119, 120, 121, 130, 143, 144
Jensen, Wilhelm 70
Johansen, John 137
Johnston, Denis 7
Johnston, Dillon 96
Jorgenson, Ib 134
'Journal' (Fallon) 62
Joyce, James 128
  Anu Productions and 171
  biographies of. *See James Joyce* (O'Brien); Joyce biography
  Borges on 107
  Dolmen Press and 96, 103
  Dublin literati of the 1950s on 49
  Dubliners 52, 103
  Edna O'Brien relationship with 6, 49–58
  European exile of 3, 132
  Exiles 136
  Finnegans Wake 1, 2, 49, 57, 97, 126, 132
  Flann O'Brien on 49
  Heaney and legacies of 35, 36, 39
  Heaney on 36
  Irish modernism and 4, 76, 94
  legacies of 107
  Nora Barnacle and 53, 55–57
  Portrait of the Artist as a Young Man, A, 51
  rethinking influence of 175
  Ulysses 7, 51, 56, 163, 172

Joyce, May 55
Joyce, Stanislaus 50, 54
Joyce, Trevor 5, 61, 67
   Syzygy 67
Joyce biography 49–58, *See also James Joyce*
   (O'Brien)
   Ellmann's editorial duties for Stanislaus
      Joyce's book and 50
   Flann O'Brien on 49
   O'Brien's *Country Girl* and 57
   politics of canon of 50

Kafka, Franz 175
Kandinsky, Wassily 132
Kane, Sarah 167, 168, 172
Kavanagh, Patrick 49, 96
Kay, Magdalena 41
KDW (Kilkenny Design
   Workshops) 138–39
Kelmscott Press 98
Kennedy, Jacqueline 134
Kennedy, Róisín 6, 111–22
'Kensington Notebook, A' (Mahon) 61,
   63–64, 65
Kerrigan, Anthony 106
Kiberd, Declan 3
Kilkenny Design Workshops
   (KDW) 138–39
King, Linda 5, 7, 125–39
Kinsella, Thomas 96
   'Divided Mind, The' 63
   Táin, The 103, 107
Kirbly, Lynne 145
Klassen, Kor 136
Klee, Paul 132
KLM 134
Knopf (publisher) 136
Kose Kanaoka 4, 145
Krapp's Last Tape (Beckett) 136
Kuhlman, Roy 136
Kuhn, Andrew 4, 6, 93–108

Ladies' Road, The (Hinkson) 11, 15–16,
   20
Lahart, Nevan 6, 111, 112, 113, 119, 122
Land Acts 76
Landscape with Horses (Marc) 143
Lane, Hugh

Dublin's refusal of paintings
   from 116, 117
separate identity for Irish art
   and 119
Lane, Temple 26
Lane Gallery, Dublin. *See* Hugh Lane
   Gallery, Dublin
'Last of the Fire Kings, The' (Mahon) 61
Last September, The (Bowen) 16
Laundry (Anu Productions) 163, 171
Lawless, Emily 2
Lazarus, Neil 178, 179
le Brocquy, Louis 103, 113, 115, 120, 121
Le Corbusier 13, 127, 132
League of Nations 128
Lemass, Seán 136
Lepecki, André 153
Let the Great World Spin (McCann) 177
Lewis, Wyndham 64
'Life to Come, The' (Forster) 81
Light of Evening, The (O'Brien) 55, 56
Limerick, Ireland 149, 150, 163
literary institutions. *See also* publishers and
   publishing
   afterlives of 93
   Irish literature shaped by 93
   literary journals 96
   literary publishers. *See* Cuala Press;
      Dolmen Press; private presses;
      publishers and publishing; *specific*
      publishers
Literary Revival 23, 76, 94, 96, 98,
   107, 155
literature. *See also* Irish-language
   literature
   experimental 75
   modernism and 1, 2
   modernism in design and 126
   private press industry and 95
   Yeats on role of models for 105
literatures, Anglo-European, medieval
   courts as origin of 2
'Little Gidding' (Eliot) 37, 65
little magazines 93, 95
Lloyd, David 4, 5, 61
   Arc & Sill 65
   Change of State 68–69
   Coupures 67, 68, 69

Lloyd, David (*cont.*)
   'Fade' 65–67
   'Lyre' 70
   '"Pap for the Dispossessed": Seamus Heaney and the Poetics of Identity' 67
   Sill 70
   Taropatch 68, 69
   Vega 69–70
loanwords, Irish language 85
Loeber, Rolf 130
Logan, Brian 150
Longford, Edward Arthur Henry Pakenham, 6th Earl of 7
Longley, Edna 62
Loos, Adolf 129
Lowe, Louise 163
Lowry, Malcolm 68
Lustig, Alvin 136
'Lyre' (Lloyd) 70

'M.' (Heaney) 45
M. H. Gill (publisher) 96
Mac Piarais, Pádraig. *See* Pearse, Patrick
MacGreevy, Thomas 63, 144
Maddox, Brenda 51
Madonna Irlanda (Farrell) 113
magazine covers 132
magazines 24, 93, 95, 96
Mahon, Derek 5
   'Image from Beckett, An' 61
   'Kensington Notebook, A' 61, 63–64, 65
   'Last of the Fire Kings, The' 61
   'Ovid in Tomis' 61, 64
Mallarmé, Stéphane 66, 103
   dance and 4, 155
   poetic experimentation by 103
   Un coup de dés jamais n'abolira le hasard 103
Malone Dies (Beckett) 136
Man of Aran (Flaherty) 111, 113
Mandelstam, Osip 5, 36
   'Conversation about Dante' 40–41, 44
   Heaney and 36, 37, 38, 39, 40, 41, 42, 43, 44, 45
   'Insomnia. Homer. Taut sails' 42, 43
Manet, Édouard 115

Marc, Franz 143
Marcus, Laura 2, 178
Martin, Randy 153
Master, The (Tóibín) 177
Matisse, Henri 117
Matz, Jesse 177
Maunsel and Company 24, 96
Maurice (Forster) 81
McBride, Eimear 4
McCann, Colum 177
McCarthy, Tom 36
McCormick, Liam 138
McCourt, Frank 150
McDonald, Rónán 94
McEwan, Ian 36
McGahern, John 179
McGann, Jerome 95
McGettigan, Charlie 148
McGinley, Bernard 51
McGlynn, Bob 149, 150
McGrath, Aoife 4, 7, 153–61
McGuckian, Medbh 65
McKibben, Sarah 6, 75–86, 178
McWilliams, Ellen 49–58
Meany, Helen 172
medieval period
   Anglo-European literatures from courts of 2
   Colum's work and 97
   Irish uncial script in 98
   literature sources in 43, 76, 118
medievalism, and Arts and Crafts movement 95
'Meditations in Time of Civil War' (Yeats) 25
Metropolitan Museum of Art, New York City 134
'Michael Robartes bids his beloved be at peace' (Yeats) 145
Mies van der Rohe, Ludwig 127, 128, 132, 138
Miller, Cristanne 24
Miller, Liam 96
Miller, Tyrus 2, 23
Mills, Billy 61
'Mise Eire' (Boland) 65
Misneach equestrian statue (Byrne) 147–48
Mo Mhórcoir Féin (Ó Conchúir) 156

modern dance 153, 155, *See also* dance
  dance plays of Yeats as example of 155
  in Ireland 154, 155
  socio-political and cultural realities
    and 154
Moholy-Nagy, László 132
Molly Bloom, in *Ulysses*
  Edna O'Brien mistaken for 56, 57
  Nora Barnacle on 56
  O'Brien's fiction and 49
Montague, John 96
  'Impact of International Modern Poetry
    on Irish Writing, The' 63
Montale, Eugenio 69, 70
Monto area, Dublin. *See* Monto, Dublin,
  setting
Monto tetralogy (Anu Productions)
  163, 173
Monto, Dublin, setting
  in Anu Productions 7, 163, 165, 171
  in Joyce 164
*Monument to Sub Minimum Wage: A Whiter
  than White Social GAMA Steak Slave
  Sandwich, A* (Lahart) 111
Moore, Henry 115
Moore, Marianne 103
Morris, William 98
Mother Ireland (O'Brien) 54
Mottetti (Montale) 69, 70
movement. *See also* dance
  theories of modernity and 153
Mulqueen, Madeline 149
Municipal Gallery of Modern Art, Dublin.
  See Hugh Lane Gallery, Dublin
Murdoch, Iris 176, 177
Murphy (Beckett) 136
Murray, Christopher 160
music
  jazz 131
  Yeats's interest in Noh plays and 155
music videos, horses portrayed in 7,
  148–49
Muybridge, Eadweard 145
My Brother's Keeper: James Joyce's Early Years
  (Joyce) 50
'My Lovely Horse' (music video, *Father Ted*
  television programme) 148–49
mythical method, of Joyce 2, 41

myths and mythology
  Celtic design and 3, 118
  classical 29, 68, 70
  dance's use of 156
  Heaney's use of 38
  heroic masculine spectacle and 111
  horse as symbol in 141, 150
  Joyce's use of 2
  Ó Conchúir's use of 154
  Yeats's use of 3, 105, 155, 160

na gCopaleen, Myles. *See* O'Brien, Flann
Nabokov, Vladimir 175
Nadel, Ira B. 51
National Gallery of Ireland 113, 115
National Gallery, London 116
national identity. *See* Irish identity
nationalism
  Celtic artistic style and 119, 120, 122
  cultural 76, 95, 120
  dance and 156
  Gaelic Revival and 76
  horses as symbols of 7
  Irish feminist modernist writers and 20
  publishing and 95
  resistance to postcolonial state and 178
Nazi Germany 126, 143
New Critics 66
New Directions 136
new modernist studies 1, 65
New Woman 3
New Writers' Press 67
New York 130, 133
Ní Dhomhnaill, Nuala 65
Nietzsche, Friedrich 19, 94
Night (O'Brien) 49
'Nineteen Hundred and Nineteen' (Yeats)
  145
Noble Drama of W. B. Yeats, The (Miller) 105
Noh plays 105, 106, 155
Nora (Maddox) 51
Nora Webster (Tóibín) 179
Nordic region, postwar reconfiguration of
  craft traditions in 138
North (Heaney) 37–38, 43

Ó Cadhain, Máirtín 80, 85
Ó Conaire, Pádraic 78, 79–80

Ó Conchúir, Fearghus 153, 154
  alternative space created by 160
  Cure 7, 156–60
Ó Conghaile, Micheál
  'Athair' (Father) 6, 75, 81–86
  queer modernism and 81
  Sna Fir 86
O'Brien, Edna
  Byron in Love 51
  Country Girl 49, 50, 52, 55, 57–58
  Country Girls, The 51, 52, 55
  Eliot and first encounter with Joyce by 52
  influence of Ellmann's biography of Joyce on 50
  Joyce biography by. See *James Joyce* (O'Brien)
  Joyce's influence on 6, 49–58
  Light of Evening, The 55, 56
  Mother Ireland 54
  mother-daughter relationships in work of 54
  Night 49
  Pagan Place, A 49
  Wild Decembers 57
O'Brien, Eugene 41
O'Brien, Flann 49, 80, 85
  Beal Bocht, An 98
  James Joyce and 49
O'Casey, Seán 128
O'Connor, Frank 177
O'Connor, Laura 65
O'Doherty, Brian 120
O'Driscoll, Dennis 39
O'Flaherty, Liam 128
O'Leary, Art 141
O'Leary, Philip 77, 78
O'Regan, Brendan 133
Object (Breakfast in Fur) (Oppenheim) 111
October (Eisenstein) 145–46
'Odysseus Dying' (Wingfield) 30
Oisin 141
'On the Road' (Heaney) 44
Oppen, George 66
Oppenheim, Meret 111
oral culture 107
'Ornament and Crime' (Loos) 129
Orpheus myth 29, 70
Ovid 41, 43

'Ovid in Tomis' (Mahon) 61, 64
Oxford University Press 107

Pagan Place, A (O'Brien) 49
painting. *See also specific artists*
  Bacon's installation at Hugh Lane Gallery 116
  horses as subjects in 7, 143–44, 145
  ninth-century Japanese 145
  Scully's permanent installation at Hugh Lane Gallery 116–18
'"Pap for the Dispossessed": Seamus Heaney and the Poetics of Identity' (Lloyd) 67
Pearse, Patrick 128
  as progressive revivalist 78, 85
  'Íosagán' 80, 86
  Irish design reflecting rhetoric of 129
  on language, style and form 78
  short story genre and 79, 80, 85
  subliminated homoeroticism of 86
Pelan, Rebecca 56
Penguin Lives series 53, 54
periodical publishing 24, *See also* magazines; publishers and publishing
Perloff, Marjorie 68
Personae (Pound) 64
Picasso, Pablo 115
Pine, Emilie 7, 163–73
Pioneering Modernism 126, 132
Piper, Billie 150
Pisan Cantos, The (Pound) 66, 69
Place, Vanessa 69
Poe, Edgar Allen 81, 128
Poems (Wingfield) 30
poetry
  collaboration between poet and publisher in 93, 96, 103
  dance-poems of Ito 155
  horses portrayed in 144–45
  lack of publishers dedicated to 24
  modernist afterlives in 5, 24, 25, 65
  typographic experimentation in 103
  Yeats's interest in Noh plays and 155
Portrait of the Artist as a Young Man, A (Joyce) 51
Post and Telegraphs, Ireland 138
Post Office, The (Tagore) 105

Pound, Ezra 1, 95
  Canto LXXIV 66
  Cantos, The 61, 62
  Cuala Press and 95
  Dante and 37, 40
  Fallon and 62, 63
  Fenellosa's book edited by 105
  Heaney and legacies of 35, 37, 41
  Hugh Selwyn Mauberley 64, 65
  'I Gather the Limbs of Osiris' 64
  Imagism and 64
  Mahon's 'A Kensington Notebook' and 63–64
  Noh plays and 155
  Personae 64
  Pisan Cantos, The 66, 69
  poetic experimentation by 103
  relevance to contemporary Irish poets of 62, 63
  Spirit of Romance, The 64
Power, Albert 129
Pramaggiore, Maria 7, 141–50
Pratt, William 54
presses. *See* Cuala Press; Dolmen Press; private presses; publishers and publishing; *specific publishers*
private presses 93, 94, 95, 107, *See also* publishers and publishing; Cuala Press; Dolmen Press; *specific publishers*
Programme for Economic Expansion (Whitaker) 136
Prometheus and Other Poems (Devenport O'Neill) 27
Proto-Modernism 126, 128
Proust, Marcel 175
pseudo-Impressionism 177
psychoanalysis 170
Public Works, Ireland 138
publishers and publishing. *See also* book design; Cuala Press; Dolmen Press; private presses; *specific publishers*
  aesthetic qualities versus commercial aspects of 98
  collaboration between writer and publisher in 93, 96, 103
  dedicated to poetry 24
  international audiences and global perspective of 105
  modernist magazines 24
  moribund state of, in mid-century period 24
  opportunities for women in 24, 95
  transcending boundaries of national context in 107
  typographic experimentation in 103
Punch 78
'Punishment' (Heaney) 38
Pushkin, Aleksandr 41, 43
Pyle, Hilary 113

queer modernism 81
Quiet Man, The (Ford) 146–47
Quigley, Mark 178, 179

Rand, Paul 136
Redon, Odilon 143
Redshaw, Thomas Dillon 103
religion 160, *See also* Catholic Church
  in contemporary Ireland 7, 154, 155
Reynolds, Paige 1–7, 175, 180
Rhys, Jean 176
Rice, Peter 134
Ricketts, C. 105
Rieger, Bernhard 125
Riverdance 148
Roche, Denis 68
Roche, Kevin 134
Rock'n'Roll Kids 148
Rogin, Michael 66
Rosc exhibitions, Dublin 107, 120, 122
Rosenstone, Robert 145
Rothery, Seán 130
Rothko, Mark 117
Rowley, Ellen 130, 137
Royal Hibernian Academy (RHA) 112
RTÉ 106, 138, 148, 156
Rubberbandits 148, 149–50
Rural Electrification Scheme 133
Russell, George William (pseudonym AE) 96

Salkeld, Blanaid 27, 65, 98
Salkeld, Cecil ffrench 98
Scandinavian Report (*Design in Ireland*) 138
'Scene-shifter Death' (Devenport O'Neill) 27
Schaefer, Karine 165

Schinkel, Karl Friedrich 127
Scholes, Robert 93
schools
   design education in 138, 139
   Irish language teaching in 129
   lack of art education in 129
   Pearse's literary work in 80
Scott, Michael 130
Scott, Patrick 120, 121
Scully, Maurice 61
Scully, Sean 116–18
   Irish background of 116, 118
   Irish modernism and 122
sculpture
   Celtic design motifs in 121
   Free State coinage design and 129
   horses portrayed in 7, 147–48
   Tatlin's installation about migrant workers 111
Sea, The (Banville) 176–77
Sea, The, the Sea (Murdoch) 177
Second Vatican Council 138
Seshagiri, Urmila 2, 4, 36, 39
'Settle Bed, The' (Heaney) 37
Seurat, Georges 143
Shadowy Waters, The (Yeats) 105
Shamrock Pavilion, New York World Fair 130
Shannon Airport, Ireland 133
Shannon, Charles 105
Shaw, George Bernard 128
'Shelf Life' (Heaney) 38
Sherman, David 26
Shields, Carol 53
short stories. *See also* 'Athair' (Father) (Ó Conghaile)
   Ó Conaire's pioneering work in 79
   Pearse's championing of 79, 80, 85
   suitability for Irish writers 78
Silence=Death Project 82
Sill (Lloyd) 70
Sligo (Yeats) 144
Sloterdijk, Peter 160
Smethurst, James 2
Smith, Michael 67
Smith, Zadie 36, 175
Smyth, Gerry 147
Sna Fir (Ó Conghaile) 86

socialism 40, 95, 98, 128, 133
Society of Dublin Painters 143
'Song for Europe, A' (episode of *Father Ted* television programme) 148–49
Sperber, Murray 146
Spirit Level, The (Heaney) 45
Spirit of Romance, The (Pound) 64
Spurr, David 12
Squires, Geoffrey 61
Stafford, Nick 143
stained glass 128
Stanford, Leland 145
Station Island (Heaney) 36, 38–39, 44
'Station Island' (Heaney) 38–39, 61, 64–65
Stein, Gertrude 95
Stella, Frank 117
Steyn, Stella 132
storytelling tradition 81
stream of consciousness 19, 65
sunt lacrimae rerum (Virgil) 66
Swallow Press 107
'Sweeney Redivivus' (Heaney) 38, 39, 43–44
Swift, Jonathan 4, 7
   Gulliver's Travels 142, 143
'Swinford Funeral, The' (Yeats) 144
Sylvester, David 116
Symbolism 94
Synge, J. M. 118, 128
Syzygy (Joyce) 67

Tabernacle (Ó Conchúir) 156, 157, 158
Tagore, Rabindranath 105
Táin, The (Kinsella, trans.) 103, 107
Talbot Press 96
Tales of Mystery and Imagination (Poe) 128
Tallon, Ronald 138
Taropatch (Lloyd) 68, 69
'Tarot Pack' (Lowry) 68
Teacup, (Cross) 111, 113
television
   horses in comedy series on 7, 148–49
   Ó Conchúir's dance project for 156
Ten Poems (Colum) 96, 97, 98
That They May Face the Rising Sun (McGahern) 179

theatre. *See* Irish theatre; *specific writers and plays*
Thirteen mini-productions (Anu Productions) 171
Thom, René 68
Thoth Tarot (Crowley) 68
Times, The 57
Tír na nÓg 141
'To His Ghost, Seen After Delirium' (Coghill) 29
To the Lighthouse (Woolf) 16
To the North (Bowen) 11, 16–18, 20
Tóibín, Colm 177, 179
'Tollund Man, The' (Heaney) 38
Tower of Polished Black Stones, A (Yeats) 105
transition (literary publication) 132
'Two Loves' (Douglas) 84
Two Plays for Dancers (Yeats) 145
'Tympan' (Derrida) 70
Tynan, Katherine 14
typography 95, 98, 103, 132, 136

Ultramarine (Lowry) 68
Ulysses (Joyce) 51, 56
   'Circe' episode of 7, 163, 172
   Monto area, Dublin, setting for 7
'*Ulysses*, Order, and Myth' (Eliot) 2
Un coup de dés jamais n'abolira le hasard (Mallarmé) 103
UNESCO International Book Year 107
United Nations Plaza New York City 134
United States Embassy, Dublin 137
United States Post Office building, Columbus, Indiana 134
Unnamable, The (Beckett) 67, 70, 136
urban planning 127, 133, 137

Vallejo, César 69
Valois, Ninette de 155
Vardo Corner (Anu Productions) 163, 171
Varnhagen, Rahel 13
Vatican II 138
Vega (Lloyd) 69–70
verbal collage 65
Verfremdungseffekt 165
Victorian era 26, 77, 128
videos

Cross's *Teacup* and Irish modernist art 111
horses portrayed in 7, 147, 148–49
Virgil 66

Waiting for Godot (Beckett) 167, 168
Walker, Dorothy 118
Walker, Robin 138
Walkowitz, Rebecca L. 179
Walsh, Catherine 5, 61
Walsh, Dearbhla 156
War Horse (Stafford) 143
Waterford Crystal 134
Weidenfeld and Nicolson 54
West, Alfred 143
Whelan, Kevin 75
Whitaker, TK 136
White Stag group 144
Wigman, Mary 155
Wild Decembers (O'Brien) 57
Wilde, Oscar 84, 105
Wilk, Christopher 126, 127
Williams, William Carlos 95, 103
Wingfield, Sheila 6, 25, 30, 63
Wollaeger, Mark 65
Woolf, Virginia 15, 16, 52
Words upon the Window Pane, The (Yeats) 7
World Literature Today 54
World Republic of Letters, The (Casanova) 1
World War I 15, 19, 20, 26, 143
World War II 1, 26, 138
World's End Lane (Anu Productions) 163
Wright, Frank Lloyd 127
Wulfman, Clifford 93

Yahoo (Longford) 7
Yardley, Jonathan 57
Yeats and the Noh (Ishibashi) 106
Yeats International Summer School, Sligo, Ireland 105
Yeats, Elizabeth 3, 95, 98
Yeats, Jack B. 113, 144
   Cuala Press and 95
   horse imagery used by 144, 145
   National Gallery exhibition of studio and paintings of 113
Yeats, Lily 3, 95

Yeats, W. B. 4, 95, 128
   'Coat, A' 62
   'Dhoya' 145
   'Easter, 1916' 68, 141, 145
   'Meditations in Time of Civil War' 25
   'Michael Robartes bids his Beloved be at Peace' 145
   'Nineteen Hundred and Nineteen' 145
   At the Hawk's Well 7, 105, 153, 154–56, 159, 160
   Cat and the Moon, The 68
   Cathleen ni Houlihan 3
   Cuala Press and 93, 95, 96, 98, 103, 105
   dance plays of 155
   decolonisation as focus of 154, 159
   Dolmen Press and 96, 98, 103, 106
   Dun Emer Press and 95
   Free State coinage design and 129
   Heaney on 36
   horse imagery used by 144–45
   Irish modernism and 94
   Irish Revival and 94
   legacies of 107
   Miller's approach to 103
   national literatures and 105
   relevance to contemporary Irish poets of 62
   Shadowy Waters, The 105
   Sligo 144
   The Words upon the Window Pane 7
   Tower of Polished Black Stones, A 105
   Two Plays for Dancers 145
   Yoro (Noh play) 155

Zeami 155
Zen, and Yeats 106
Zeus myth 68

www.ingramcontent.com/pod-product-compliance
Lightning Source LLC
Chambersburg PA
CBHW021827300426
44114CB00009BA/360